"Wonderful, heartwarming and possibly the best thing to come out of Facebook." —Emily Giffin, *New York Times* bestselling author

"[An] incredible story. Inspiring and winning, Sam and Anaïs's tale is a testament to the power of sisterhood as well as the way social media can positively affect lives." —*Booklist*

"*The Parent Trap* on steroids, with higher stakes . . . These sisters were cheated out of a lot of years and adventures together—but their outlook is downright inspiring." —*Glamour*

SEPARATED @ BIRTH

a true love story
of twin sisters
reunited

anaïs bordier and samantha futerman
with lisa pulitzer

BERKLEY BOOKS
New York

BERKLEY

An imprint of Penguin Random House LLC
375 Hudson Street, New York, New York 10014

Berkley trade paperback ISBN: 978-0-425-27615-0

The Library of Congress has cataloged the G. P. Putnam's Sons hardcover edition as follows:

Bordier, Anaïs, date.
Separated @ birth: a true love story of twin sisters
reunited / Anaïs Bordier and Samantha Futerman; with Lisa Pulitzer.
p.   cm.
ISBN 978-0-399-16816-1
1. Bordier, Anaïs.   2. Futerman, Samantha.   3. Adoptees—Biography.
4. Twins—Biography.   5. Sisters—Biography.   6. Family reunification.
7. Intercountry adoption—Korea (South).   I. Bordier, Anaïs.   II. Title.
III. Title: Separated at birth.
HV874.8.F87   2014   2014028560
362.734092'3957—dc23

PUBLISHING HISTORY
G. P. Putnam's Sons hardcover edition / October 2014
Berkley trade paperback edition / September 2015

PRINTED IN THE UNITED STATES OF AMERICA

10 9 8 7 6 5 4 3 2 1

Cover photographs of the authors © Anaïs Bordier and Samantha Futerman.
Cover design by Andrea Ho.

*Penguin is committed to publishing works of quality and integrity.
In that spirit, we are proud to offer this book to our readers;
however, the story, the experiences, and the words
are the authors' alone.*

Penguin
Random
House

This book is dedicated to
orphans and adoptees everywhere.
May they always have love, family, and happiness.

contents

ANAÏS

the first time
i caught a glimpse of her

Saturday, December 15, 2012, was the most incredible day of my life. On this day, while sitting on a double-decker bus near Oxford Circus, shivering from the winter rain and rushing to the warmth of my shared flat in Finsbury Park, I discovered there was a young woman in America who looked exactly like me! Her image, a screenshot from a YouTube video, had been sent to my cell phone by a friend. The young Asian woman so closely resembled me that she had to be my double!

The day had started out like any other: an early morning wake-up followed by two cups of strong French coffee and a few bites of a croissant. I wanted to stay in bed and out of the rain, but I had an important mission—to find fabrics for my designs that I would be presenting in the Central Saint Martins graduate fashion show in the spring. All final-year students at the University of the Arts London's Central Saint Martins College of Art and Design would be presenting six pieces in May, and in ninety seconds, each of our collections, which had taken an entire final year's worth of energy, would be up and down the catwalk. But when this requisite was behind me, I would receive a degree in fashion design from one of the top fashion schools in the world. Alexander McQueen, John Galliano, and Stella McCartney were among its distinguished alumni.

I was well on my way to having the drawings/design portion of my portfolio ready, so I could now start collecting my fabrics. Christmas break was looming, however, and I had a lot to do. After breakfast, I went to Soho and looked over the excellent inventories at my three favorite fabric stores, secured a few swatches that I really liked, and was settling myself on the bus back to my flat when my cell phone buzzed. It was a notification from Facebook, alerting me that a friend, Kelsang, had posted something on my wall. I opened my Facebook wall immediately, only to have my breath taken away. There in front of my eyes was a screenshot of a presumed stranger, but whoever she was, she had the same eyes, the same skin, the same hair length and color, the same nose, and the same smile as me.

My Internet connection on the bus was really bad, so I couldn't do any more investigating until I got home, still twenty minutes away. I was in complete disbelief. I was adopted from South Korea as an infant and raised in France, so all my life, I had wondered if there were people out there who looked like me. The girl grinning back at me on my Samsung Galaxy looked so much like me that I thought one of my artistic friends might be pranking me. They were all very creative, and could manipulate images with ease, and they all loved a good laugh, so it was reasonable to think this could be a joke. Every possibility of who this girl might be consumed me for the remainder of the ride. Was she a doppelgänger? Was she a relative? Was she real? Was she an impostor? Did she know about me?

When I finally got home, I ran straight to my computer. It turned out Kelsang had been surfing through YouTube videos when he had stumbled upon my look-alike. She was an actress in a short video called "High School Virgin," a staged comic piece where she was playing the role of a teenage tease. The entire video was only four minutes long. My "double" had a forty-second speaking part, but as none of the four actors was credited, I didn't have her name. The more I watched the video, the more I thought I was looking at myself, except for the American-accented English. (When I speak English, I do so with a British accent.) But other than the accent, I could not find a single difference that would distinguish one of us from the other. All I could find were the similarities. Who was she? I knew I needed to find her.

I got in touch with Kelsang as fast as I could and asked him how he had come across the video. He told me he had been doing some research, and it had popped up on the right side of his computer screen. The female character had looked so much like me that he had posted her picture to my Facebook wall for me to see. I didn't ask him what he was researching that would bring up a title called "High School Virgin," because that was his business, but I was thankful that he had. I love everything about Kelsang. He and I have been friends since my second year at Central Saint Martins. He is Tibetan, came to school with more experience in fashion than I did, and is always teaching me personal fashion tricks.

Part of my intrigue with the mysterious American stemmed from the fact that I was adopted. I don't have any siblings and I don't resemble anyone in my family, including my European parents, Patricia and Jacques Bordier. My mother is blond-haired and blue-eyed, and my father is as French-looking as they get. Even though there is a neighborhood in Paris with a very small Korean population, it was nowhere near Neuilly-sur-Seine, where I lived. I knew other Asians, but I didn't look very much like them, either, although people joked that we all looked alike. A lot of French people tend to think of all Asians as Chinese.

I had one Korean friend, but she was eight years older. She had been adopted, too, and coincidentally she was also named Anaïs. We went to the same Catholic school in Neuilly, Institut Saint Dominique. When we had glasses on, we looked quite similar. Anaïs was like a big sister to me when I was growing up, protective and kind. We had become friends when I was five and my mother had come to pick me up in the schoolyard at dismissal. She called my name, so the other Anaïs turned around, too. Our mothers started talking, and it turned out the other Anaïs had also been adopted from South Korea. It was nice to have that in common with someone.

Throughout my life, I had always hoped to find someone who looked like me. I'm not sure, but it might be a common theme among adopted children to speculate on who could be in your family. Being an only child, too, I probably fantasized about these things even more. When I was very young, I had an imaginary friend I called Anne. My mum didn't know about her until the mother of one of my school friends told her. "I didn't know Anaïs had a sister," the mother said. My mum assured her that I didn't. A lot of only children had imaginary friends, but I was longing for a sibling, not just a best friend. I didn't just want a permanent playdate. I wanted someone I could relate to in physical appearance. But I had never found anyone . . . until now.

I watched "High School Virgin" at least ten more times, convinced the Asian actress was somehow related to me, maybe a half sister or a cousin. When I showed Marie, my roommate, the video, she was as blown away as I had been. We both agreed that the girl looked slightly younger than me, but identical in every other way. Marie was great at computer sleuthing and tried various searches that might lead to an identification. But, like me, she came up empty.

Over the next few days, I sat at the kitchen table with my laptop open. I wanted to contact Kevin Wu, aka "KevJumba," the Chinese-American humorist and director of the video, but I worried that a message would get lost amid the fan messages on his Facebook page, or in the comments on his YouTube videos. "High School Virgin" had more than two million views and fifteen thousand comments, so how would he see mine?

Wednesday evening, I had happened to have dinner with my friend Oliver, who claimed to be a physiognomist, someone who supposedly can assess a person's character by his or her facial features. I was anxious to get his reaction to the mystery girl. "She has to be your sister!" he exclaimed after seeing her picture. "You look exactly the same." He was insistent that I find a way to get in touch with KevJumba, but this kind of encouragement made me more scared than excited. Who knew what I would find out? I wasn't ready for rejection, and I had to entertain that rejection was a possibility. This girl might not have any interest in me whatsoever.

On Thursday, I was taking the Eurostar to Paris for Christmas break. Before I headed out that morning, Marie had me pose the same way the American was postured in her screenshot, and she snapped a couple of photos of me. She wanted to create a split-screen photomontage of the two of us for comparison purposes. Even before my train pulled into Paris, her creation had been posted on my Facebook wall. Looking at us side by side, I could only be in total awe of our resemblance.

My father picked me up at Gare du Nord. Although he knew I was perfectly capable of taking the Metro the four miles home, he didn't want to wait that long to see me. When we got to our flat, I was so anxious to show my parents Marie's photomontage, I didn't even stop to say hello to Eko, our American cocker spaniel, who was jumping at my legs as I raced to the dining room table to turn on my laptop. My mother was disappointed that I hadn't given the dog a warmer greeting, but I knew she would forgive me when she saw what was so compelling. Turning my parents' attention to the photomontage displayed on my laptop, I waited for them to react.

"So . . . what are the differences in the pictures?" I asked.

"Well . . . first, you are more tanned in one," Mum guessed, pointing to the American girl's photo occupying the top half of the screen. "And heuuuu . . ."

"And . . . it . . . is . . . NOT . . . ME!" I jumped in.

"Exactly what I was going to say, it's not you in this picture!" Mum smiled. It was probably too embarrassing to admit that she wasn't able to identify her own daughter.

Over dinner, I explained that my friend Kelsang had uncovered a video with a dead ringer of me in it, then showed them the forty seconds of "High School Virgin" that featured her. They were both amused by the video, despite the abundance of American cussing. But they also came up with lots of reasons why this girl could not be my sister. My father told me about a Korean actress he was familiar with who looked just like me. He had been watching Korean movies in his free time and had come across this particular woman in several films.

"You can always find people who look similar," he reasoned.

My father is an amazing person and incredibly smart, but in this case, I had to disagree with him. "This girl and I don't look similar—we look exactly the same!" I insisted. I didn't want to be talked out of my fantasy, and I wanted my parents to indulge me, not try to dissuade me, even if they were trying to protect me.

My mother explained that she had addressed the option of adopting twins when she first signed on with Holt International Children's Services, the adoption agency that handled my case. She had told them that if twins became available, she would happily adopt both of them. That was even a question on her application: *Would you take twins?* She told me that there would have been no reason to separate me from a twin sister, if I had been part of a pair. They had a copy of my birth record, too. It said "single birth," and my parents had full faith that it was correct.

My mother's point was strong. The more I thought about it, the more I talked myself into believing that this girl was not my twin or even a relative. Any further mention of her was simply for fun and done in a joking manner. I had a doppelgänger somewhere in America, and that was that. Even so, I continued to surreptitiously check KevJumba's Facebook page, Twitter feed, and website every day, still hoping I would come across the girl's name.

By the end of Christmas holiday, I had stopped searching, although I still thought about her. As much as I accepted that our similarities were likely coincidences, I was still haunted that she could be someone in my birth family. What if she had already discovered me at some point and hadn't really cared to pursue it? Maybe she knew about me, and hoped I would never know about her. I also reasoned that if I had been born a twin, I would have known it in my heart via some telepathic longing. But I had never had emotions like that . . . until now.

My curiosity was piqued enough for me to do a little research about my birthplace, Busan, a huge port in the south of Korea. With more than three million people, it was the second-largest city in South Korea, complete with an abundance of skyscrapers, plenty of seafood, and a tourism industry built around the beaches.

My parents had taken me there on a family vacation when I was seven years old, determined to show me my roots, but I was too young to really appreciate it. Now I was fascinated to learn the city had a huge Russian Mafia presence, the largest in all of Asia. I wondered if perhaps I could have some Russian blood. There was also the possibility I had American blood. Camp Hialeah, a U.S. military base in Busan until it closed in 2006, had had several hundred U.S. servicemen stationed there. It was a well-known fact that U.S. servicemen often abandoned their Korean wives and children when their tours of duty were over. Maybe I was part American, and my birth father had been in the service, then abandoned my mother? I started imagining different scenarios, but in the end, who cared if I was part Russian or American by blood? Patricia and Jacques Bordier were my parents and the only parents I cared to know.

By the time I got back to London, I had put my American "twin" to the back of my mind. When mid-February 2013 came around, I was back in full work mode. I had to get some toiling fabrics, and I was on the bus heading to Woolcrest in Hackney accompanied by Kelsang and Lucas, another friend of ours. Out of nowhere, Kelsang mentioned he had seen the "American girl" again in the trailer of a soon-to-be-released American movie called *21 & Over*. I immediately typed the name of the film into my cell phone, hoping I could find her in the cast. Sure enough, there she was. Samantha Futerman!

I was beyond excited. Now that I had her name, I Googled her, and the first thing that popped up was a link to her profile on the popular Internet movie database IMDB. The picture of her on that website looked as much like me as her cameo in "High School Virgin." Next to her photo was the biggest shock of all—her date of birth, which was the same as mine: November 19, 1987! I froze. I thought I had probably read it wrong, transposing it in my mind to what I had hoped to see. But when I looked again, it was still reading, "November 19, 1987."

"KELSANG!" I screamed across the bus. "The girl from the YouTube video, she was born November, 19, 1987!"

"So what?" Kelsang asked, not understanding the importance.

"So, *I* was born on November 19, 1987," I explained. Could she be my twin sister? Her name was very American, "Samantha Futerman," so she must have been adopted, too. Now that I could see her closely, I could see details that I hadn't seen before. *Mon Dieu*, she even has the same freckles on her nose as I have! By the time I got off the bus, I was beginning to feel faint.

On the walk to school, I was a wreck. I called my parents to tell them what I had learned. My mother gasped when I told her about the shared birth date. "Do you think she could be your twin sister?" she asked in disbelief.

My dad called back later but he was skeptical. He told me he wanted to look up "Samantha Futerman" himself to see what he could find. Five minutes later, he called back saying she wasn't my twin, as he had found a website that indicated she had been born on the first of November, not the nineteenth. He admitted several sites had said "November 19," but he needed me to be aware that there were other "facts" that contradicted the date I chose to believe. We hung up with him locked into the idea that it wasn't possible for Samantha Futerman to be my twin.

The day was so strange. I was feeling completely turned

around. I think I was in shock, but I just didn't know it. When I finally settled into the studio and started working on my collection, spreading my fabric out on my worktable, I still kept staring at Samantha's photo on my laptop as I obsessively reread her IMDB profile. I was impressed to see that she had been in several films, some of them big, including *Memoirs of a Geisha*, an adaptation from a huge international bestselling book, which I had seen with my mother when it came to France when I was seventeen. Samantha played a young Japanese girl named Satsu, the older sister of the lead role. At the time, she did not jump out at me as my doppelgänger. She was heavily made up to look Japanese.

My studio mates were hard at work, but at the risk of being annoying, I simply had to communicate my excitement. "That girl is born the same day as me, and she's adopted, too!" I'd blurt out whenever the urge hit me. I had no proof she was related to me, but it was making complete sense in my head, and I was compelled to share. People could draw their own conclusions, but I was already convinced.

Things started getting even freakier really fast. Lucas directed me to several more YouTube videos he had discovered that featured Samantha, pointing out that she and I had the same inflection and delivery in our voices. No video of Samantha's blew me away more than the one titled "How It Feels to Be Adopted . . . I Am Sam." It was a humorous three-minute skit of Samantha being questioned about her feelings about adoption. Friends were asking her purposefully naïve questions, such as . . . was she from South or North Korea, how come she didn't look like the rest of her family, and if she felt sad and alone because her birth parents had given her up. She reveals that she has two American brothers, one of whom we meet in the video. Did this mean I had two American brothers, too? At one point, she dresses up as Little Orphan Annie and belts out the song "Tomorrow." I found it incredibly amusing, but more important, it was my confirmation that we were twins. Her mannerisms, her voice, even her sense of humor . . . were mine.

I raced home to the safety of my computer, where I started sending the "How It Feels to Be Adopted . . . I Am Sam" video to everyone I could think of. Enlisting friends, I also launched my massive campaign to figure out a way to get in touch with Samantha Futerman, putting all my faith in social media. We were unsuccessful in locating a Facebook page for her, but Kelsang did find her Instagram on his cell phone. We went through all of her pictures, with me feeling a little guilty at the depths of my snooping, but it was so much fun! We found very recent pictures of her on a trip to Korea. One of them had her posing with a woman she identified as her foster mother. She looked very happy to be with her.

Next, we found "Samantha Futerman" on Twitter. She had been tweeting a lot lately, so I got to spy on her back-and-forth conversations. As paradoxical as it sounds, I was discovering her both slowly and quickly, all without her knowledge. Someone suggested we try working backward to find her Facebook page by finding a relative of hers on her Twitter, then seeing if we could locate that person's Facebook page. If we were successful, we could hope to find a "Samantha" in that list of "friends."

We chose a Twitterer named "JoFuterman," searched the name on Facebook, opened Jo Futerman's "friends" inventory, and had a match! Someone named "Samantha" was on Jo's list! I clicked on her name, and up came the same photo we'd seen on her Instagram. I had found her! Most of her information was private, but I would find a way to contact her, no matter what I had to do. Flying to America crossed my mind, but I would save that as a last resort.

I started composing a message with what I thought was just the right tone: not too scary, not too funny, something that would not freak her out and put her off, but would be serious enough to attract her interest.

Finally, I sent a friend request with the following message:

Hey, My name is Anaïs, I am French and live in London. About 2 months ago, my friend was watching one of your videos with Kevjumba on youtube, and he saw you and thought we looked really similar . . . like . . . VERY REALLY SIMILAR . . . we were making jokes, about it etc. (I'm always being violent with people and hitting them too hahaha)

Today, he saw the trailer of 21 & over and told me he saw you again, I then checked your name on the cast, stalked you A BIT, and found out you were born on the 19th of November 1987.

I checked more of your videos (which are hilarious) and then came upon the "how it feels

to be adopted" . . . and discovered you were
adopted too.

So . . . I don't want to be too Lindsay Lohan,
well . . . but . . . how to put it . . . I was
wondering where you were born?

I was born on the 19th of November 1987, in
Busan but my papers were made at the Holt
Children's Institute, so "officially" I was born in
Seoul. My Korean name is Kim Eun Hwa. I arrived
in France the 5th March 1988, so 3 months later.

You can check my Facebook if you want to check
the pictures and the videos. It's more obvious on
videos . . .

Let me know . . . don't freak out . . .

     Lots of Love

     Anaïs

I absolutely had to get her attention. I needed her to answer
me in any fashion she wanted, but I needed her to know I was
looking for her.

2

SAM

the day a french girl landed
on my lap . . . top

When I got out of bed on February 21, 2013, I believed that my entire day was going to revolve around the premiere of a movie I was in, a major release called *21 & Over*. This was my third year living in Los Angeles, doing the acting/waitressing thing. When I wasn't in a role or auditioning for one, I worked as a waitress in an upscale brasserie in Beverly Hills. Being cast in films like *21 & Over* was a good reminder that I was progressing in my career and not just chasing an empty dream.

The premiere that night was a red carpet event. Being the total spaz that I am, I don't really like walking the carpet. I find it completely nerve-wracking and not in the least bit appealing. I know it would be more fascinating if I liked the glamour of galas like this, but the truth is, I get uncomfortable, probably because I feel like it's crazy that I'm even at these stylish parties, with all the Hollywood heavy hitters. Even when I get dressed up, I feel like I should be on the catering staff, passing hors d'oeuvres, as I do in my financial supporting role of "waitress." I always find myself eyeing empty drink glasses, wondering if I should put them on a small round tray and take them to the kitchen.

This was the second red carpet event of my career. My first one, the opening of *Memoirs of a Geisha*, had definitely been an experience—glamorous, thrilling, and terrifying all at the same time. I don't remember many details, except that the food was incredible. I ate and drank myself to the point of delirium and left the party the happier for it.

The premiere of *21 & Over* was being held at the Westwood Village Regency Theatre, which added to the extravagance of it. This grand old movie house, formerly the Fox Theatre, has hosted some of the biggest premieres in the history of Hollywood, including those of the Harry Potter franchise. I was a huge fan of Harry Potter, but I could never be cast in the films—when J. K. Rowling sold the rights to Warner Bros. in 1998, she stipulated that the cast be British, except parts whose nationalities were identified in the books. As she didn't have any Asian Jewish female characters, that eliminated me. But, just being in the same venue as the opening of such a monumental film series made me look forward to it.

All the stars of *21 & Over*, including Miles Teller, Justin Chon, and Skylar Astin, were going to be in attendance. We had loads of fun filming together. Justin and I even went bar-hopping after set, tossing back beers while bonding over being Asian-American actors.

Like most mothers today, mine was cursed with contemporary-reference dyslexia and kept getting the name of the film confused. But I know she loves me, and getting the movie's name right wasn't the most important thing in the world. She had raised me with love and support, and I honored her for that.

The day of the premiere was also my father's birthday. He was turning . . . old. Little did I know that on his special day, I would soon be getting a huge gift of my own, one my whole family would enjoy for the rest of our lives.

I woke up early on the twenty-first, "early" generally falling between the hours of eight and ten a.m. I headed over to my girlfriend Lauren's apartment to have my nails painted. Lauren was a hostess at the restaurant where I waitressed, and we had become close friends with our shared crude senses of humor. Being a Jersey girl, I would be a complete disgrace if I stepped onto the red carpet without a manicure, and Lauren had offered to be my nail artist for the gala. Around eleven, while we were chatting and doing my nails, a Twitter message from someone I didn't know popped up on my iPhone. "Hey Sam, my friend Anaïs sent you a message on FB, check it ☺ (it might be in the spam box)."

Normally, a stranger contacting me via Twitter or Facebook would creep me out. I had all my Facebook settings set to "private" in order to avoid these strangers reaching me. However, this time for some unknown reason, I pulled up my Facebook page to see what this was all about. I didn't have a message from an "Anaïs," so I checked my friend requests. Right there, about one square inch in size, I saw a picture of myself. My first thought was . . . Great, a creepy KevJumba fan saw me on his YouTube channel and made a fake Facebook page of me. Kevin had a massive YouTube following and very dedicated subscribers, so it wasn't out of the realm of possibility. And with all the "catfishing" out there, who's to say what the truth was. But I clicked into the picture anyway. That's when I realized it was not a picture of me. It was an actual . . . girl . . . a real live girl named Anaïs who looked exactly like me. As I clicked around her profile, I learned that she was twenty-five and lived in London.

I saw that we shared a birth date, but for some reason, it didn't register as something significant. It was more like, Oh yeah . . . same birthday . . . hmm . . . weird. I showed Anaïs's friend request to Lauren, who was still painting my nails, but neither of us knew what I should do about it. Finally, again for some inexplicable reason, I decided that Anaïs was legit, and I accepted her friend request.

Just as quickly as I had friended her, I wished I hadn't. I rarely accepted strangers into my world, and I was already regretting my haste in this decision. Excusing myself from Lauren's polishing, I went over to her computer and changed my Facebook privacy settings immediately. This way, Anaïs would have only a restricted view of my profile, which made me feel much more secure. Just because she looked like me didn't mean I had to let my guard down.

A second or two after my settings were fixed, my phone alerted me to a Facebook message from this very Anaïs who I was trying to keep at arm's length. Anaïs Bordier. Just when I thought I was at a safe distance, here she was again. I felt strangely calm as I decided to see what she had to say. It was almost as if there was some divine intervention guiding me toward someone I was destined to encounter. I had no other explanation.

I didn't know what to think about the girl's message. She was awesome, and I loved her "Lindsay Lohan" reference to *The Parent Trap*. In that movie, Lindsay Lohan plays both sisters in a pair of identical twins separated as infants and raised on different continents. I knew Anaïs was implying that somehow we could be identical twin sisters, too, separated at birth and raised on different continents. Her message seemed too sincere to be a joke. In the pit of my gut, I could feel how possible it was that this could be true.

Now that we were Facebook friends, I had access to her photos and albums, and I got right to examining them. I had to make sure she wasn't a poser, making up a phony identity. Anaïs was also "secure" in her settings on Facebook, which was a sign that, like me, she took her privacy seriously. Her photos all looked legitimate. What was most impressive about them was that she looked . . . just like me. Not like a cousin, not like a doppelgänger . . . like a mirror image of me.

I started scrolling around her albums for a while. The similarities I was discovering in the pictures were uncanny. In one of them, she was looking at a menu in some restaurant. A commenter had written facetiously, "I want this and this and this," seeming to indicate that Anaïs always wanted to taste everything. That was just like me. I always want to try every single item on the menu, and announce it in an overly excited manner. Even more bizarre, she had freckles just like me, even though Koreans having freckles is highly unusual. I always thought mine were the result of spending too much time lying in the Jersey Shore sun, working on my Snooki tan. Could my freckles be genetic? In a recent Halloween photo of Anaïs, she was dressed as an amazing black bird with crazy wings, which, according to a comment, she had made herself. I loved Halloween, too, and like Anaïs, I usually chose the funny animal costumes, despite the tendency for women to dress one degree sluttier for trick-or-treating. When I was finished with my cyber-stalking, I took a screenshot of Anaïs's Facebook page and texted it to Justin Chon, the star of *21 & Over*, for his opinion. "Dude, that's your twin," he wrote back. Even though that same thought had slightly grazed my mind, it hadn't truly occurred to me. I like to protect myself, so even if I believed it was probably true, I didn't admit it. Instead, I kept my composure and continued to investigate, and by "investigate," I mean that I sent the screenshot to all the people I knew, so that I could get their opinions on it. What can I say? I like teamwork.

The opinion I valued most was that of my friend Kanoa. He was one of my best friends in Los Angeles, even though I'd only known him a few months. Justin had introduced us and we became close really fast, sharing our funny stories about acting school and commiserating about having to support ourselves as waiters. He was also an ethnic actor. He was hapa, an ethnically ambiguous blend of Chinese, Caucasian, Hawaiian, and a bunch of other races. Whatever they are, he is gorgeous.

Kanoa's opinion was really gentle and comforting. He didn't want to say if he thought I had a twin, but he anticipated that I was likely in shock from being contacted by this French look-alike, so he asked me if I was okay. I really appreciated his sensitivity, especially after Justin's surprisingly bold yet likely true pronouncement. I wanted other opinions, too, especially those of my two older brothers, Matt and Andrew. I told them not to tell Mom and Dad, thinking that would make the situation too big, but I wanted them to check out the pictures and tell me what they thought. Typical of my brothers, they didn't give me much. Their responses were, "Wow . . . weird"—they were always so predictably generic.

The thread of texts with my friends that ensued was insane. Justin was particularly relentless in his insistence that Anaïs and I were twins. "Sam, that's your twin. She has to be. It's your twin. She's your twin. Twin. Twin. Twin. Twin."

Finding a long-lost twin only happens in the movies. Like in *The Parent Trap*! It didn't happen in real life. Just that past summer, I had been to Korea on a "roots" tour with my mother, and I had had the opportunity to see my birth records at the adoption agency that handled my case in Seoul. There had been no mention of a twin. According to the official record, I had been born alone, a singleton. The document said that my mother had given birth to a daughter two years earlier, so that might mean I had an older sister, if I believed it. That information had been added to the record at a later date, so it was even more suspect than the other information. Who knew what, if anything, was true?

A few weeks earlier, I had been out with a friend named Robyn. She had gone to Korea to find her birth mother. They had a reunion, and when they did a DNA test, it turned out they weren't a biological match. The birth search had been wrong, based on incorrect information, so Robyn and the woman had briefly thought they had found each other, only to be wrong. In Korea, very few birth mothers are brave enough to actually come forward, so Robyn had been feeling lucky. I couldn't even fathom her sadness when they discovered the truth.

From my search, I knew I had a birth mother who had no interest in me making contact with her, so I let it go for now although I still hoped that day would come. Now, me having a twin? That was completely inconceivable. Yet, I couldn't get rid of the thought. I mean, she could be my twin. She shared my birthday, and we looked exactly alike. Stranger things have happened. But what if she wasn't a twin or even a relative? My head was spinning.

I had to write back to Anaïs, but how do I respond to a message like the one she had sent me? What to say? "Hey. LOL. This is crazy! ☺. Ttyl?" I just didn't have a response.

3

ANAÏS

waiting for first contact

The role of social networking in the world today cannot be appreciated enough. By the networks and their available applications, we communicate our ideas, stay informed, market our merchandise, share our photos, present our opinions, and absorb enormous amounts of knowledge, some so trifling we are confused as to why we ever needed it. We stay connected with friends, and we find friends we have lost touch with by way of a few key word searches. Without social networking, I would never have found Samantha Futerman.

There is an upside and a downside to the connectedness on the Internet. As great as it is to communicate with people all over the world, we get overly accustomed to instant gratification. We become used to the immediacy of it all. Write a blog and get instant feedback. Post a tweet and watch it get retweeted again and again. Post something on Facebook and see how many friends "like" it in a matter of minutes. After I sent my message to Samantha saying we might be twins, the most important message I had ever sent in my life, I expected an instant response. Instead, I found myself waiting . . . and waiting . . . and waiting.

In anxious anticipation of Samantha's reply, I knew I wanted the moral support of my friends. Kelsang offered to have a "waiting for contact" pizza party at his flat, and I gladly accepted his invitation. Kelsang and his flat mates, and our friends Rafa, Angel, and Marta were the ideal distractions. Takeaway pizzas from Pizza Hut sounded good to me. Everybody in the room was almost as excited as I was. We all kept refreshing our Twitters and Facebooks, making sure we didn't miss anything that might come in, even for a minute. To keep the waiting fun, we drank lots of wine, ate our pizza, and spent the time laughing and joking. But the levity didn't calm me down. I was a bundle of nerves.

The more time that passed without any response from Samantha, the more my doubts and insecurities started to surface. Everybody else was still hyped up, but my focus was on what could be going wrong. I had already factored in the time zone differences, and as it was seven o'clock in the evening here in London, it was about eleven in the morning for Samantha in California. If she was anything like me, and I assumed she was, she would have gotten up fairly recently, and she would be checking all of her social media. So, why wasn't she writing back? I was suddenly alarmed that she wouldn't see my message, or worse, she would but wouldn't answer. On Facebook, you could see if somebody had read your message, so I was watching my computer screen, waiting for the pernicious "seen at blah blah time," but it never appeared.

I waited at Kelsang's until well after midnight, but no reply from Samantha. By now, it would be late afternoon in California, so it would be almost impossible for her not to have logged on. It crossed my mind that she could have a Facebook privacy setting that would allow her to see my friend request without my knowing. If that was the case, and she wasn't responding, there was nothing I could do about it. There was also the possibility that it had gone to her spam box, so my request would be equally doomed.

I was exhausted, emotionally and physically. Waiting was only adding to my anxiety, and although I knew what I was waiting for, Samantha lived in another world. Having expectations about what she would do with my friend request was getting me nowhere. All I could do was go home and get into bed. I still couldn't stop obsessing about her—I watched Samantha's videos a thousand times before falling asleep.

Where was she? What was she doing at this moment? Those were my first thoughts when I woke up on Wednesday, February 20, 2013. My probable twin was out there somewhere, over there in America, and I was feeling energized. When I talked to my parents, I promised to send them some of the amazing pictures of Samantha I had found on Instagram. Mum seemed to be getting really excited about the idea of what she could discover from the photos. Dad was not as enthusiastic, although he encouraged me to send on what I had found.

Obviously, if I had a long-lost twin, this was going to

impact more than just me. The dynamics of our entire family would change. Theoretically, my parents would suddenly have another daughter. Wait a minute . . . that would mean I had two sets of parents. Would I have to explain to four people that I wanted a tattoo? Who would Samantha's parents be to me? Who would everybody be to one another? I adored the set of parents I had. Would I have to share them with Samantha now?

I generally don't give away my feelings for others, but my parents are incredible people, and I cannot imagine life without them. They are my real parents, the ones I argue with and admire at the same time. They are loving, thoughtful, and kind. What if I didn't like Samantha's parents? What if Samantha didn't like my parents? What would our parents be to one another? Would everybody get along? What would we do about holidays and birthdays? Spend them all together, or alternate houses, like married couples do with in-laws?

I was probably getting ahead of myself, but slowly the idea of having a twin started to really weigh on me. I lay in my bed paralyzed, contemplating all the possible relationships and scenarios, and as of yet, the Futermans were only strangers. They didn't even know about the Bordiers. Bringing myself back to the present, I looked at Sam's Twitter again, hoping to find something I might have missed the day before. I called Mum to let her know I was still doing okay, and she suggested I send Samantha a message asking if she had been born in Busan, like me. Samantha had not yet answered my Facebook request, so my biggest fear remained that she might never answer me, no matter how many messages I sent her.

I was glad I had revisited Samantha's Twitter. This time I looked at older tweets she had been posting during her trip to Korea the previous year. She had written that her biological mum was from Busan! There was one more clue that we were twins. I called Mum back to tell her, followed by Dad, followed by everyone else I knew.

There was still the problem of Samantha not having seen my message, so I spent a little longer trying to find out what she had been doing over the past twenty-five years. Social media like Facebook and WhatsApp have made it so amazingly easy to spy on people through the cables and plugs that interconnect us all. Technology brings voyeurism to a whole new level, and I was so happy to have this tool at my disposal. In her photos, I could see that she liked to wear amazing costumes and her boyfriend was really, really tall. She seemed to be a very happy, fun, and playful person, except in one photo, when she was about seven or eight, where she seemed a little lost. She was with her two older brothers, and she was holding a baby in her arms. But she wasn't looking directly at the camera and smiling, like her brothers. I don't know why that picture struck me, but it did.

I was really indulging myself in Samantha's childhood when my fears returned. She was never going to accept my friend request, because now I was convinced it had gone to her spam mailbox. I didn't want to send her a message in any public forum, because Samantha was an actress and therefore vulnerable to stalkers, people like me. I didn't want to post just anywhere for the whole world to see. Already, my friends and I had added her everywhere we could—Instagram, Twitter,

WhatsApp, etc. We even became followers of her YouTube channel.

It was two p.m. by the time I could finally get myself out of bed. I didn't go to school. I was exhausted and hugely disappointed that I hadn't heard back from Samantha. I felt really bad about skipping. "Waiting to hear from your potential twin" did not make the list of excusable absences, but I didn't care anymore. I only wanted to discover more things about Samantha and who she was. I would have flown to Los Angeles to locate her, doing the best I could with the hints I was picking up from her Instagram. I felt like I was a detective, slowly putting pieces of her story together.

Kelsang could sense my trauma and despair. He was sweet enough to invite me to a movie, even though he had a lot of work to do. We went to see *Beautiful Creatures*, perfectly cheesy for the occasion. After the movie, I checked my phone to see if there was anything new. Samantha still hadn't answered, so, dragging Kelsang with me, I went to French Connection UK to buy my mum a silk top for her birthday. Then we went back to my flat for burgers. In the hour and a half of shopping, and the trip back to my place, there was still nothing. The long, emotional day had left me with more questions, no answers. The things running through my head were wild. What if she is not interested? What if she doesn't want to know about me? What if she thinks I'm a crazy teenage fan obsessed with her? What if she never discovers the message? I was going insane. Kelsang and I talked about if we should tweet her, but again we decided against it. After Kelsang left, I got back into bed, ignoring my exhaustion in favor of watching the videos of my "twin" again. I fell asleep with the image of Samantha fading into my dreams.

By morning, I was feeling downright schizophrenic. I'd watched the videos so many times, I couldn't even tell the difference between Samantha and me anymore. Everything was merging and mixing. The videos seemed real and time was distorted. It was crazy. I had learned so much about Samantha's life in the past few days that she was no longer just an image to me, but a real, breathing person who was walking somewhere on Earth at this very moment. She was moving about, making decisions about what to have for dinner, maybe reading lines for a part, but she was right there with me. The trouble was, I was the only one who knew it. It was like reading a book and slowly unraveling a character, bringing him to life in your imagination. However, I could see photographs of her, and she was made of flesh and bones.

When Kelsang came over for breakfast the following morning, we got right on my computer only to see that Samantha was tweeting. Knowing she was online, Kelsang used the opportunity to post a personal tweet with a mention of her and her handle, which would automatically go to her "Mentions" tab. My heart was pounding as he tweeted instructions for her to go to her spam box on Facebook, where she would find my message. I panicked as soon as he did it. Worried that it could look too spam-like, I asked him to remove it immediately, which he did. I came up with another idea, to send her a message on her YouTube channel. Kelsang shot me down when he told me he had already tried this tactic. But I did it anyway. Next, I composed a message to her that I was determined to deliver somehow. "Oh, good morning, I am your twin sister, Cheers." Never mind. It was a little too bold, and there was no way I could think of to get it to her and be taken seriously.

It was time for me to go back to classes. I was right in the middle of the final collection, and missing the previous school day was catastrophic enough. Technically, this was the year you rarely slept, ate, or had any fun, except for discovering a novel sewing technique that could save you three hours of work, or should I say, gain you three hours of much-needed sleep. Even if all my focus was on Samantha, I had obligations in London and I had to get back to work. Only three days had passed since I had sent my Facebook friend request, but it felt like twenty-five years. Nothing else mattered but hearing from Samantha. I wanted to know that she had received my message, but even more I wanted for her to answer it. I was feeling so vulnerable that I wanted to be home in Paris being comforted by my mum and dad. They would have supported me in a way that only parents could.

Right now, I was feeling overwhelmed with frustration and uncertainty. It was like I was imprisoned somewhere, trying to yell at someone who couldn't hear me, and had never heard of me, and wouldn't know if I were dead or not. It was almost unbearable, knowing about Samantha and knowing that she had absolutely no clue of my existence. I just wanted her to see me, to see my message and to react. Whatever the reaction was, I just wanted her to know I existed. All I could do was wait.

My friends were waiting, too, feeling my stress. Everybody wanted a resolution, and some took matters into their own hands. Without me knowing it, my friend Maxence twected Samantha from Paris, telling her to look for a message from Anaïs on her Facebook, and then open it and read it. Lucas posted an Instagram photo of me with a handwritten note on the bottom—"Check your spam box." He thought something handwritten would look friendlier than a computerized message, and he was thinking Samantha might not even know there was such a thing as a Facebook spam box.

And then it happened! In a life-changing instant, two notifications from Facebook popped up on my phone that Samantha had accepted my friend request and read my message! I was at school in the studio with my friends when I found out. "YAY! YAY! YAY! YAY!" I shouted, crazily jumping around the studio. "She read it! She read it! She read it!" Everyone erupted in cheers. I didn't know it yet, but the winning communication had been Maxence's tweet from Paris. That was the one that had gotten Samantha's attention. What I knew was that contact had been established, and I couldn't have been more elated.

4

SAM

right in the palm of my hand

Now that I had confirmed Anaïs's friend request, I was really at a loss for what to do next. There was no way I could say the photos I had seen in her albums didn't look like me and dismiss her as delusional. I didn't simply agree that we looked alike. I thought she could be my reflection in a mirror. It was beyond comprehension. My birth records said I was a singleton, and I had never felt otherwise in my heart or spirit, yet the photos of Anaïs were saying something else. We were born on the exact same day, so she couldn't be a younger sister, or a half sister. Well, I guess technically we could be half sisters, if we shared one father, who had made babies with both our mothers in Busan about the same time. . . . Never mind. It was not worth going there. But how could I respond to a message that read, "Hey, we might be twins?"

I know it might sound strange, but I didn't want to get too personal, and I was very short on time with the hour of the premiere closing in. For some reason, I decided to send Anaïs my birth records, what I thought was a good first step. I already had a separate photo of each page saved on my phone from my trip to Seoul, so it would be really easy to just forward them to her. At 12:03 p.m. precisely, I sent a photo of one page via Facebook messenger. This way, she could see if it matched hers without us having to make personal contact. If it didn't match, no harm done—we'd both go our separate ways, two Korean adoptees who once crossed paths with each other in a Facebook message, in the throngs of people who inhabit the Internet.

"Thank you," came a reply from Anaïs exactly ten minutes later. Wow, she was really on it. "I've just looked through the document, so it says 1st of 2?!?!?!?!" She had misunderstood. "1st of 2" referred to our birth mother having a younger sister, not that I was the first of two children. I felt too uncomfortable to correct her, so I just sent the second page right away, hoping she would understand.

My birth records seemed to only encourage her. "I just had a heart attack," she wrote, followed by some emphatic HA HA HAs. "I will send you my documents, too." Apparently, seeing my birth records had supported the possibility that we could be twins, although she didn't mention anything specific. I really wanted to communicate more, but I just didn't have the time at that moment. "I'm actually getting ready for the *21 & Over* premiere," I wrote back. "Sorry I haven't been super-responsive. CRAZY. I will talk more I swear. We are totally twins."

There. We had both called each other our twin. Anaïs was a complete stranger living five thousand miles away from me, and yet we might be identical twins? I sent her the final page of my record, which had information on my birth parents, although none of it was confirmed.

According to the document, my birth parents had met each other through their relatives and had been married since 1985. My birth father was twenty-nine when I was born. He was from Kyŏngsang-bukdo, a province halfway between Seoul and Busan. After high school, he moved to Busan to find employment. He did military service and then returned to Busan. When he married my birth mother, he promised to support her family as well, which put them in "needy condition." When my birth mother conceived her second child—me—she and my birth father decided that adoption would be the best choice for my sake. It was their hope that I would be adopted by a good family. My Korean name was listed on the top left corner of this page—Ra-Hee Chung.

I waited for Anaïs's reply. She wished me luck at the premiere and said that she would send me her records when she got home. "I guess we'll have a lot more to talk about," she finished. Now I had to focus more on my primping, although it was hard. Everyone was coming to my house at four p.m., and it was already one thirty. Lauren was doing a great job on my nails, using tiny brushes to make them a matte floral print. I was feeling confident enough to put on four-inch heels— which would make me five two—for my walk on the red carpet. During most of the primping, though, I was imagining what it would be like to be a twin.

At 1:57 p.m., Anaïs sent me a collage of photos of her from when she was young. Her resemblance to me when I was that age was even more startling than our current similarities, although we were still very alike. We briefly discussed being short. Anaïs told me she was 1.53 meters, so I had to have her convert that into feet. When the conversion was complete, we both came in at around four ten, short in either measurement system. I've been petite all my life! Maybe this was why! Twins are tiny! And squished! And like to hold hands!

Anaïs also sent photos of her birth records from her adoption agency, Holt International, which, oddly, was not the same as the one that had handled my case. It didn't make sense that twins would be sent to different agencies. We also had different surnames. Anaïs's surname at birth was "Kim," and mine was "Chung." Maybe our birth mother thought it would be easier for us to be adopted as singletons? If it were me giving up my children, I'd want them to stay together.

A lot of the information in Anaïs's records didn't match mine, but I had discovered during my roots tour that Korean birth information for adoptees was unreliable. For starters, unwed birth mothers might not provide truthful information because of their shame. In Korea, the stigma of being an unwed mother is so enormous that it is nearly impossible to raise her children alone. There is little government support, and the disgrace blankets the entire extended family. The children, as well as the mothers, are basically outcasts, forced from the family and ostracized by family, peers, employers, and anyone who knows their situation. Being a single mother can cause permanent loss of employment, housing, and social status. Ninety percent of infants relinquished for adoption are born to single mothers.

Many unwed mothers make it to birth homes where they can stay during the later stages of their pregnancies. After they have given birth and their babies are safely surrendered to foster care, they can escape the stigma and return to their lives because nobody knows their secret. When they are interviewed for the birth record, they can say anything they want, as there is no corroboration required. They could even choose not to register the birth at all, if they were giving the child up for adoption. Many don't want to be found—with the way society shames them, the price is too high. The more untruths they tell, the less likely they are to be tracked and accountable. Sadly, it is a really dire situation for these women. But I am aware that South Korea is making progress—painfully slow progress, but progress—to accept and support single mothers.

Besides the problem of untruths, another problem with the birth records is accurate translation. Translating from Korean into English or French is not straightforward, especially because of the different alphabets. Anaïs's record had inconsistencies from one page to the next. First, it stated that she had been born "full-term, natural delivery." One page later, it said she had been born "premature."

Our mothers' first names were different. As for our birth fathers, there was a surname on my form, but it had been filled in at a later date by an intake worker, claiming that my mother had come back after some time to provide more information about my father. The space for Anaïs's father was blank. My form mentioned an older sister, same father. Anaïs's form said that she was her mother's first delivery.

According to Anaïs's birth record, her birth mother had graduated from high school, was twenty-one years old, and worked in a plant. Her marital status was "unwed." Her birth father had also graduated from high school and also worked in a plant. He was twenty-eight and "unwed." The history of the pregnancy was quite detailed. When the natural mother went to a movie, she met the natural father. She was involved with him for about three months and became unintentionally pregnant. The natural father transferred to another job, and then the communication between the natural parents was cut off. The natural mother did not learn of her pregnancy until she was six months pregnant due to her irregular menstruation. She continued to work, but hid her pregnancy by binding her abdomen tightly. She left the plant fifteen days before she gave birth to the baby. As she could not bring up the baby adequately by herself "due to her unfavorable circumstances," she referred the baby to Holt, an international adoption agency, for adoption in view of the baby's "optimum future."

Other things on our birth records were also different. I weighed 5.3 pounds at birth, and Anaïs was 4.85 pounds. If we were full-term singletons, these would be considered low birth weights, but not extraordinary. Term Asian newborns were typically smaller than term Caucasian babies, and how "full-term" we were had not been established with any accuracy. One thing both records agreed on—we were single births. There was no indication of a twin birth on either record. Still, we had to be twins. We might have sounded like we were teasing when we said to each other, "Dude, we are so twins," but I think we both felt it without a shadow of a doubt.

I couldn't do much about this incredible situation at the moment. But, in these first two hours of contact, everything was beginning to fall into place. It's funny. In the thick of life, I sometimes think nothing will ever work out for me. Maybe it's the self-indulgent, feeling-bad-for-myself routine, but finding out I might be a twin changed everything. Maybe everything I had gone through in life so far was leading up to this very moment. If I had gotten bigger acting roles earlier in my career, maybe Anaïs might have spotted me sooner and this moment might have gone down already. But what if I hadn't been ready and able to handle having a twin? I had to assume timing was part of a master plan. Anaïs and I agreed that we would talk more in the next few days, and that we should *definitely* Skype!

Once in the car, I did what every person in L.A. does: started calling people. I called my dad first. "Dad, I'm a twin!" I blurted out when he answered.

"What?" he asked in dismay, thinking I was probably pranking him on his birthday, something I never fail to do. To convince him I wasn't kidding about a possible twin, I told him I had pictures of Anaïs to show him my evidence.

Next, I called my mom, who I knew would be on her way home from work. I shouted into the phone, "I'M A TWIN!"

"Hold on, I'm pulling over," she told me.

I told her not to worry, I'd talk to her more when we each got home.

Once at my apartment, I sent the profile picture of Anaïs to my family and friends even before I started on hair and makeup. My dad called me minutes later. He was initially pretty skeptical, especially as he is also a huge football fan and the Manti Te'o catfishing scandal was the hot sports story in the news. My father was worried that the Anaïs person might be an impostor. "Well, Sam," he said, "you don't look exactly alike." But after I sent him the pictures of Anaïs as a baby, he became more convinced. In fact, being an accountant, he came up with a statistic. "Okay, there's a ninety-one percent probability you are twins," he decided.

My mother was supportive, as always, although despite her excitement, her maternal instinct made her want to protect me. She told me not to get my hopes up prematurely, because she didn't want me to have them smashed if it turned out not to be true. I also sensed sadness in her, but I wasn't quite sure what it meant.

My friends were mind-blown by the news, as were my agents. My talent manager, Eileen, went nuts when she saw the screenshot of Anaïs. She had been my manager since I was ten, and she was like a second mother to me. Another of my agents at the time, Domina, didn't think it was true. When she finally believed me, she told me she knew a producer at *The Ellen DeGeneres Show*. "Do you want me to contact her?" she asked me. Agents, always working the angles!

The meeting point for those going to the premiere with

me was my place. I lived in an inexpensive, three-bedroom, two-and-a-half-bathroom apartment in midcity. The half bath was nasty. It had no natural ventilation, and when the vent fan was on, it smelled of mold. Black dust covered the walls of the laundry room. The woman who lived upstairs had a dog that barked every time it heard keys jingle. We never saw her walk it, but the carpet on the stairs going up to her apartment smelled of piss. The stove was greasy, and there were dead silverfish all over the walls. Our landlord was an adorable little old man, like liver-spots old. He liked to tell us romantic stories of traveling around the world to win his wife's heart. Because of his advanced age, getting him to fix things wasn't the easiest, so our apartment had a lot of maintenance issues, but we tried not to complain and made it as nice as it could be via IKEA.

My roommate was named Lisa. We knew each other briefly in New Jersey. We balanced each other very well. She couldn't cook, so I'd make dinner, and she'd clean up (she was obsessively neat). It was the perfect arrangement.

By four o'clock, everyone was in my living room—Kanoa, Justin Chon, Kevin Wu, Eileen, and a producer named James Yi. They had all been on the thread of text messages that had been going back and forth all day about the French girl. By the time they got to my apartment, everyone was in a weird state about it, and we couldn't stop discussing it. "I'm a twin . . . twin . . . I'm a twin," was all I could say.

How did I focus? Strangely, walking down the red carpet took my mind off the intensity of maybe having a twin. The thought of Anaïs relieved me of feeling self-conscious in front of the cameras. The awkward feeling I always got on the carpet, that I didn't belong, was trumped by knowing that across the world, there was someone just like me. Even in all the excitement of the entire evening, I kept checking my phone for messages. I was supposed to be charming and schmoozing, but all I could do was think about this girl, this French entity on my iPhone.

At some point in the evening, I posted a picture of me with Kevin on the red carpet. My brother Matt was the first to send a comment, "No, everyone can clearly see that's not you, that's @Anaïsfb." Anaïs commented next. "Oh, wow! I look fantastic in that dress!" I was feeling pressured. It was too soon for a comment like that. For the first time, I felt this was moving too fast. Anaïs's comment, certainly meant harmlessly, made me feel weird. You're invading my personal public space! I'm not ready to take this relationship to that level yet. What next? Are we going to confirm it on Facebook? Of course, I didn't respond. I just held on to my feelings to process them.

I headed into the theater to watch the premiere, but I kept thinking about Anaïs. I didn't socialize much the rest of the night. At the premiere party, I tossed back a whiskey on the rocks, my social aid to calm the nerves. Anaïs's picture, her Facebook message, and the reactions of my family and friends kept playing in my head.

The next morning, I woke up facedown on my bed opening one eye at a time, pretty groggy, slight headache, but that was to be expected after a few drinks. By the time I got my second eye opened, I remembered I had a long-lost twin! I was barely conscious, and she was already on my mind. I reached over and grabbed my cell phone to make sure it wasn't a dream. It opened up to Anaïs's Facebook profile. There she was, staring right at me. Her eyes . . . my eyes. Yup, it's true. She's my twin.

I jumped into the shower with just enough time to get ready for my first audition of the day. It was a dramatic part, and I had to be prepared to shed some tears in the third scene. After everything that had happened the day before, my emotions were free-flowing, so that wouldn't be a problem. Besides, I had a lot of energy that needed to be released. Sometimes, as an actor, you just have to take all the crazy energy and use it.

I truly was an aspiring actress in L.A. Part of me was really uncomfortable and annoyed with how seriously other actors took their "craft" and lifestyle. But the other part of me secretly enjoyed it, even if it was just because I got to make fun of it. People in L.A. could be so insanely pretentious— hiking in the hills around the city with full makeup and short monologues tucked into their yoga pants; green juice refrigerators in organic clothing stores; vegan/gluten-free substitutes available at every restaurant; and community tables at Starbucks packed with skinny vanilla latte–drinkers reading screenplays on their open laptops. These were not stereotypes, they were fact. I didn't mind it, because I had made some great friends in Los Angeles, and I was pursuing my dream. And for the record, I have never hiked with full makeup and audition lines tucked into my yoga pants, and if I ever do, punch me in the face.

I climbed into my car and headed for the audition, alternating my memorized lines and my twin's face/my face/my twin's face in my head. When I got to the casting office, I ran up the stairs to the audition waiting area and took a seat. No sooner was the audition over than I headed home to prepare for my next audition. For this one, I had to change my hair, makeup, and wardrobe to look older. When I was ready, I drove toward Santa Monica, again mixing the lines I had memorized with thoughts of the French girl and what I would say the next time we communicated. Should I "poke" her? Is there a three-day rule, like with boys? The ball was in my court. The audition in Santa Monica went well, but I wouldn't hear for a few days.

I wasn't obsessing over the auditions. I just wanted to sit behind the wheel, listen to music, get home, get into bed, and stalk Anaïs on Facebook. No sooner had I turned on my phone when up popped a message from Anaïs. Weird, she was already reading my mind.

"Hey Sam, how are you?" it read. "Hope everything is fine! I've seen some pictures of your premiere, you were super pretty! Can't wait to see the film now, haha! I'm going back to Paris tomorrow for the weekend for my mum's birthday. I'll try and find a few more documents, but my mum scanned pretty much everything already of what I've sent you." A few seconds later another message that included her Skype name popped up. "Whenever you want a little Skype session HAHAHA."

Ha ha ha, ugh! I wasn't sure I was ready to Skype yet. Time to drive home in traffic, which was the perfect excuse not to message her back immediately. I had to think this all through. I called Eileen to talk about how the audition had gone, but we talked about Anaïs instead. When I told her that Anaïs and I might Skype, she told me to hold off, to give it the weekend. She wanted to talk to some people first. I could tell she was already angling to control the story, with my best interest in mind, of course.

I actually felt a little relieved that I could postpone the Skype session with Anaïs, not sure if I was ready. Back home, my friends had all sorts of opinions about the inevitable Skype call. The consensus was that I should do it, and I should tape it. At first, it sounded like a great idea. But the more I thought about it, the more I felt as though it would be exploitive for both Anaïs and me. This was very private, and it was really only about the two of us. Why was I waiting to talk to her? Why was I letting other people weigh in? She was my twin! Not anybody else's! This was my life. On the other hand, it might be good to have it documented for posterity's sake. We would have it forever.

Conflicted, I called Kanoa to talk it through. When I told him that a lot of people had business suggestions for me about this story, he told me to think it through and do what I thought was right. He was spot-on, and I really needed to hear someone I trusted say it. Yes, the story could be a great business opportunity, but I had to make my own choices. I decided I was going to Skype Anaïs. I just couldn't do it tonight. My life had me working a full shift at the restaurant after a full day of auditions.

When I finally got home from the restaurant, I sat down at my computer to compose a message to Anaïs.

Anaïs! I am doing well (kind of true). Still
processing all this crazy information (yeah, that's
true). The premiere was great! It was definitely a
crazy day ☺ (input smiley face because you're
uncomfortable and don't know what else to say)
it'll be weird when you see the movie . . . cause it
will be you . . . but not . . . cause it's me . . . but
you . . . (input humor because you're
uncomfortable, and it makes it better.)

Ok! Great! I'll have my mom and dad take
pictures of my baby stuff. They live in New Jersey
and I'm in Los Angeles, so it's a bit far . . . but I'll
get it to you! (well . . . you made the effort. I
should, too.) Yes, please! Let's Skype! We will have
to figure out a time because of the time
difference.

How are you? How is your family processing this
information? Are you doing okay?

Love Sam

After I sent the message, I plopped onto my bed, curled
up under the covers, and logged on to Facebook. I looked at
Anaïs's pictures again and again, going back into her past as
recorded by her and her closest friends. It was literally a time-
line of all these years apart, up until the very moment she
made first contact. I could see the moments right there in the
palm of my hand.

5

ANAÏS

nothing is like family

Growing up, I wanted for nothing. I attended some of the best schools in Paris, traveled around the world, summered in the South of France, learned to play the piano, and had years of classical dance and horseback riding lessons, as many other kids from the wealthy suburbs of Paris do. But there was always a curiosity, a secret longing, to find another person who looked like me.

I can't say I didn't struggle with being of Korean heritage in a community as déconnectée, "disconnected," as Neuilly-sur-Seine. When I was a baby, a doctor who lived in our apartment building asked my mother what language I would be speaking when I started talking. My mother was appalled at his ignorance. "French, of course!" she told him, asking him what language he thought I would be speaking. Even though he was a doctor, he assumed I would miraculously know Korean just because I was born in Korea. My mother was right to think he was awfully narrow-minded.

When I was in kindergarten, my family was living in Belgium. I would go to friends' houses for playdates, where I would find myself being served white rice by mothers proud that they were "accommodating" me. This was well-meaning but insulting at the same time. Even now, people in my town who don't know me assume I must be a maid or house cleaner when they see me in the elevator of my parents' apartment building, where they have lived only a couple of years. In Neuilly, a lot of the household help comes from South Asia, and there are not so many Asian-looking people in the area. But I am not foreign. I speak French, I eat French, and I dress French. France is my homeland, and I am as French as my parents.

February 22 was my mum's birthday. I really wanted to see her and my dad. I just wanted to be with them. Sam had posted a few more images on Twitter and Facebook, and it was all becoming real. She was there. She was tangible, and we had exchanged messages. Some of her Facebook postings were mentioning her father's birthday, so even he was becoming real. How cool was it that her dad and my mum had almost the same birthday! Just one day apart.

During my first call to them since the discovery, I had been almost crying, because I had finally made contact with Samantha. During the second call, I had been shouting at Mum to send my birth records as fast as she could, so I could send them to Samantha. Sam had sent me hers, and I wanted to send her mine. By the third phone call, I was out of my mind with glee. I told Mum to send me some of my baby pictures, so I could share them with Sam. My father was becoming quite moved by the whole thing, even though he had been the last holdout. I was his little girl and his only child, so he was having a hard time imagining two identical "me"s.

My father had come from a large family. He grew up on a small farm in the central Loire Valley in a tiny village between the cities of Orléans and Chartres. My grandfather, Gaston Bordier, was a wheat farmer. With his wife, Madeleine, they had five children, my father being the oldest boy. He had an older sister, two younger sisters, and a younger brother. He loved growing up on the farm, and he worked alongside his father wherever he needed help. He wanted to go to university, travel, learn languages, and maybe become an academic. He was a bit of a perfectionist. Everything he undertook, he wanted to do well. His first job was with Air France, but he went to school at the same time. When he finished his studies and passed all his university exams, he held various executive positions, which later gave him the idea of having his own business. He finally took over a leather goods company, which he positioned in the luxury segment.

My mother was hardworking, too. She was the perfect right-hand woman when my parents purchased the business. She grew up in Troyes, a beautiful medieval city in the Champagne region southeast of Paris by one hundred kilometers. Her father, Jacques Wach, was a successful accountant. My grandfather and my grandmother, Simone, had two children. My mother was five and a half years older than her brother, Gilles.

Gilles is now a monsignor in the Catholic Church and runs a seminary that he established himself outside of Florence. My mum has a great story about how young my uncle had been when he knew he had a calling from God. The family used to go to church occasionally, although they weren't particularly devout. They had a country house near Troyes where they went in the summers, and one day after mass, my mother saw Uncle Gilles in the garden near the house. He was five years old at the time. He had taken all my mother's dolls and arranged them so they were all looking toward him. He was wearing my grandmother's black skirt like a robe and was performing Mass for the dolls. My mother ran to get my grandmother, who asked him what he was playing.

"*Non*, Maman, I'm not playing," he said. "I will be priest one day."

As he predicted, my uncle was ordained into the Roman Catholic Church. John Paul II performed his ordination in 1979, when my uncle was twenty-three years old. When I was baptized, it was Uncle Gilles who did the honor.

My mother enjoyed a pampered girlhood. She rode and jumped horses, beginning at age twelve. She even had her own horse. When I began riding at age eight, she would often ride with me. Every summer in her youth, my mother's family went to the South of France, either to the Mediterranean or the Atlantic Coast. Mum was really smart and well educated, and attended university in England. She met my dad at a party in Paris. It was love at first sight. They had many things in common, and they knew right away they had found their partner for life.

My parents were married in 1976 in Troyes. They wanted to start a family, but not right away, not before they had a good financial standing. When they tried to conceive a baby several years later, they were unsuccessful. They immediately turned to adoption, as they decided not to go through infertility treatments, my mum knowing she would be just as happy with an adopted child, and wanting a family more than anything. She and my father decided they wanted a child from Korea, and Korea only. My mother said it was in her heart. She wasn't sure why, but she felt very, very strongly about it. My father felt the same way. He even started to teach himself Korean in anticipation.

My parents didn't realize that being this particular about a country was going to be problematic. In France, there is a specific process for adoption. First, social services needs to agree that the applicants are suitable to be parents of an adopted child. When they are approved, a couple must decide if they want to adopt domestically or internationally. My parents chose to go through a specific association, Amis des Enfants du Monde (AEM), Friends of the Children of the World. When my parents said they were only interested in a baby from Korea, the agency was upset, saying a child is a child wherever he or she is from.

My mother was not dissuaded. She told the representative if the application didn't go to Korea, she and my father would find another adoption agency that would accommodate them, so Korea or nothing. It was very important to her that she feel a connection with her child's birth country, and for no explainable reason, her connection was with Korea.

My mum had put a lot of thought into her decision. She was making a choice not just for the baby in infancy, but for that child's entire lifetime. In her opinion, parents adopting internationally hadn't always prepared themselves for the added hardship involved in raising a child from another country here in France.

In slightly less than two years, my parents got their authorization. Just before Christmas in 1987, my parents got word from AEM that their baby girl had been born, weighing in at 2.2 kilos (about four pounds, thirteen ounces), and measuring forty-four centimeters long (about seventeen inches). The first physical exam report said I was "cute and tiny," although I wouldn't be arriving in France for six months. Their first photo of me was sent to them when I was four days old, newly transferred from the private clinic in Busan to the Holt Institute in Seoul, the adoption agency in Korea that worked with AEM in France. A few days later, my parents got a second, more official photo of me, with a matriculation number, and my Korean name, Kim Eun Hwa. In Korean, Eun means "silver," and Hwa means "flower."

A few weeks later, the agency sent a picture that showed a sizable strawberry-colored vascular birthmark on my head. These unsightly growths, called hemangiomas, are fairly common on newborns and are usually cosmetic. My mum, wanting to make sure it wasn't something of great concern, took my photo to my future pediatrician, and he reassured her that it would disappear completely by the time I was nine years old.

Now, it was time to pick a name. There were a lot of little girls named Anaïs in the South of France, where they spent a lot of time, and the name worked for them for very special reasons. For one, "Anaïs" was popular in the South of France, and I was from the southern part of Korea. For another, "Anaïs" was a near homonym to "Hanae" (pronounced Hana-e), the word for "flower" in Japanese. That would complement the fact that my Korean name used "flower." Yes, "Anaïs" had a lot of meaningful interpretations that made it the perfect choice.

The initial information given to my parents by the agency in Seoul was that I would be arriving sometime in May, six months after my birth. Therefore, my mother felt no need to rush to furnish my nursery and stock my drawers. Suddenly, on the last Monday in February, a woman called and said I would be arriving on a flight that very Saturday. My mother was in a panic, as she hadn't prepared my nursery yet. All her friends came forward to help her find a crib, clothing, diapers, formula, toys, blankets, and everything else that the new baby would need. My crib, which was shipped to the house, arrived in fifteen complicated pieces, so there was another scramble to find someone to help my father build it. Thanks to their friends, everything was done in five short days.

On March 5, 1988, I made my grand arrival. I was one of four children from Korea who were landing at Charles de Gaulle Airport that day. Two of us were infants, myself and another little girl the same age. The other two were older, a two-year-old girl and a seven-year-old boy. We were accompanied by one employee of the Holt Agency, who had been assigned to deliver us.

I was sleeping soundly when I was taken off the plane. My mum said that when she took me in her arms for the first time, she bonded with me immediately. In that second, she knew she was holding her own child, born from her own heart. According to Mum, I suddenly opened my eyes and looked at her, then smiled before closing them again. She said that I was sleeping so deeply during the car ride home, she had to pinch me to see if I was still breathing. As for my dad, he was nothing but really happy!

I love the story my mum tells about when we first arrived at the apartment as a family of three. We had a six-year-old apricot poodle named Twist, who wasn't sure if he was thrilled to meet me or not. My parents didn't want him to get too close to me, fearing germs. In fact, Mum and Dad were so nervous that I would contract some weird germ that they put white lab coats over their clothes to give me my first bottle. My mum's covered her festive red turtleneck and stylish black-and-white slacks, and Dad's hid his snappy casual blue button-down shirt, black sweater, and jeans. Every moment was captured in photos.

From the stories, I apparently opened my eyes with a little bit of panic. My mum said I had that worried *Where am I?* look. She tried to give me my bottle but when I didn't drink, my dad took over. He was quite proud that he had been successful until I started crying, as the formula didn't agree with me. My parents called a neighbor, who was a pediatrician, and he told them about a special milk that was available. I was about to grow up in France being lactose intolerant. Talk about a difficult road ahead.

My mum remembers every one of my "firsts." I took my first steps on my first birthday. On my first Christmas, we had a white tree decorated with white bulbs, Santa ornaments, and a red bow tied to the top. I wore a red dress and a white blouse and received my first doll from Santa, a boy doll in a blue pajama. I named him Baby Gilles in honor of my uncle. Of all my dolls, he was my favorite, and I carried him in a backpack everywhere I went. He is still in my room today.

For the first three years of my life, my parents and I lived in Neuilly-sur-Seine, ranked as one of the wealthiest communities in France. Nicolas Sarkozy, the future president of France, was the mayor of Neuilly at the time of my arrival. He often had breakfast at the little Café du Parc bistro on Rue de Chézy right near my school. My mother would sometimes see him there when she stopped in for coffee after dropping me off in the mornings.

Partly because it was so beautiful, Neuilly was home to a lot of well-known people—actors, writers, athletes, politicians, and diplomats, all living there in relative privacy. The wide boulevards that Neuilly is known for were once part of the grounds of the Château de Neuilly, home to King Louis Phillip I. Neuilly also had the Bois de Boulogne, the second-largest park in Paris; the American Hospital of Paris, renowned as one of the best hospitals in France; and the headquarters of the *International Herald Tribune*, now the *International New York Times*. It was a fantastic place to live, because it was so close to the heart of Paris, yet far enough to be a refuge of peace and quiet.

Exactly one day after my third birthday, we moved to Brussels. My father had taken a job as a general manager at a cosmetics company, with a territory covering Belgium, the

Netherlands, and Luxembourg. My mother threw me a small celebration with a cake at school, but the next day, we were in the car, heading to Belgium. Dad had found us an amazing, beautiful duplex in the center of the city, fifteen minutes from his office. It was two hundred square meters, more than two thousand square feet. The open staircase to the upstairs level scared me, but I loved the terrace that overlooked Cinquantenaire Park. I made my first snowman on that terrace.

My mother loved the apartment, although she hated the move. We didn't know anybody, and the weather was dreadful. Things got better the following Easter, when all the parents of my preschool friends were renting houses on the North Sea. My mother found a rental for us, too, figuring it was our one chance to make some friends. She was right. We all had a great time in Knokke, a seaside resort about seventy miles northwest of Brussels. She liked our new home better after that.

I liked Brussels from the start. My favorite thing to do was to dress up in costumes, my interest in style manifesting itself early. I especially loved my sequined Harlequin getup, and I would walk around town wearing it as I hauled Baby Gilles on my back in his baby backpack.

My school was friendly and warm. When I learned one of my teachers was having a baby, I was so impressed that I needed to share the news with my mother. "Maman, you will never guess what is in the belly of Madame!" I exclaimed when I got home.

"I guess it's a baby," my mum answered.

"Was I in your belly, too?" I asked her in curiosity.

Mum's answer confused me. "Anaïs, you were always in my heart, but there was another woman who gave birth to you. You were made in another woman."

"What other woman?" I demanded. How on earth would that work?

"This woman couldn't be your mother, so she gave you to us," my mother continued.

I didn't have any more questions. The concept was too strange, and there was nothing else I could ask.

Not long after that I started to realize what my schoolmates meant when they said, "You don't look anything like your mother." They were saying, "She can't be your mother. She is blond with blue eyes, and you are Chinese." I still didn't know what to make of it. One afternoon, I came home from school totally distraught. "Was I abandoned? Did you find me in the garbage?" I asked my mother. I had seen a news story about a baby being found in the garbage in the Philippines on TV, and a boy at school, who had probably seen the same story, said that this is what probably happened to me—I was abandoned in the garbage, and my mother found me there.

"No, Anaïs, you were never abandoned," my mother assured me. "The woman who gave birth to you, she immediately gave you to us. You were never abandoned. Look, we have a picture of you at four days, right after you were born."

I didn't ask any more questions, but this abandonment thing didn't go away just because my mother shared a picture. This boy had really riled up feelings in me, and I didn't know what to do or think. I loved my mother more than anybody, but who was this other mother she was talking about? And why wasn't I with her?

For the first time, I felt really lonely inside. I tried to appear like I was taking the information in stride, but I had a pain that was hard to describe. It still stays with me to this day. No matter how I looked at it, I couldn't shake the feeling that something had gone wrong at the very start of my life. My birth mother couldn't keep me, so I must have been a problem for her. My parents really wanted me, but had they been able to conceive a child of their own, they wouldn't have needed to adopt me. The feelings were difficult and complicated, and nothing I wanted to share. I loved my parents, but voicing my loneliness was impossible. Instead, I worked on burying it.

Most of the time, I didn't worry about what my birth mother meant, as I was completely happy with my real mother. I did have a temper, and I could be in a bad mood if I had a night of strange dreams. I also had strong anxiety and sad moments for no reason. Sometimes I sensed that I had been ripped off from something, but the feeling was so bizarre, there was no way I could have put it into words. There is a picture of me I posted on Instagram, a young me playing with my two dolls, Baby Gilles and another one. It is hard to find a childhood picture of me without Baby Gilles. It went well beyond that he was my favorite. I never left him behind. I had to carry him everywhere, and if by chance I forgot him, I was panicked that he might disappear forever. He was my constant wherever I went, and we needed each other. Nobody was going to rip me away from Baby Gilles.

My family stayed in Brussels for three and a half years. When my father was promoted, we had to return to Neuilly, which made me very unhappy. Although he left for Paris in February 1994, my mum and I stayed in Brussels until the school year ended in April. I was learning to read, and Mum felt I needed all my lessons, so I would be at my grade level when I got back to Saint Dominique. There, I was one of the best readers in my class, which, of course, made my parents proud.

Returning to school in France was like being the new kid. I didn't really have any friends, and my classmates were all bonded and not really looking for anybody else. I missed my schoolmates in Brussels and the system we had of entering the classroom in twos holding hands, kind of like in the Madeleine books. At Saint Dominque, it was every kid for himself. The good news was that I was not the shortest child in my grade, as I had been in Brussels. There were two girls who were both two centimeters (almost an inch) shorter than I was, and we became instant friends.

Starting at a young age, my mum had me enrolled in a lot of extracurricular activities, which I loved. I tried piano, ballet, and horseback riding, and I wanted to do everything to the best of my ability, sharing the same kind of drive with my dad in that respect. If I wasn't motivated, I lost interest fast. In piano, I needed the challenge of a competitive recital. My father bought me an upright early on in my playing, and with lots of practice, I advanced nicely. But once I reached a level where there were no more recitals, I was done. The same thing happened in ballet. The dance school was right next to my school, and I loved going. I was at ballet class practically every day, steadily advancing my level. But one day my ballet instructor appointed another girl to a competition I wanted to be in, and I quit.

Horseback riding was good as long as I was improving and striving for a goal. My mum and I took advantage of the horses for hire in the huge park with a state-of-the-art equestrian center near our apartment, so if I wasn't at a lesson, we were trail riding or practicing in the ring. I rode from the ages of eight to fifteen, but when I fell off a horse and broke my arm, I had to take a leave. When I was healed, I was only willing to ride again if I could be on the competitive team, and as that required too many hours away from my studies, I gave up horses, too. If it wasn't competitive, I wasn't interested.

When I was seven and a half, my parents took me to Korea for two weeks during the Easter holiday. The objective of the trip wasn't to reconnect with anybody—it was for pure pleasure, visiting the country, eating the food, speaking the language, seeing the people, and touring the sites. The flight was endless, more than twenty hours in transit, but I made friends with a small Korean boy seated in front of me. One of the stewardesses gave me the Korean Air logo pin with the tiny wings, which my mother keeps stored in a treasure box of mementos in the apartment. My parents were excited to show me the country of my birth. They had never been there, either, and my dad was really looking forward to practicing his Korean.

In Seoul, we stayed at the Hotel Grand Ambassador. The hotel had a huge buffet with food from different countries. Some of my memories are from the journal I kept in a tiny little spiral notebook, which I called "Voyage en Corée." I wrote in it faithfully throughout the trip, even though the entries were very short. I was also the illustrator, drawing everything that struck me as worthy, from the plane's window to the kind of cars people were driving. My entries briefly touched on my viewings of a palace, a prison, a temple, Korean dances, and some beautiful moons. It was a Korean travel guide on a shoestring. I even practiced my script handwriting.

I was too young to fully appreciate the idea that this was the country of my heritage. The trip was more emotional for my parents than it was for me. The Korean people were fabulous and welcoming. Some people in the adoption agency in Paris had told my parents that it might not be a good idea to bring me there, because the people feel humiliated that they cannot take care of their own. We found that they couldn't have been more hospitable toward all of us.

Upon our return, my teacher invited my parents to make a presentation about Korea to the class. Mum and Dad created a slide show and brought all the trinkets and souvenirs we had bought, including a *hanbok*, the national costume. I modeled it for the presentation. It was gorgeous, with beautiful vibrant colors, a great big skirt, a tiny jacket, big sleeves, and embellishments of ribbons. The presentation turned Korea into a real place for my classmates, who had been prone to think everything Asian was either Chinese or Japanese. Many of them hadn't even heard of Korea. They asked my parents a lot of questions, confirming their curiosity.

A few days later, someone who wasn't in my class said on the playground that I was Chinese. One of the boys in my class corrected him. "Anaïs isn't Chinese," he said. "She is coming from Korea." I finally had an identity that other people could now understand and they would not lump me in with all Asians anymore. I know that they didn't mean any harm by it, but they didn't really know or care about what country you might come from. Some French kids were snobby, too, especially at my school, which was almost exclusively French. It was hard to pinpoint exactly what made me uncomfortable, but Neuilly was filled with rather conservative families who could trace their ancestries back for generations. Some of the teachers had been at the school so long, they had instructed the mothers and grandmothers of my classmates. French schools were strict and competitive with rigid, old-fashioned ways. In Belgium, we wrote with pencils, but here we had to use quill pens. Although I was ambidextrous, I tended to use my left hand, but the French educators were trained to encourage us to be right-handed. Parents were really invested in having their kids be the best at everything and applied lots of pressure. I was a good student because I had a lot of pressure on me, but it was a lot of stress.

In sixth grade, I had to choose between English and German for my second language. I knew a little English, as I had spent three weeks in London when I was eleven. I had stayed with my Japanese-American friend Miku and her family. Miku had a Japanese mother and an American father. We had known them in Belgium, but they were now living in the Wimbledon area, southwest of London, which had a thriving expat Korean community. It was my first time living in a neighborhood with people who looked something like me, and it was great. We ate lots of Korean food and went to lots of places that had Korean takeaway, something we didn't have in Paris. The children had folders of tiny Korean stickers, another novelty for me. The stickers were colorful, glittery, weirdly shaped animals or Korean characters that we did not have in France. Besides the thrill of being in a Korean community, I also learned a little English.

When the time came to choose between German and English, I wanted to study German, despite my previous exposure to English. But then *Harry Potter and the Goblet of Fire* happened. I had read the first three installments in French, but I wanted to read the fourth one the moment it came out, which meant it would only be available in English. At eight thirty a.m. it went on sale for the midnight release in New York, and I went to WH Smith booksellers at Place de la Concorde to wait. WH Smith was the one English-language bookstore that I knew would be carrying it, and one half hour later, promptly at nine, when the doors opened, I headed straight to the stack of books, grabbed my copy, and made my purchase. I spent the summer reading it in English with the help of a French/English dictionary. By the end of the summer, my English was pretty good, and I opted to take English as my second language. There were going to be other Harry Potter books coming, and I had to be prepared.

When I was fifteen, I wanted to change my birth date from November 19, 1987, to March 5, 1988, the day that I first arrived in France and my life started. We called it my "Arrival Day," and it was far more important to me than my actual birthday. On March 5, we'd always go to Samo, our favorite

Korean restaurant on Rue du Champ de Mars. We loved to order the bulgogi, Korean BBQ. We'd eat out on my real birthday, too, but not necessarily at a Korean restaurant. I just liked my Arrival Day, the day I became part of my real family, better.

In Saint Dominique's secondary school, which is equivalent to American high school, the academic pressure was insane. Classes were from eight a.m. to six p.m., and we had a four-hour test every Wednesday to train us for the baccalaureate, on top of our schoolwork and tests from our regular classes. Besides the academics, there was also the annual theatrical production. In my baccalaureate year, the equivalent of a senior year in high school, I designed the whole set, from conceiving how it would look to doing the drawings we would work from. It was so fun, I considered doing something with theater professionally. However, my parents were not very enthusiastic about that. They thought child actors and models were exploited and advised me to wait until I was eighteen if I wanted to pursue anything with theater. I also liked acting and being onstage, but I was entering art school and didn't see the point. I always thought that I would catch up with cinema at some time, either in costume design, set design, or acting. I loved going to the movies and the theater, but there weren't many roles available for Asian-looking people.

Right until I graduated from Saint Dominque, I was vacillating between medical school and art school. When my biology teacher heard I was considering art, he tried to talk me out of it, convinced I was meant to study biology. My test scores were so high, he hated to see me pursue anything else.

There was a feeling that for good students, the better career choices were engineer, politician, doctor, or attorney, so why would you go to art school?

My mother wanted me to become a doctor. She thought it would be a good profession for me, and it would offer me a steady and secure income. She also knew it would allow me great flexibility to choose where I wanted to work. Surprisingly, it was my father who helped her accept that I was going to art school. He thought I would be disappointed with medicine, either doing research with very little money for my lab or being a general practitioner and finding it boring. He knew I was passionate about art, even if I had to be a starving artist. He believed it would make me happy for all my life, even if I couldn't make a living from it.

I am happy I went to design school. I got to meet a lot of people from all over the world, and it was from there that I found Samantha. It was my destiny. Otherwise, I wouldn't have been in London, so I wouldn't have met Kelsang, so he wouldn't have known to show me KevJumba's video, and I might have lived the rest of my life never knowing Samantha existed.

6

SAM

we. are. family. get up,
everybody, and sing!

When I was a kid, I always wanted my parents to get another child. I wanted a younger sibling, someone to take care of, despite the fact that I loved the attention and glory of being the one and only baby girl. And let's be honest, Asian babies are cute. Naturally, as a baby and little girl, I got a lot of attention, not only from my family, but from friends of the family and strangers as well. I'd be lying if I said that I didn't enjoy it. Still, a sister would be cool. I was always envious of the girls who could wear their big sister's clothes to school and then get into a fight with them about it at recess. I certainly wasn't going to wear my brothers' cut-off shirts and smelly sneakers. They didn't even fit!

I really wanted a little sister, so I could paint her nails and do her hair. I wanted someone to look up to me, and I wanted to give her all my wise knowledge. Being a little girl myself, I'm pretty sure I didn't have much knowledge, except for how to tie my dance shoes properly and how many times in a row I should brush my hair to make it shiny, something I learned on the many sleepovers I attended, where my friends and I watched the movie *Now and Then*.

Of course, if I were going to get a little sister, my parents would have to "buy" her, too. At times during my childhood, I joked to my parents that they had "bought" me, although I never resented that I was "at cost" to them, and I was never angry that they wanted me because I was a girl. In fact, I actually didn't find out that they specifically wanted a girl until I was much older. But, if they hadn't wanted a girl, I wouldn't be here today, so how could I be mad at them for that? I never felt like I was a purchase. But, I guess in some sense, joking is a passive-aggressive form of confrontation. Sometimes you need to laugh at a situation and call it out for what it really is. But the truth is that my parents wanted another child to love for the rest of their lives, and that was that.

I don't think I ever imagined having a twin. I mean, as I got older, I wanted to find someone who looked like me. Yes, a lot of Asians look alike. There, I said it. But I had yet to find someone in the world who I thought looked just like me. I'm incredibly short and have a really strange profile, freckles, boobs, and a butt. These aren't the typical Korean attributes. Not that my brothers have a striking resemblance to my parents, either, but I never even had the option to look like someone. How would I know what to expect? What wrinkles am I going to get? At what age will I start to get fat? Will I have spider veins? I had no model on which to base my theoretical "aging" scenario.

As a kid, I remember thinking about my reflection. When I looked in the mirror, I didn't see a small Asian girl. I saw a small white girl. I aspired to have the blue eyes and blond hair like seemingly everyone else in Verona, New Jersey. Yet I wasn't disappointed when I looked in the mirror. I guess my image of beauty came from my family. When I imagined myself being beautiful, it was looking like my parents and my brothers. But my reflection brought me back to reality. I never imagined being able to stand across from someone, look directly into her eyes, and see myself.

I have always known that I was adopted. It is like knowing that the grass is green and the sky is blue. Some parents choose a particular time or an "appropriate" age to tell their children that they are adopted. But, for me, there really wasn't a chance that I wasn't adopted—my parents are a different race. It was never a problem for me, because it wasn't presented as such. My mom was my mom, my dad was my dad, and my brothers were my brothers.

Adoption was always part of the Futerman family plan. My parents discussed it early on in their relationship. The idea appealed to both of them. They say it wasn't for any altruistic reason. They weren't looking to help a "poor orphan" somewhere. They just wanted to have one or two biological children and adopt one or two more. Little did they know, they would end up with bratty me—and maybe a French "plus one."

And so the plan went. They already had two biological sons, my brothers, Matthew and Andrew, when they started the process to adopt a third child. Apparently my mom had been putting Andrew's baby clothes into storage boxes when the feeling hit her that she wasn't done. Either that or she was manifesting the beginning of her mild hoarding syndrome— not legit, just diagnosed by a couple of perceptive individuals, myself included. My parents began with a domestic adoption agency, Catholic Charities, but they were told the wait could be eight to ten years, and they didn't want to wait that long. Their sons were both under the age of six, and they wanted their next child to be relatively close in age to them. As this was going on, Matt made a new friend at preschool, an adopted Korean girl. My parents liked the idea of adopting a child from Korea and asked the girl's parents how they had gone about it.

My parents were told about Spence-Chapin Adoption Services, and they took the recommendation. At the agency, the intake person explained the adoption procedures, paperwork, and parental age requirements so clearly that my mother was scared that she and my father might not qualify. Next came the discussion regarding fees and expenses. Now my parents were not only scared but shocked. The costs were very high, between New York agency fees, Korea agency fees, foster care fees, airfare for the baby, and airfare and fees for the baby's escort. At the time, babies were "escorted" to the parents' home country. Few, if any, parents actually picked up their child in the country of birth. My parents weren't poor, but they weren't rich, either, and they wondered if they could really afford it. There were also the eighteen years of costs to raise me, and college tuition . . . but, hey, I think it was a safe business investment. My parents did, too. They took a second mortgage on their home in Verona, to pay the expenses.

Spence-Chapin was extremely thorough. The social workers not only talked to our family pediatrician, but they investigated our neighborhood to be sure that a Korean child would not have trouble living there. There was a family meeting at the agency with my parents, Matt, and Andrew. My parents also attended one or two group meetings with other potential adoptive parents, which, they said, felt like group analysis. All of this, of course, was to prepare them for how the arrival of a Korean baby would change, and add to, their family dynamics.

My parents filled out mountains of paperwork. Because they already had two sons, it was mentioned that they could request a daughter, and although there was no promise, every possible effort would be made to see this happen. It was also mentioned that considering their ages—my dad was in his early forties, my mom was in her late thirties—Korea would not approve another adoption later down the road. So, my parents' initial plan of "one or two biological children and one or two adopted" turned into "one adopted." They requested a daughter and began the wait.

Less than a year after starting to work with Spence-Chapin, my father received a phone call that their baby had been born. He ecstatically located my mother to tell her it was a girl. Although I had been born in November 1987, my parents first heard about my birth in January 1988.

To announce my arrival, my father sent bouquets of pink flowers to both my grandmothers with a card that read, "It's a girl!" My maternal grandmother was working in a small children's clothing store at the time, and the owner of that shop sent my parents the entire girls' display from the window.

My paternal grandmother, meanwhile, bought every pink item of clothing she could find.

Then came the scary news. The social worker called my parents to say that the Korean agency had reported that I had a serious birth defect, so serious, in fact, that my parents could refuse me and take the next baby available. My parents were thinking . . . eleven fingers and twelve toes . . . no face . . . half panda. To be certain my parents understood what they were getting into, the agency in Korea sent them three pictures of me, one where I was being held by my foster mother, and two where my arm with the "serious birth defect" was circled and highlighted with arrows. My mother has since been told that this strawberry patch was once considered a sign of bad luck in Korea, but we are not sure if it meant bad luck for the child or the parents, or if this is even the truth. A medical report was forwarded to our pediatrician, and the "serious" defect was nothing more than a raised strawberry patch birthmark, known as a hemangioma, on my left arm. Our doctor assured my parents it would be gone before my second birthday.

My parents did not delay with the adoption. In my mother's heart and mind, I was her baby, even if the hemangioma had been problematic. My foster mother wrote my mom and dad a letter in Korean, which the social worker translated and read to them over the phone. It said that I was her first foster child, and that she never put me down, but always carried and cuddled me. She warned them that I had my days and nights confused, and although I would fall asleep eventually, I preferred to be held on her shoulder to do so. How unbelievable to have been loved so much by my first caretaker.

My parents had a wait of more than two months to finally meet me, so they had time to prepare my nursery, set up my crib, and baby-proof the house. Mom also received her special gift from Dad—whenever a baby arrives in my family, my dad buys Mom a piece of jewelry to commemorate the event. For Matt's birth in 1982, Mom got a diamond band ring. For Andrew, born in 1985, Dad gave her a diamond necklace. When I was born, she got a gold bangle bracelet with bits of jade and emerald, the green gems chosen to represent Korea.

On March 21, 1988, my parents, accompanied by my two brothers, drove to New York's John F. Kennedy International Airport to await my arrival. It is so strange to think that only two weeks prior, six time zones away, a French couple was picking up a little Korean girl at Paris's international airport—a baby born the same day as me.

Throughout the adoption process, my mother's motives were transparent—she wanted her third baby, end of story. She hadn't worried about taking care of a third one, as she already had a supremely supportive, loving family. What my mother didn't tell me until very recently was that the night before I arrived in New Jersey, she had a major panic attack. Suddenly, she felt guilty that she had subconsciously been "stacking the deck" to ensure herself a daughter. She also feared that bringing me to New Jersey was selfish and not the best choice for me, that she wasn't as capable of taking care of three young children, that our town would not accept me, that I would have no friends. Overcome with anxiety, she fell to pieces, crying uncontrollably in the shower. She managed to pull herself together for the trip to the airport on very little sleep.

My parents had informed their families that they wanted the day of my arrival to be private, i.e., no grandparents or other relatives, just the two of them and my brothers. After a suitable time of bonding with me at home in Verona, they would then invite small groups of the family to visit. As is typical with my family, nobody listened or complied because that plan sounded really boring. My paternal grandmother, my father's brother, and my maternal grandparents all "happened to be at JFK airport" that day. It wasn't all bad. There were little coin-operated TVs attached to chairs in the waiting area, and my grandfather would plunk in quarters so my brothers, then six and two, could have something to keep them busy.

Nine other adoptive families were also waiting for this flight. Suddenly a plane was spotted out the window of the terminal, slowly taxiing in their direction, and just as suddenly stopping. My brothers jumped from their TVs and glued their faces to the window. Let's be honest, they were thrilled to see an airplane so close—they didn't jump out of their seats in anticipation of my arrival.

All nine families watched and waited. Most of the passengers had already deplaned at another gate, so only the nine Korean babies and one medical student, the escort, remained on board. One escort taking care of nine babies all the way from Seoul . . . a fourteen-hour flight! I would have hated being on that plane. Oops, I was.

There was a social worker from Spence-Chapin waiting with the families, who explained that only one family member could go aboard to collect the baby. My father jumped to attention. He was the first in line to board the plane, but the last to come off. He had to go from baby to baby, searching for the wrist bracelet that said "Futerman," so it had taken him a while to find me in the far back, bundled in a yellow knitted ensemble complete with matching booties with appliquéd butterflies, handmade for me by my foster mother.

When my father finally emerged, he was beaming so proudly that in photos his broad smile could be seen even under his massively oversized Super Mario mustache. He held me facing forward so that everyone in the family could see me. Grand entrance, indeed.

Mom said I wasn't alone in being fashionably dressed—all the babies wore adorable little outfits and looked extremely cared for and loved. When Dad and I reached her, I looked right into her eyes with the biggest, most beautiful smile she had ever seen, and all of her fears from the night before disappeared. I looked so confident and self-assured, as if I recognized the whole family and immediately knew that they were mine. I'm still amazed how in a matter of seconds, I took complete control of the family, and I was only four months old. I was theirs, and they were mine, and everything couldn't have been better.

My mother got to hold me for a brief moment before the grandmothers descended on me, and I was passed around from grandma to grandma to grandpa to uncle. The pictures we have from that day are awesome reminders of the monumental event.

Everything at JFK did not go completely smoothly. As my mother relaxed into comfortable mom-under-control mode with her (now!) three well-behaved kids, my brother Andrew took on the power challenge. He had gotten it into his head that the families could pick the baby they wanted from the airplane. I was as bald as Daddy Warbucks, but Andrew had seen some of the other parents come off the plane with babies sporting really cool hairstyles, and he wanted one of those. He had a special liking for one with a tiny Mohawk. My mother was mortified, having been trying to impress the social worker with how "perfect" her family was. But now she was carrying Andrew like a football tucked under her arm out of the airport while he screamed, "I didn't want that one, I wanted the one with the Mohawk!" It was my day, but Andrew was trying to steal the attention. His middle-child syndrome had begun.

From JFK, the family went back to my maternal grand-parents' house, where lunch and a baby shower were held in my honor. My mom said that the days that followed were busy, crazy, and wonderful, the love she felt for me growing boundlessly. It wasn't always easy. There were days when she was overwhelmed with the needs of three children. Laundry quadrupled in the basement. My brothers, while loving me immediately and taking great pride in playing with me, also acted out. Matt had never been easy when a new baby came. Several weeks after Andrew had been born, he wanted to know, "When does that kid go back?" So, Matt acting out for attention when I came home was not a surprise. Andrew also had his moments. His best came when my father was going on a business trip. Mom told him Dad would be going to the airport soon. Andrew looked at her with total horror and asked: "He's not getting another kid, is he?"

I was two years old when I was formally adopted on

March 22, 1990. Four months later, on July 17, I became a U.S. citizen and received my Certificate of Citizenship. Pictures of that day show me at a huge family barbecue in my backyard on the Fourth of July. I am dressed in a fun red, white, and blue outfit. I have a fleeting memory of my mother trying to pose me next to my brothers for photos, although all I wanted to do was climb on the swing set. I wore the same patriotic dress at the swearing-in ceremony thirteen days later. That event even made the front page of the local paper, the *Verona–Cedar Grove Times*. Mom had sent them a little announcement, expecting it to run in the "Births" column. Instead, a reporter came to the house for an interview with her and a picture of me, dressed in the outfit and waving an American flag. My mom still has several yellowed copies of the paper.

When I was growing up, my mother used to read me stories of adoption. My favorite one was *The Mulberry Bird: An Adoption Story* by Anne Braff Brodzinsky. I loved hearing about how the single mother bird came to the decision to give her baby boy bird to a family of birds that could better take care of him. I loved the happy ending. I could always sleep well after that.

Some adoptees have a real *aha!* moment when they realize what it means to be adopted: that they were taken from or given away by their parents and raised by others not in their genetic lineage. Because I didn't look like my parents, I didn't need such enlightenment. Adoption was just a part of my life, and my definition, and my vocabulary. I think my parents did it right. It wasn't an issue or something that I did wrong, it just was.

My mother taught me that my birth parents loved me

very much, and that they had given me up because they wanted me to have a better life. I believed it, and I still do now. Whether or not my birth mother's intentions at the time were bad or good, she gave me up because she couldn't provide for me. That is love. Yes, she didn't raise me, but she could have flushed me down a toilet or left me in the trash to die, but instead, she brought me somewhere with the hope that I would have a better life.

Not that I didn't have my share of awkward moments about my identity. At times, people would stop my parents and say things like, "Oh, your child is Chinese . . ." Most people, especially my schoolmates, just assumed I was Chinese or Japanese. The kids in my school didn't really know where Korea was. When I told them I was Korean, they said, "Where is that?" and I shrugged and replied, "Near Japan?" To be honest, I didn't really know myself. But it didn't matter. They just said, "Oh, okay," and that was that. They dropped it, so I did, too.

On one of my early birthdays, my mother found me in my bedroom hiding under my covers, quite distraught. "Do you think that woman ever thinks about me?" I asked her.

Mom knew exactly who I was talking about. "You can call her your mother," she told me.

"You are my mother," I said.

"Okay, your birth mother," Mom corrected. "And yes, she does think about you. She just couldn't keep you." At the time, my parents believed that my birth mother had been fourteen years old when she gave birth to me, the same age Matt was now. "Look at your brother," she said. "Is he old enough to be a daddy?"

"No," I agreed.

"Well, your mother wasn't old enough to be a mother to you."

Mom's explanation satisfied me. I thought about my birth mother from time to time, but even though I didn't dwell on her, I worried about her. I wondered if she was safe, had enough to eat, had a place to live, things that I had but wasn't sure she had. I was Sam Futerman, Korean, yes, but ultimately American.

My parents tried to encourage an interest in Korea, but never forced it upon me. They were exceptional in reading my wants and needs. When I said I wanted to do martial arts, they enrolled me in Tae Kwon Do. Andrew also took lessons, which made it that much more compelling. I never wanted him to be too many levels ahead of me. Every year, the Tae Kwon Do studio would throw a Korean party, where they served Korean food. They also offered Korean language lessons, which I tried for a while, but lost interest. Why would I want to study more after school was over? I liked Tae Kwon Do for the rubber knives and nunchucks, and looking cool in front of my brothers and their friends.

I had a Korean friend, another girl from my class at school. My mother liked that I could share a Korean heritage with at least one other person. She and Dad offered to enroll me in a true Korean school in nearby Fort Lee for weekend studies, but I wasn't interested. I just stuck with the Tae Kwon Do and the Korean food to satisfy my cultural appetite. I fully accepted that I lived surrounded by Americans in a predominantly white neighborhood. I identified myself as an

American, not a Korean, and very few people ever made me feel like I was an outsider.

Verona, my hometown, is eleven miles from Manhattan. It is a cute little village around two miles wide, with a big park featuring a man-made lake. It also has an amazing corner deli near the middle school, where I would always eat the #7 sub, a delicious sandwich consisting of ham, salami, provolone, tomato, onions, shredded lettuce, oil, and vinegar, with a "mudslide," fries with cheese and gravy, on the side. But despite this Jersey delicacy, my favorite part about Verona is the abundance of pizza places and nail salons. As you drive down the main drag, Bloomfield Avenue, you will be flanked by Ray's Pizza, Paradiso Nail Salon, Nail Story Spa, Capri, Verona Pizza, Tiara Nails, Nail Art II, Anthony Franco's, and Frank Anthony's, two different pizza parlors—not kidding. Many scenes from HBO's hit series *The Sopranos* used Verona as the backdrop. It is an upper-middle-class commuter town, with lots of Hondas and Toyotas, and well-kept houses on quarter-acre yards.

The only house I ever remember living in is the one where my parents still live today. It's an old three-story, East Coast Tudor with wood floors, dark windows, and lots of creepy creaks and sounds. The dark was scary, as were the hallways and stairwells. I would always picture seeing someone not in my family coming out of the darkness.

For a long time, my brothers and I slept on the floor in my parents' room, which was the third floor, a gabled attic converted into a master bedroom. To reach it, we had to go up a staircase far narrower than the staircase between the first and second floors. My parents had the bed, and the kids had the floor. I hated when I had to sleep in the spot at the foot of the bed close to the stairway, but by standard sibling sleep rotation, that was where I ended up. When Dad was away on business trips, at least two of us got to sleep in bed next to Mom.

My father traveled internationally for work quite a bit and would be gone for a couple of weeks at a time. Although two weeks might be an exaggeration, it was definitely an eternity. I really didn't mind when he left, because that meant more room in bed with Mom, and I knew he'd bring me home a cool present. I'd always get a beautiful doll or a dress from overseas.

My father is a certified public accountant. He was born in Brooklyn, New York, but he grew up in Flushing, Queens, where the family moved when his little brother, Robert, was born. The two boys were five years apart. My grandfather Jerry was a printer, and my grandmother Lillian worked as a bookkeeper. They owned a co-op, although they always dreamed about buying a house. My grandfather died of a heart attack when my father was twenty-four.

My mother also grew up in Queens, but in College Point, not Flushing. She was the oldest of Jack and Dorothy Urban's two children. Her brother, my uncle Daniel, was ten years younger. My grandfather worked many different jobs, his last being a manager/supervisor for a company that made baseboard heating and swimming pools. I never really knew what my grandfather's occupation was until my parents told me after he passed away. All I knew was that he made me cool wood carvings and taught me how to fire a shotgun in the woods. My grandmother had some part-time jobs, usually at the post office, to make extra money for Christmas. The family lived in the first-floor apartment of a two-family home, which they rented from the couple who owned the house and lived upstairs. My mom was so fond of them, she called them "aunt" and "uncle." When they died, they stipulated in their will that my grandparents could buy the property at the price they had paid many years earlier.

My parents met at Queens College night school. My mother was earning her graduate degree in English and creative writing with a minor in the legend of King Arthur. My father was majoring in accounting. They met in the same communications class, and then dated for four years. The fact that my father was Jewish and my mother was Catholic did not affect the relationship, nor did the fact that my father had been married before and had a young son named Jeremy.

My father proposed to my mother at a New York Mets game at Shea Stadium, the same place he had taken her on their first date. My mom loved him, so she had learned to enjoy baseball, and this day was a doubleheader. Dad put the engagement ring in a box of Cracker Jacks that he had bought previously and resealed with a hair dryer. During the game, he went to the concession stand and returned with a soda and the "loaded" Cracker Jacks box. My mother didn't like Cracker Jacks, however. She took the box and put it under her seat, forcing him to insist she open it, pretending he wanted some for himself. The ring was right on top. They were married at Saint Fidelis Church in College Point in 1976, the same year the Bordiers were married in Troyes, France. My parents' first apartment was in Queens, across the street from a New York City garbage dump. The bedroom was so small, it could just fit the bed. My father worked for Sony Corporation, and when the headquarters moved to New Jersey, my parents moved, too. They bought a tiny Cape in Pompton Lakes, not too far from Verona. Mom worked as a secretary for Mobil Oil Corporation in New York City, so she commuted until Matt was born, when she became a stay-at-home mom. Eventually, they moved to Verona to have a yard big enough for a play set and a house big enough for the children to have their own rooms.

My bedroom was my fortress. That didn't mean I still didn't sleep with either the TV or the light on. I used to have nightmares about wolves and rabid guinea pigs, and the light helped. I think the guinea pig thing was guilt, because I went through about four guinea pigs in one year. Our house was a menagerie—fish, dogs, birds, rodents—but I was never great with animals. My parakeets and hamsters didn't end up well, which always made me feel really bad. I would lose interest in about a month and forget to feed them. Luckily, my mom would do it for me. My room had a bluish-purple wall-to-wall carpet and a beautiful cherry bedroom set that I had found by going to every furniture store in existence.

My parents were great about letting my room be my space, and I loved perfecting it. My brothers were slobs, and their rooms reflected it, but my room was my sanctuary, my place to let it out if I was upset because someone was mean to me at school, or when I was older, because I didn't get a part that I had auditioned for. I would go upstairs, close the door, and cry by myself. I was constantly rearranging my bed and dressers to find the perfect fit and energy. I was always making improvements, so much so that I thought I would be an interior designer.

Growing up, I was a "mommy's girl," always wanting to be held in her arms. From there, I could look up into her beautiful blue eyes. I also loved her pale Irish skin and her ever-changing shades of reddish-blond hair. I remember my dad would dye it for her in the kitchen sink. He would dye his own hair—his mustache and his eyebrows—in the guest bathroom off of the dining room, but for whatever reason, Mom's hair was done in the kitchen.

My mother was my hero. While she was the nurturer, I knew if she said "no" on something, I could convince my dad to take my side. He was the man of the house, and then it was two against one. My dad taught me how to have thick skin and a sense of humor at the same time. He wasn't home a lot, but my brothers and I never resented that. It made it a treat and more exciting when he was. We would see his headlights in the driveway at the end of the day, and we would run to hide. My hiding places were never great. Sometimes, I would crouch in plain view and cover my face. Not smart, but I was under pressure. Dad always went along with it and made me feel like gold. Then, he would pick me up by my feet and dangle me in midair. When he kissed me, his mustache would scratch my face.

My brothers have always been my protectors and my support. We grew up with lots and lots of screaming, wrestling, and putting each other in headlocks, but all in good fun. They never made me feel like I didn't belong. Most of the time, we all forget that I didn't come from my mother, too. Granted, I didn't have the experience of living with my birth mother, so I don't know how a connection like that would differ. But I did come from my mother. I came from her heart, her hopes, and her wishes. A lot of babies are "mistakes" or "surprises," but my parents had to sacrifice a lot to get me.

My brothers taught me how to survive in school, how to win video games, and how to play every kind of sport. If their friends weren't available, they could force me into learning how to be "Player B" on Duck Hunt or Donkey Kong, or teach me how to play H-O-R-S-E or stickball. I was like their pet. But I wanted them to think I was cool, so I learned what they wanted me to. If I didn't want to play with them, they would come into my room to get me. My mother told me to just ignore them and they would go away. Sometimes it worked, sometimes it didn't.

Matt and Andrew have very different temperaments. Matt is quiet and introverted. While Andrew and I were running around the house playing, Matt was locked away in his room doing his own thing. He wasn't an attention seeker, although I think he sometimes resented that Andrew and I demanded so much attention and got it. Matt wanted to be recognized for his accomplishments without marketing them. He is very artistic. He used to make amazing cartoons and doodles. I looked up to him and wanted him to be proud of me.

Andrew was a typical middle child—wild and needy. He was a troublemaker in school beginning in kindergarten. I remember my mother having to go to the principal's office many times to sit with him. When I got to middle school, I was known as "Futerman's sister," and all the teachers would tense up when they figured out I was related to Andrew. Sometimes

I would pretend he wasn't my brother. After all, we didn't look alike, so it would work until they saw Mom picking us up after school together—damn it! He always meant really well, but he just couldn't execute. He also has a hot temper, just like my dad. Despite all of this, he and I are best friends.

In our childhood, Andrew and I did a lot of the same things. When I started dance classes at age four, Andrew decided to take jazz and acrobatics classes at my dance studio. In his shining moment during one of our recitals, he was supposed to lift one of the girls in the dance number, but instead he dropped her onstage. When he decided to audition for a Christmas play in the community theater in the neighboring town of Montclair, I told my mom that I wanted to audition, too. I was either going to be in the play or dragged around like a tote bag, so it made sense to try for a part. Luckily, we both got the roles we wanted. He played a Christmas elf and I was a Christmas angel. And so my acting career began.

As we entered middle school, our relationship became a bit more separate. We were in band together, but I didn't want to be embarrassed by him anymore. If he did something stupid in first period, I would hear about it by lunchtime through everyone else. One time, he superglued his hand to his face, and all I could think was that he was ruining my life. I was starting to really like boys, and to me, it seemed like Andrew was messing up my chances.

I remember one night sitting at the top of the stairs in our house, listening to my parents arguing about something. I was spying, trying to hear what was going on. My parents fighting was devastating and elicited a really intense sadness in me. But I stayed anyway, in need of hearing them find a resolution. Matt came out of his room and saw me, so he stopped, sat down, and put his arm around me. He didn't say a word because he didn't have to—that wasn't our relationship. He would never try to talk me into feeling okay. Even though it was such a simple gesture, I knew he was letting me know that he was there for me.

Not that we didn't have our misunderstandings. One time, Matt, Mom, and I were in the car, stopped at a red light. We were talking about adoption, and my brother said, "I don't understand why you would adopt kids, if you can have your own." I didn't even know what to say. I sat frozen and speechless in the backseat. I was really upset.

When we got home, I flew into a rage, complaining to my parents about what Matt had said and going off about how close-minded and stupid I thought he was. My parents looked at each other, smiled, and then let out a slight chuckle. Had they not heard what I just said? What *he* said?!

"Sam, it's a compliment," my father explained. "Matt doesn't even think of you as being adopted." I thought about that until I figured out what Dad meant. When Matt said he didn't know why someone would adopt, he wasn't including me in the pool of children who had been adopted. He considered me his biological sister, as much as he and Andrew were biological brothers. Wow. Dad was right. I changed from outraged to honored. It was a moment I'll never forget. Dad wasn't trying to save Matt from my wrath; he was just being wise.

In sixth grade, I tried Little League baseball on the boys' team. Softball was for girlie girls, and I already played baseball in the back of the house with my brothers. I wanted to make the point that girls could play baseball if they wanted to. Plus, my dad was the coach. So there I was, on a team full of boys and one little Asian Jew girl. I played right field, benchwarmer, flower picker, but at least I was on the team. In the outfield, I could practice for my dance competitions solo, without too many people noticing.

I was also a dancer growing up. I took tap, jazz, ballet, and lyrical. I hated ballet—too many rules, not enough creative expression. Not only did I have to listen to classical music, I had to have my hair in a bun and a leotard with no skirt. Jazz was much better. I could dance around and do jazz hands, and our costumes for the recital were always embellished with feathers and fringe. Sometimes, I would wake up in the middle of the night from muscle pains, hysterically crying. Mom would kneel next to me, put a pillow under my knees, and rub them until I fell asleep again. There were even times when she would let me stay home from school. Yeah, she is definitely my hero.

Mom drove me to three or four dance classes a week, Tae Kwon Do, Little League practice, play practice, French horn lessons—everything. I'd come home from school, eat a bowl of soup, get changed, and head to dance class, which lasted from six to eight p.m. Then, I'd come home, eat macaroni and cheese, pretend to do my homework, and go to bed.

I was always very dramatic. When I was mad at my parents, I would throw myself on the kitchen floor and scream. ("I won't have goodie bags at my birthday party!") My mom called these my Samantha Meltdowns. One of my first encounters with the spotlight was memorable, but for the wrong reasons. I was playing the ingénue in the elementary school's annual Thanksgiving play, and I was too terrified to excuse myself to use the bathroom. So I ended up having an accident . . . onstage . . . in front of my entire class. I mean, I guess I could say I was just marking my territory. I knew I'd be an actor for life.

I began summer plays when I was just eight years old. I was a chorus dancer in my first production, *Guys and Dolls*. The following summer, I did *Bye Bye Birdie*, again as a dancer. I was always a dance captain and in the chorus. By the time I was twelve, I was training at the Paper Mill Playhouse's Summer Conservatory. The Paper Mill Playhouse is a highly regarded regional theater in Milburn, New Jersey, that often casts big Broadway stars. I would spend two months there in the summers, where classes began at ten a.m. and ended at five p.m. I got to perform on the main stage in such shows as *The King and I* and *Miss Saigon*. This exposure eventually led me to my talent manager, Eileen, who saw me in the conservatory showcase. My heartthrob was Leonardo DiCaprio. I went to see the movie *Titanic* as soon as it came out, and not long after, my walls were plastered with posters of Leo. I spent hours listening to the sound track my mother bought me. I would put on the music, stand on my bed, and stage the action with my dolls, throwing them into the "water," my bluish-purple wall-to-wall carpet. My other favorite movie-based reenactment was based on the film *Outbreak*, which my parents allowed me to watch at a very young age for some unknown reason. All of my stuffed animals had all died of Ebola virus. I would always come downstairs to reveal the bad news in person. Mom would follow me upstairs to find them all laid out in the morgue, which again was on the floor, with little blankets over their bodies. Grim, but an honest delivery.

In high school, my zest for acting revved up. During my freshman and sophomore years at Verona High School, I would go into Manhattan to audition for commercials, TV shows, print, and film. My mother would pick me up from school; have my head shots, résumés, and lines in the car; and drive me into the city. The expenses involved were substantial— gas, tolls, parking—but Mom paid for it all. Once she even had her car towed, so that cost more than $250. When I was fifteen, I landed my first feature film. I was ecstatic! It was called *The Motel*, and it was an independent film written and directed by Michael Kang, who is still my friend and mentor today. My second big part was a role in *Memoirs of a Geisha*. I was sixteen, which meant I needed a parent present while filming. Mom quit her job as a preschool teacher to travel back and forth to California with me. She always put her kids first.

My junior year, I transferred to the Professional Performing Arts School (PPAS), a public high school in Manhattan that required an audition for admission. Kids from all over New York City wanted to go there, and the competition was tough. Trumpeters, saxophone players, dancers, choir singers, kids of every race, every shape, and every size were waiting for their turn on audition day. I had my three-ring binder in hand, filled with the songs I knew by heart. I was called into a bright pink room with a man on the piano and a teacher behind the desk. I did my

88

thing, walked out, and let out a big breath of relief, and an even bigger one when I was accepted a few weeks later.

The PPAS was on Forty-Eighth Street between Eighth and Ninth Avenues. I would wake up every morning at six, be on the bus at 6:50, be in the city at eight, and walk the few blocks to school. We had academics every day until one fifteen. The rest of the afternoon was dedicated to performing arts classes, a different emphasis each day. Mondays it was vocals training; Tuesdays it was acting; Wednesdays was song preparation; Thursdays it was acting; and Fridays it was movement. At three fifteen, we were born free. I would walk back to the bus stop and take the 3:55 bus home, arriving in Verona at four forty-five. The spring had longer days, as they included rehearsals for the spring musical. I would have rehearsals until ten. My mother would drive into the city to pick me up, sometimes as late as eleven. On some nights, I would just stay in Manhattan with friends. I spent my lunch breaks in Times Square, searching the Swatch store, sampling Sephora products, and drinking Jamba Juice from one of their takeout bars. Fifteen years old and the city was mine.

The school let students take time off to be on location for a movie or TV show, if they landed a role. We had kids doing *The Lion King* on Broadway who would leave at one fifteen in order to make "half-hour curtain call," a theater expression meaning a half hour before the curtain goes up and the show begins. I learned how to be a performing arts kid, a biz kid, and so much more. It was my first time being completely immersed in an incredibly racially diverse environment. There weren't many Asian students, but it didn't matter. Everyone looked different, everyone dressed differently, and it was great. We were performers, stretching and honing ourselves as artists. It was awesome. In my senior-year production, I was Milky White the Cow in *Into the Woods*. I got to dress up as a cow and die onstage, to this day one of my favorite roles.

I had always felt as comfortable with myself as any other teen did. I was obsessed with boys and whether or not I was getting fat. Sometimes, though, I was curious about my Korean heritage, especially as I started to learn about makeup, which forced me to look at my facial features more carefully. Still, being Korean didn't make me that interested in Korea. When my father offered to take the whole family on a trip to Korea, I didn't really want to go, so we went to Cancun, Mexico, instead.

I finally did go to Korea. I went with my mother when I was twenty-four. We had received a brochure from the Spence-Chapin Adoption Agency with information about a roots tour of the country, an annual event that brings Korean adoptees and their families to their birth country. "Korea's many sights, sounds and tastes will enrich your journey," the brochure seduced. My mom convinced me that the timing for this one was probably going to be the best it would ever be, and the fact that I would be traveling with her made it that much more appealing. It was quite expensive, which worried Mom, but we signed on.

We traveled to Korea with two other families, also with adopted Korean children, and assembled into a much larger group in Seoul, with adoptees from all over the world. We spent time at the Social Welfare Society (SWS) and visited a mothers' birthing center in Daegu. Ten expectant mothers were there at the time, and another group had forty-five adoptees and their parents. It was a very enlightening and emotional experience for me. It was humbling to see the attachment the birth mothers had for their babies. They were incredibly concerned about where their infants would be placed and if they would be loved. Some wanted their babies to be sent to the United States, assuming they would be well taken care of there. Others wanted their babies to remain in Korea so they would be able to reconnect with them in the future, if they wanted. As an adoptee, I was able to realistically accept the possibility of how much my birth mother must have loved me.

I was genuinely moved by the difficult circumstances this group of women faced. These women were able to stay in these birthing centers for more than a year—from the time they knew their condition to a few months after delivery. This way, they could tell their families they were ill or depressed and were seeking treatment for anything but pregnancy to disguise the real scenario. During our visit, the young mothers ranged in age from sixteen to twenty-six. Being in their presence gave me a much deeper understanding of the love between a birth mother and her child.

It was an incredibly telling and moving experience. We could ask the birth mothers questions. Someone wanted to know, "Why wouldn't you want to see your child again?" to which the unanimous answer was that they would want to see their child again, but Korean society stigmatized the single mothers so much that it was almost impossible to make that happen.

Some of the women asked us questions. "Do you love your adopted children as much as your biological children?" My mother stood up. "I have two biological sons, and I love them exactly the same as my daughter," she said. "Samantha is as much my child as the boys are." I started to realize how much love and thought went into giving up a child for adoption and for choosing to adopt. To see my own mother stand up and speak so passionately made me proud. I cannot speak for my birth mother, but I imagine that she had given me up out of love. And although the focus had always been on my birth mother, it triggered thoughts of my father, and whether he ever thought about me, or even knew I existed.

While in Korea, I also witnessed an adopting family picking up their new son, a boy about two years old. It was heart-wrenching to watch this little boy separate, perhaps for good, from the couple who'd been his foster parents for those two years, a time in which everyone involved had clearly become very attached. The boy and his foster grandfather were bawling their eyes out as they hugged for the last time. Once again it reminded me how loved these children really are. Adoptees often feel they have not been loved, because they have been "given up." But during this trip I learned that this is a myth. We have been loved by so many people, starting with our conception.

7

ANAÏS

first skype call with samantha

I was getting to know Samantha without her necessarily knowing how much I was snooping. I saw her baby pictures and her pictures from her trip to Korea. I learned about her life from "How It Feels to Be Adopted . . . I Am Sam," but that was her as an actress, so I had to decide how much of her character was how she was in real life. Discovering a person through social media is insane. There were pictures and snippets of dialogue, but there was not yet common ground. Our histories up until this point had been completely separate, and all of a sudden, we were becoming spontaneous best friends, only on a hunch that we might be twins separated at birth. I found it somewhat difficult to think of topics to bring up during our messaging sessions—after all, she was someone I knew absolutely nothing about, but with whom I felt identical.

Messaging each other definitely was the best first approach: First, I wasn't self-conscious and felt protected in the anonymity of typing as opposed to face-to-face communication; and second, I could think longer about what I was going to put down on paper, or should I say, type on the keyboard. I even had time to review and edit anything I said, in case it sounded weird or wrong. On the other hand, writing can be very puzzling, as people express themselves differently with their choice of words, and therefore a written message can still be misunderstood in the nuances. Further complicating matters was that English was my second language, making it even more nerve-wracking.

Those first few days, Samantha and I kept things fun and general. I told her I was an only child, I was in my final year of design school, and I liked to go to bed late, so she needn't worry about the eight-hour time difference between us.

The idea of "seeing" Samantha in a Skype call was floating somewhere in my field of neurons, but I guess I was trying to ignore it. Of course, it had been the first thing I had hoped to do: see this potential twin of mine instantaneously—flesh and bones—in French, *en chair et en os*. On Facebook we could "chat," and interact at the same time, compared to letters or even e-mails. It fascinated me how immediate Facebook chat was, like an instant snapshot, although it still wasn't face-to-face. I was desperate to actually get a look at Samantha "live," although I was reluctant to ask her if she wanted to Skype, as it's not something I could invite someone to do on our first "meeting." It was like a date. You can't rush it, but must patiently wait for just the right moment.

After a few Facebook chats, I finally mentioned Skype very casually and gave Samantha my Skype name, in case she was interested in talking that way. I started getting anx-

ious when four and five days passed without her doing anything about it. But at last, she suggested we set a time. I had
no idea if she felt as excited and terrified as I did. I was mostly
terrified, but in a very good way. "That's going to be the weird-
est experience ever!" I wrote in my response to her.

We set up the call for later that night, February 27, at
ten p.m. for me in London and two p.m. for Samantha in
L.A. I made sure I gave myself plenty of time to get home and
be in front of my computer. I wasn't going to wear anything
particularly special. I had on the same V-neck sweater that I
had worn to school. As I was counting down the minutes
until our call, I got a message from Sam that she had a last-
minute audition she had to attend. She assured me she still
wanted to have the call, but we needed to push it off a few
hours. I was really disappointed, but at least it hadn't been
canceled, only delayed.

The fact that all my flat mates were out made my evening suddenly lonely. To fill in the downtime, I tried working
on some of the designs for my project. The pending Skype
call had me rather distracted, but I still did my best to cut,
sew, and draw, even though I'd have to start everything all
over again, because I was not concentrating at my best. Time
passed extremely slowly. Every time I looked at the clock,
only a few minutes had gone by. A few hours more to wait . . .
fine . . . totally fine . . . I was fine . . . yes . . . fine . . .

So many questions were racing through my head. I guess
I was mentally jumping for joy, because physically my body
was warring between petrified and soft as a mollusk. I was
eager to see if Samantha and I were alike for real, and if she

could be my real sister, or if I had just dreamt it and wished for it too strongly. When I had seen her in her YouTube videos, I had started building a personality for her based on all her acting personas. I was also creating a character for her based on my own personality. We are twins, after all. It was like a dance of contradictions, salsa or a waltz—you put a foot forward and take it back, then you turn, but in the end, you stay in the loop.

Everything I was thinking, I was almost immediately taking back. She must be like me personality-wise—wait, no, this is stupid, you don't even know if you are identical, or twins. Maybe you fantasized it. No, I did not. I will check on Facebook if she still exists. We were identical babies. Come on, have you seen our pictures? No. I am being schizophrenic. Oh, no, wait, she is real. Her Facebook is still there. Phew. Breathe. Okay. What time is it? It is two minutes later. Great . . . She was definitely small, as she had asserted in one of her videos, and I was really small, so that was a match. . . .

I had no idea what the Skype call would be like. I had agreed to let Samantha tape it, knowing she wanted to show it to her family. How long would the conversation last? How long would she want it to last? Was she as excited as I? Or was she just being polite with me? Will she be alone? Will she be interested in me? Maybe she will not like me . . . but if she's my twin sister, she has to like me, because I already like her, even though I do not know her. Can I make a joke, or is it too soon? I should have made a list of subjects and organized them in the order of significance. Maybe she will be like a superstar actor and talk only about herself? What if she is a bitch? Nah, I am not one, so . . . But we are different people, and twins can be different. Will she think I am crazy? Will she be dramatic? Actors can be very dramatic, right?

Finally, at 12:29 a.m., two and a half hours after our scheduled call time, Samantha sent me a Facebook message that she was about to log on. Seconds later, I heard the little *boink* sound Skype makes when someone on your contacts list logs on . . . without a doubt, Samantha.

"EEEEE," she typed in the message box.

Right, I thought, she is as crazy as I am. And, she likes to use onomatopoeia like me, too. She is quintupling her letters. She is anxious, and I have proof on my screen. These quick observations made me feel much more comfortable. This was going to be great. Argh . . . trouble with my Internet. Five, four, three, two, one. I was hugely relieved when I heard *tuti du titu di tu di*, the sound of a Skype call ringing!

Why is my Internet connection so slow?! It was definitely not working at normal speed. Maybe it was because Samantha was calling from L.A., so many time zones away. Something was coming into focus on my screen. I SEE MYSELF PIXELIZED! It was unbelievable. It was me, but wearing a white lacy blouse with short sleeves! Even pixelated, we look so identical. Wait, she is moving. Wait, she looks so nice. She is smiling. She looks happy. Oh, she is giggling. And so am I. I can't believe it. This is really it. We are reunited!

Houston, I hear something! She is about to speak! Who will talk first? My Internet connection was failing me at the worst time ever. Just when I thought it was going to cut off completely, it stabilized. Thank God. I was about to start my end of the conversation with a swear word, which I wasn't sure was appropriate. Although I'd soon find out anything goes with Samantha. We are very similar in our liberal use of cuss words.

"My connection is really bad," I finally told Sam, making me the first to speak.

"Oh, my God, you're European!" I heard her squeal.

I could even see her bringing both her hands to her face in disbelief. I guess my accent caught her off guard. And we both broke into giggles. I knew I was French, but it was funny to hear myself referred to as "European."

The first few minutes of the call were surreal. I felt like I was floating on a cloud, like time had frozen around me, around us. Time and space did not matter anymore, because we were on opposite sides of the earth, talking at the same time. In the first moments, we were even talking in different languages. When Samantha asked me, "How's it going?" I answered in French! "Ça va" came out without me even thinking about it. "This is a really weird experience," I said.

"It's sooooo weird," Sam agreed, and we started giggling again. Our answers were almost time-delayed, because we were paralyzed in looking at each other. Sometimes I felt self-conscious, like I was talking to myself in the mirror and someone walked in on me while I was doing so. I was so blown away, it was difficult to remember all of the questions I had for her. Seeing her made me forget everything. On the other hand, I didn't struggle for something to say, like I had feared. The conversation just went naturally, one question after the other. It made sense. We were talking like two people who knew each other and enjoyed spending time together. It was like building a relationship in an accelerated amount of time. From the outside, it could have looked like a video in fast-forward, but for me, time was suspended. I never wanted this Skype call to end. Never!

"I know this is really strange. I don't know where to look," I said to Sam, feeling awkward about looking directly at her.

"OMG!" I heard Sam exclaim. "This is so weird. We're like *The Parent Trap!*"

"I know," I giggled.

"What time is it there?"

"It's midnight thirty," I told her. "Yeah, it's daylight for you, and it's completely night here."

We went through all kind of subjects—jobs, studies, life, childhood, boyfriends, how I had found her, tattoos (What? Who has a tattoo?), medical information, surgeries, freckles, small hands, food tastes, etc. I'd gone into the call completely exhausted from the long days I had been spending on my designs, but now, I was suddenly energized. I did not want to go to bed for fear Samantha might disappear, or that it would turn out that this was a dream and when I woke up, she'd be gone. On a funny note, I had to go to the loo badly, but I was fighting as hard as I could to hold it, because I could not detach my eyes from her. I will never let her go, I thought.

At some point, my flat mate Rory came home, at almost the same time as Samantha's roommate Lisa. Rory was a bit embarrassed to be disturbing us, his mouth wide-open as he realized Samantha was on my screen. He tiptoed into the kitchen, poured a glass of water, and then tiptoed back to his room, trying not to be noticed. On Sam's screen, I caught a glimpse of Lisa in the background. She even talked to me for a bit. Sam's room looked nice, too, but a bit messy. My room wasn't all that tidy, either. I liked her taste in fashion, too. Her blouse was something I would probably wear in the summer. Then I remembered, even though it was February, it was always summer in L.A. I was so satisfied that I could now picture her much more precisely.

Well, we had to hang up eventually. Sam was going to meet a friend, so we had to end our call. She said she had a headache and was feeling overwhelmed and tired, and I was drained, too. I had completely lost track of time, so I thought it was really cool that we had talked for ninety minutes . . . wait . . . more than three hours? I really had lost track of time. I had had an easier time talking with Samantha for three straight hours than I often had talking with friends I knew well. We reluctantly said our good-byes but promised to talk again the next day. I went gliding and sliding into my bed, all emotions gone from my body. As much as I wanted to share this experience with my parents, it was almost four a.m., so it would have to wait for morning.

So much was happening in such a short time, eliciting all sorts of new emotions I had never felt before. I couldn't even describe them, but my life had just changed, and any fear I had of not being able to make a connection with this stranger disappeared. There was no reason to be scared anymore; even though I didn't have absolute proof, I had found my sister.

I had no idea what would happen next, but I felt I had just reached a huge turning point and was waiting to see how the elements would come together. My world was completely turned upside down. I had **no landmarks**, and I had just talked to my possible twin sister, **at the other** end of the planet. It was almost the next day in London, and she still had an afternoon to go through. Time and space did not exist. We were not just connected electronically anymore; we were humanly connected now. We had just proven to one another that we were each real, existing and breathing, moving around the same dimension and not living in parallel worlds at all. What was she doing next? Where would she go now? What would she eat? How was she feeling about all this?

At least now I knew I was not dreaming. As I let myself fall onto my bed, I was thinking . . . Right . . . so I am definitely not schizophrenic . . . I pinched myself a few times to be certain I was not fooling myself. I was sinking into my bed and was waiting for something to happen, my body to charge, my brain to load. It was like a video game . . . LOADING . . . you have just refilled your lives and are ready for the next level. Talking to Sam was like talking to someone you had just fallen in love with. After just three hours, I knew I loved her already.

8

SAM

faster than the speed of wi-fi

Seeing Anaïs on Skype was unreal. I mean, we had to be twins.
I had never seen anyone who looked even remotely like me, let
alone my exact mirror reflection. She had my laugh, my freckles, and that profile. When she turned to the side during that
first Skype conversation, I was blown away. I stopped for a
second and freaked out inside.

But what if we weren't sisters? What would that mean?
Would it mean that dinosaurs really walked the earth with
Jesus? I mean, that's how crazy it felt, right?! There was no
way we weren't related. But I guess there are no guarantees
in life.

If we were sisters, then maybe Anaïs would have medical issues similar to mine. Maybe she would know where her
freckles came from, and her dry skin, and her eczema! What
if she was lactose intolerant?

Being adopted and being asked to fill out a medical history form at the doctor's office was always sad in a way. I'd come to the part of the sheet that asked if I had any family members with cancer, heart disease, diabetes, etc., and I would draw a big cross on the section and write "N/A." I had no medical history. I didn't know if my mother had or has had breast cancer, or lung cancer, or sensitive skin, which meant I didn't know to watch out for these things. I could never be prepared, and it made me a hypochondriac. Every time something was remotely wrong, I'd assume the worst . . . I'm dying. Then I'd go on the Internet and type in my symptoms, and it was confirmed. Instant death. It was so ridiculous. These websites were crazy. Headache? Check. Sore throat? Check. Stomachache? Check. Rash? Maybe.

Perhaps now I would finally have a medical history, or at least have someone to share my hypochondria with. It turned out that Anaïs and I had experienced very similar nerve disorders at around the same age. For me, it was during the fall of 2011, pretty soon after I moved to California, and I thought I was dying! For a time, I had phantom pains in my right foot, which was thought to be nerve damage in my leg. After much testing, it turned out to be nothing, just my nerves sending mixed signals to my body, which translated into pain. My body wanting attention—rude. Anaïs also had phantom pains, except hers were in her back and neck. The only conclusion to reasonably come to is that we are both insane.

Our Skype call really got us thinking about our similarities. Over the next few nights, I couldn't wait for our calls to take place again. I was becoming an Anaïs Bordier addict—I couldn't get enough of her, and I was getting the feeling that she couldn't get enough of me, either. I guess you could say that we were becoming self-obsessed. All I did was talk about her to all my friends, which luckily didn't seem to bore them, and I wouldn't have cared if it had. Anaïs was my new focus in life, and thankfully everyone around me seemed to be just as excited.

Being in Hollywood, of course, meant that I got bombarded with suggestions of how to turn our story into a moneymaker. From the moment I first heard from Anaïs and told people that I might be a twin, my friends and agents started thinking, project! That first night, at my premiere of *21 & Over*, all I heard was, "We gotta make a movie. WE GOTTA MAKE A MOVIE!" That kind of chatter almost overpowered the incredible event that was happening in my life! "You should record it, if you talk to her!" someone said. "Don't miss that! You should record it!" said another. I wanted everyone to SHUSH! I agreed that making a movie about it would be cool, if it turned out that we were twins, but for now, SHUSH! I was going through something crazy, something insanely wonderful, and I wanted to be present in the immediate moment of ecstasy, not planning a project.

My manager told me to delay talking to Anaïs. She had some things she wanted to think through before the call took place. I, on the other hand, wanted the event to be totally private, Anaïs and I alone. I didn't want our moment to be corrupted or exploited by intrusions, especially not by the business that provided my livelihood.

On the other hand, when I thought about it, I imagined how cool it would be to have the moment recorded, even if it was just for personal use. When I asked permission from Anaïs, and she said it was okay, I downloaded a recorder. I am so glad I did, so relieved. In real time, the moment we first "saw" each other has no words; it was simply indescribable. But, having recorded it, I can watch that moment again and again, and I can share it with my friends and family.

In addition to taping the Skype call, my friends and I were floating the idea of making a documentary. I was still up in the air about whether or not we should commercialize the whole crazy happenstance. I know how ugly Hollywood can get. There are some really bizarre reality shows that do nothing but exploit their subjects, and I didn't want that for Anaïs and me. I especially didn't want to scare Anaïs away. I started weighing the pros and cons and soliciting everyone's opinions about it. Should Anaïs and I make a movie? Should I just write a screenplay about it, but not make a documentary? Should I really film our interactions? What could we do with all the footage? How would the documentary look? Would it be like old pictures of us and memories of our childhoods? We didn't even know for sure if we were twins. Finally, Anaïs and I decided to go forward with the documentary idea, although we'd proceed cautiously.

Deciding to do something like a documentary with someone you had never met was strange. Essentially, I was entering into a business plan with someone across the world in order to share our most intimate moments with anyone who would watch. I mean, that's weird, right? Why on earth would Anaïs and I take an important moment like this, tarnish it with cameras and cameramen, and then release it to the world? Well, being an actress and being in the business, I was very aware that the events unfolding before me were completely extraordinary. Doing the documentary was also doing something creative and possibly even therapeutic at the same time, which was a huge upside. In a way, it was giving us a means to express and process the crazy information that had come out of nowhere. Not many people have something this insane happen in their lives.

We decided we wanted to do a full-length documentary rather than something shorter. We would start by filming our getting to know each other, which would be through our video blogs, video diaries, and Skype conversations. The film crew would then follow us as we made preparations to meet in person for the first time.

We really wanted to capture our families on film, too. As much as Anaïs and I had been through, our families were going through their own emotions. Our parents were still very fearful that we might end up with an unfathomable disappointment, but they were also excited, knowing how identical we looked, and how we shared the same birth date and birthplace. They had a lot of questions, but they were totally willing to believe we were related and had found each other. My parents were fully on board for a documentary. My mother had been around the business since I was a kid, so she didn't mind the cameras, and my dad's a ham. Anaïs's dad was the most reluctant about the project. The Bordiers are very private people and not accustomed to Hollywood voyeurism. They didn't say they would absolutely not participate, but they were not enthusiastic. Anaïs knew her father was just being protective.

French culture is very good about keeping people's private lives private, much different from the disrespect for privacy in the United States.

As soon as we gave the project the green light, I got to work finding a production crew. I had just filmed a movie in Hawaii with Justin Chon, Kevin Wu, and James Yi called *Man-Up!* The three of them had been with me when I first heard from Anaïs on premiere night, and now they wanted to be on board for this project. Kanoa wanted to join in, too. Justin would be our executive producer, and Kanoa, James, and I would be producing. My manager also came on board as a producer. James set up a $40,000 budget to cover the small crew's trip to London—housing, flights, and food; postproduction costs; and the camera equipment. Now we had to raise the money. We all knew the level of excitement the story could attract, but that didn't guarantee big sponsorship. We reached out to a few private investors and organizations, but we couldn't find anything substantial, and the last thing I wanted was to sell our life rights to some Hollywood studio that would turn our amazing story into the Asian *Parent Trap*. If we were going to share our lives, I wanted us to do it right and make it authentic, not embellished and not from the perspective of a Hollywood producer with dollar signs in his eyes.

I was anxious to get to London, not wanting to wait another moment to meet Anaïs. If it were a matter of finding a cameraman, I would just shoot it on an iPhone if I had to, but I wanted to get going already. But Anaïs had also been considering the timing. She thought that maybe, if we could wait until mid-May, I could be there to see her fashion show at Central Saint Martins. She said the show was always a huge deal, an extravaganza, where the students created the most spectacular outfits imaginable.

Anaïs's parents were coming to London to attend the event, so that would be an added bonus for me, my chance to meet them as well. I asked Anaïs what she thought if I invited my parents to London, too, and she loved the idea. A full-blown event, if they agreed. Anaïs and I would meet first, of course, not as family units, but just the two of us, and then we would introduce our families. Already, Anaïs's mother was anxious to contact my mother to introduce herself.

The production crew liked the idea of the London trip in May, because it would give us enough time to fund and organize the documentary. I reluctantly agreed, curbing my disappointment that I would have to wait almost three months to actually meet Anaïs in person. In the meantime, I continued to *virtually* meet her pretty much every day on Skype, as we bided our time until we could actually hug and poke each other's noses in person.

As for raising the money, the team finally landed on the idea of crowdfunding to gain our production financing, which now seemed like the only way to do it. Social media had played such a huge role in Anaïs and me finding each other. Why shouldn't we crowdfund? I knew that there was potential for our story to go viral, which meant a lot of exposure and perhaps a lot of donations.

Kanoa and I considered a few crowdfunders, primarily Kickstarter and Indiegogo. Finally, we decided to go with Kickstarter, the largest and best-known crowdfunding platform out there. First, we read all the tips about the website and talked to friends who had run successful campaigns using it. The familiarization process was filled with long nights of the production crew and me sitting at my dining room table, mulling over ideas for the documentary's title and a name for our production company. Finally, we decided to call the film *Twinsters*. It was a decision made over a few drinks after sitting for hours at my dining room table. We wanted to merge some words together and coin a term. Twin . . . sisters . . . twins . . . twinsters. Aha! As for the production company, we settled on the name Small Package Films. Once we had our names and set up our project, I wrote the plea for funding:

> Why we need your help!
>
> We are firm supporters of the social media world, which includes crowd sourcing & funding platforms like Kickstarter! Without the world of social media, Anaïs & Samantha may have never been able to connect!
>
> We plan to gain the entirety of our budget through this Kickstarter campaign. Creating a documentary can be very expensive, especially when you are traveling to Europe! Your donations will help us to fund production expenses, which include: travel, equipment rental/insurance, crew expenses & a DNA test for Samantha & Anaïs. They will also cover our post-production expenses, which include hiring a sound/picture editor, a graphic designer and everything in between.

As the launch date approached, we were feeling the pressure. We didn't know if it was possible to raise that much money, and at the last moment, we decided to downsize the dollar amount to $30,000 and be frugal with our budget. We needed to raise the $30,000 in three and a half weeks, leaving us with two weeks to process the funds and still get us to London by May 16, in time for Anaïs's fashion show. The rule with Kickstarter is if you reach your goal, then you keep the money, minus a 5 percent commission and some payment charges, and if you don't reach your goal, then you forfeit it all. Only slightly more than half the projects succeed.

The night before the launch, I was up all night working on last-minute details. At seven the next morning, we were officially under way. Within a few minutes, our first donation, $100 from Eileen, came through. After that, the money started flowing. By nine, we already had something like $2,000, and by the end of the day, we had raised around $5,000. It was insane. I never expected people's generosity toward a project for which there was very little in it for them, except to see an artistic endeavor come to fruition, happen so quickly. At the rate we were going, we'd need far less time than the twenty-eight days we had allotted.

Then followed the interest from the media. This part had me worried even before the launch, on account of Anaïs's trepidation about making our story public. She was far more private than I, and I was worried that media bombardment might scare her off. I woke up the next morning to e-mails, Facebook messages, Twitter messages, and Kickstarter messages from reporters from every major news network. Several of them had even tracked down my father and called him at work to get more details on the story. I wasn't sure what to do! I hope they are not harassing Anaïs! was my first thought. When I checked in with her, sure enough, a reporter had contacted her, too. There were people messaging her Facebook friends and trying to call them by telephone. This was what I had been scared about: people intruding into Anaïs's life. Luckily, Justin's publicist was willing to field the media, so that was a relief.

One outstanding task was finding a cinematographer. Justin suggested Ryan Miyamoto, a friend of a friend. After watching an old reel on his website, I was overly impressed. Plus, he was dang cute, too. He looked like a Hawaiian Ken doll. Not too shabby to have around for several stressful weeks, eh? And he was available to leave the following week and spend some time away from home. He was the first and only option.

Now, it was time to get serious about planning the trip. We found a short-term rental in Shoreditch big enough for the entire crew. The final itinerary would include a day at the Harry Potter studios. After all, Anaïs and I both love Harry Potter.

Just as everything was falling perfectly into place, I got a message from a professor of psychology at California State University–Fullerton, who was a world leader in twin studies. Dr. Nancy Segal was also the director of the Twin Studies Center there. She had written several books on the subject of twins separated at birth, including *Born Together—Reared Apart: The Landmark Minnesota Twin Study*, published by Harvard University Press in July 2012, and *Someone Else's Twin: The True Story of Babies Switched at Birth*, released in August 2011 by Prometheus Books.

Not long after Dr. Segal contacted me, I went to meet with her on the Fullerton campus, which was only thirty minutes south of L.A. She has been studying twins for a long time. She was a fraternal twin, which made her interest and passion in the subject that much more personal. Her library was massive and had hundreds of books that could shed an enormous amount of light on all the possibilities of my situation with Anaïs. She was also doing a huge study on unrelated look-alikes, which was really fascinating, but fear-provoking in a certain way. It made me realize that although it was improbable that Anaïs and I were not twins, it was a possibility.

I was thrilled when Dr. Segal offered to lend her expertise to us. She even said she would coordinate a DNA test for us. Anaïs and I had been talking about doing this since our early communications, but we didn't know the best way to go about it, so Dr. Segal's offer was fantastic. She had a relationship with Affiliated Genetics, a laboratory in Salt Lake City, Utah, that provides a range of DNA tests for government agencies and private clients. The DNA result was the crucial piece of information still outstanding. Anaïs and I were already convinced we were sisters, but the truth lay in the test. We wanted to be together through the whole DNA testing process. We'd allow ourselves to be filmed receiving the results, but we weren't sure if we would be alone or have our families with us. We'd work out those details later. Dr. Segal would also do testing on each of us to discover our psychological and physiological similarities and differences. She even offered to let us film her lectures and do an on-camera interview, and all her contributions would be free. Anaïs and I gratefully took her up on her offer.

Dr. Segal reviewed Anaïs's and my birth records. She appreciated the similarities, that we were born on the same date and in the same city, and that we looked so much alike. The only doubt in her mind, she said, was that we had been managed by different adoption agencies, which is unusual for twins. Dr. Segal gave me two DNA test packets, one for me and one for Anaïs. She told me the test generally took three to four weeks to complete. However, when she explained our situation to the lab, they agreed to rush it for us.

Anaïs and I had originally wanted to both take the test and see the results together in London. Because the timing wasn't going to work out, we changed the plan to collecting the samples together on Skype and then getting the results together in London. Dr. Segal agreed to keep the results confidential until Anaïs and I were together. She would give us the results live over Skype.

Until the genetic testing was complete, Anaïs and I were only hypothetically twin sisters—two girls born on the same day, in the same place, who looked almost exactly alike. However, I never imagined we weren't sisters, not from the moment I saw Anaïs's picture. If it came down to that we weren't siblings, it was going to be even stranger. Everything up to this moment had been perfectly aligned, had perfectly fallen into place. There was no way that it couldn't be true. I didn't know true love yet, but I was certain this was what true love must feel like. When you know, you just know, right? By this time,

113

we had decided if it turned out that we were not twins, we would still be friends. Anaïs was the only other person who understood what this particular experience had been like. The hopes, dreams, thrills, and even wary calm about the entire situation was only known by the person who was so often staring back at me through my laptop screen, Anaïs. It's like being in a race. You know what to expect; you know the track; you know the rules; you know where the finish line is; you know the spectators are there; and you know you are not only hoping to win, you are absolutely going to. You've pictured it in your mind, and you focus on that alone. You hear the crowd cheering you on. There will be glory when the ribbon hits your chest, and you throw your arms in the air, but at the moment, you are just anticipating it, just breathing. You can't plan for the worst. You have to keep your eyes forward, be there in that moment, and when the gun goes off, run full speed ahead.

And I did.

9

ANAÏS

dna test

On Tuesday, April 23, at ten p.m. London time, two p.m. L.A. time, Sam and I were going to simultaneously, via Skype, swab our cheeks to collect our samples for the DNA test, which would prove or disprove we were twins. If we were twins, the test would even reveal if we were identical or fraternal. A DNA test performed on monozygotic twins will return results with 99.99 percent similarity. However, DNA from non-identical (fraternal or dizygotic) twins will generally be about 50–75 percent similar. For many twins, or families with twins, the only way to know for sure whether they are identical or fraternal is through DNA testing. By now Sam and I fully believed we were identical, but why not prove it within 99.99 percent probability, just to silence the doubters, although, in truth, there really were no known doubters left.

Ten p.m. was about the right time for dinner in Europe. We eat our last meal of the day much later than Americans do, but we usually keep it quite simple if we are eating in—a small plate of something, a little wine, a little dessert, and we are satisfied. Marie and Lucas were with me the night of the simultaneous swab, so they were right there in it with us, making it festive and fun. Right on schedule, Sam Skyped me saying she was ready.

Sam and I had been waiting to share this moment together for at least two weeks. The test itself was only going to take seconds, but we could make it bigger and better with some pasta and, of course, some wine! I might have had an American identical twin, but I am French!

It was funny that Sam and I were both using our kitchens as the test site. Looking at Sam's from her laptop camera, I was impressed by how bright, yellow, and cheery it was. It seemed to me everything in L.A. was always drenched in sunlight and pastels, whereas everything in London was gray or darker, especially this time of year. Sam picked up her laptop and gave us a quick tour from her seat by rotating her webcam a wobbly 360 degrees. When we got to where the kitchen meets the living room, I could see the sun shining through the vertical blinds. Here in London, it had been pitch-black for a few hours now, although thankfully, the days were finally starting to get long enough to tell that spring was here.

Marie returned the favor of Sam's laptop tour and took Sam around our kitchen with my laptop webcam. My kitchen is very functional and white, but we do have enough room for a fairly large white round table and four chairs for dining. As the camera panned by me, I was standing over the pasta pot making sure it didn't cook longer than al dente. When I heard Sam calling out to me, I turned around, smiled, and said hello back. Lucas opened a bottle of white wine and poured each of us a glass . . . well, not Sam.

It almost seemed like she was at dinner with us, as we placed the laptop so it was pointing right at the table when we finally sat down. We French take our dining very seriously, so if our need to have a sit-down dinner before the DNA test seemed strange, it really wasn't. My only wish was that Sam could have actually, not virtually, been with us in person.

Sam wasn't alone, either. Once in a while, I could see her turn away from her webcam to talk to Ryan, who was there to film. Sam looked so American in her green plaid shirt. I loved everything about her, especially her positive attitude. She is always smiling, happy, and bubbly. I was wearing a horizontally striped white-and-black sailor shirt, so she probably thought I looked really French. The two of us were much quieter than usual, and for the most part, Marie and Lucas did the talking. When Sam would talk, Lucas would say our voices were so similar that if Samantha spoke French, he wouldn't be able to tell who was speaking.

"You should have cooked the same thing, and we could have eaten together," Marie said to Sam into the webcam as she took a seat at the table. Marie also spoke English with a heavy French accent, although she was more fluent than me. Sam and Marie had seen each other on Skype before and seemed to get along really well, which made me feel very comfortable. I liked that my friends were into my potential sister. In fact, it was really important to me, as it kind of validated me that Sam would surround herself with the same kind of people I tended to choose.

Sam was watching us as we started eating our spaghetti topped with a perfect spoonful of red sauce and the Parmesan cheese I had just finished grating, complemented by a bottle of red wine chosen by Lucas. "It's weird that French people eat with both hands," she remarked, meaning that we hold a utensil in each hand throughout the meal, not switching the fork, the way Americans do.

"OMG!" Sam exclaimed. "You guys are going to think we're so rude when we're eating together." Marie joked that the American way wasn't rude, it was all cultural. I thought the whole thing was pretty funny. We were all laughing when Marie made her observation about a similarity in our laughs, much like Lucas had pointed out the similarities in our speaking voices. "When you two laugh, it's exactly the same. It's crazy!" I had never thought about it before, but she was right.

We put out theories about how it would be possible for us to still be blood relatives in the event we weren't twins. Neither of us had ever had contact with anyone in our birth families/family, so all bets were off. "Our biological dad slept with two women?" I put out there first, pouring myself another glass of wine.

Marie thought that was hysterical. "At the same time?" she chortled, but I told her not at the same time, although the same day.

Sam had the grossest idea of all. "Or, if two brothers and two sisters did it, and then they got pregnant and they each had a kid . . ." Sam and I always went off on crazy, weird tangents whenever we had the chance to muse about how we came to be related. If we weren't twins, we were going to be related, no matter how much we had to use our imaginations. We meant that much to each other already.

The conversation turned to the intense media coverage our story had been getting. Marie said everybody in London was talking about us, and Sam and I knew it was getting coverage in South Korea. Since the launch of the Kickstarter campaign, reporters from around the world had been trying to track us down. Lucas asked Sam how big the story was in the United States, and Sam said it was being talked about on all the major networks besides being all over the Internet. I really hadn't anticipated this kind of attention when I had first contacted Sam. I still wasn't any different than I had been on that day in February. It really was crazy.

At one point, the Skype call froze. I could hear Sam and Ryan talking, but I couldn't see anything. Ryan was asking Sam, "Is it weird to see a French version of you?"

"Why'd she have to be French?" I heard Sam say as she broke out laughing. She was always teasing me like that, saying I was "soooo French!" She once told me that when she first heard from me, she had this image of me being totally stereotypically French—snobby accent, wearing a beret, and riding a clunky bicycle with a basket, a French baguette tucked under my arm. That's okay! I thought she was soooo American. I imagined her wearing T-shirts and baseball caps, and drinking one-liter cups of Starbucks coffee, walking in the streets with sunglasses on her way to the mall. I imagined her being super-easygoing, saying, "Heeeeey, guyyyys," in an American accent, gossiping with her girlfriends at pajama parties, and talking about boys on a baseball field after she had finished cheerleading.

After dinner, it was time for us to do the DNA test, "live" and together. "I'm gonna brush my teeth and be right back," I told Sam. (Turns out Sam and I both have a penchant for brushing our teeth several times a day!)

"It's like Christmas!" Sam said, unwrapping her envelope that had come from the lab. She started getting silly and put it on her head, and I did the same. I think we were both so anxious that we were trying to add some levity to the business of proving we were twins. Spiritually and emotionally, we were already there.

Sam and I were both nervous. At least the task at hand was simple—all we had to do was each collect a small amount of saliva from the inside of our cheek with our swab, then put what we had collected on the card provided and wait until it dried.

The instructions weren't complicated, but the results were so profoundly important that both us were very anxious about getting started. What if the slightest error in sample collecting made the whole trajectory from start to result go horribly wrong? I took it very seriously when Sam said, "Make sure you don't touch the little circles, because it says in the instructions that you have to use the swab, and swab your mouth on both sides, and press it onto the circles for like twenty to thirty seconds . . ."

I was beginning to feel self-conscious with my friends staring at me, like when your parents are watching you at

Christmas as they try to see your reaction to a gift they've given you. Four months earlier, I hadn't known Sam existed. Now we were four swabs away from being long-lost sisters touched by a miracle. My friends still thought the swabbing was unnecessary.

"Honestly," Marie said as Sam and I did our one-two-three-GO! "You guys really don't need the test. You are just the same. You even make the same faces."

Sam and I talked about a lot of other things we had in common. Both of us had had our wisdom teeth removed before they had even erupted, we could both raise one eyebrow, and we had the same fat big toe. We hated leaving the house without brushing our teeth, no matter how many times a day that might be, we had a phobia about being touched by the shower curtain, and we both preferred Coke to Pepsi! We each had a Napoleon complex and needed to sleep ten hours to promote our creativity and eat the rest of the day. Also, when either of us gets overwhelmed, we take a nap. These things were not going to come up on our DNA test.

We absolutely had the same sense of humor, too, although Sam was even more of a prankster than I am. "What if on the space to mark 'sex,' I wrote 'YES'?" she joked, borrowing from *Austin Powers*. We even goofed around about switching the names on the samples. Sam invented a scenario for us if we went onto one of those less-than-dignified American talk shows to get our results in front of a live audience. "The host comes out to the side, and he's like, 'And the results are . . . YOU ARE NOT TWINS' and everyone is like 'OHHHH!'" We both knew that wouldn't be the case, but what if it was? I couldn't even fathom the disappointment I would feel, and it would all be captured on camera.

The truth was that I really liked the idea of having a sister. I had grown up as an only child, and having a sibling was what I dreamed about most. Almost everybody I knew had brothers and sisters. I didn't care which sex my sibling was, brother or sister. It was always changing. Sometimes, I wished I had an older brother, because he would protect me, or I could date his friends. But sometimes I wanted an older sister, so she could show me how to dress up and put on makeup. Or I wished for a little sister, so I could show those very things to her. I had a best friend, Jonathan, who is still one of my best friends. He is thirteen months younger than I, and he is my *frère de coeur*, "a brother of the heart," like what Americans call a "blood brother." He's like my little brother, and has been for close to twenty years. He only had a mum—no brothers, sisters, or father. We were each other's siblings at heart.

Most of the time in my childhood, I wasn't that lonely without people my age at home. I had friends and activities, and hanging out with older family at holidays was fine, as I loved them all. But I was always expected to behave like an adult. Plus, old people just thought in very old ways. They didn't think the way I did or relate to my point of view. Older people were always living in the past. With Sam, I had a sister and a comrade. And she came with brothers, but I would have to discover more about them later.

Now it was time to seal our packages and ready them for posting. We had just signed off on our witnesses—mine were Marie and Lucas, and Sam had Ryan—when all of a sudden,

Sam stood up and put her hand over her heart. "Ready, Anaïs?" she asked me. She started to recite the Pledge of Allegiance to the United States.

"*Nonnn!*" Marie shouted at her. "We don't do that!" Marie, Lucas, and I began to sing "La Marseillaise," the national anthem of France.

"Nooooo!" I could hear Sam shouting back, trying to do the Pledge louder than "La Marseillaise." I think we won, because we were three against one, and we were singing really loudly. Lucas had to leave, so Sam, Marie, and I were left to discuss what would be a good place in London for us to get our results, now that our tests were sealed away. We were trying to think of someplace exotic or clever. Marie put forward someplace famous, like in front of Westminster Abbey, which made Sam think of Buckingham Palace. Marie topped that with her suggestion of the London Eye. "You get to the top, top, top, and when you can see all of London, that's when you should get the results," she said.

Sam and I nixed that idea. We didn't like Ferris wheels—another thing we had in common. We didn't care if Marie thought our fear would be mitigated by the fact that the Eye went so slowly. What would really go slowly was waiting for the results of the DNA test. We had launched our sisterhood already, but everybody likes to have her proof. We left open where in London we'd do it. We still had a few weeks to decide that. It was just fun to run ideas, because it made everything seem that much more inevitable.

10

SAM

our numbers match

Wednesday, April 24, another ordinary day, except that I had just swabbed my cheek the night before to see if I had a DNA match with a person who had grown up across the world. Taking a DNA test felt like such a strange thing to do. It was this big moment in my life, and yet, it was just Wednesday. It was really intense, and not intense, all at the same time. On the outside, it was like any other hump day, with me running around L.A., but inside my brain was cranking. I am not sure how Anaïs felt about it. She seemed to have a much more casual attitude. I mean, we were doing this DNA test that would affect the rest of our lives, and while I sat nervously waiting on Skype, she insisted on first sitting down with her friends to a dinner that lasted almost forty-five minutes—so French. I now understand it was her way of coping with the intensity of the situation, but at the time, I thought it was odd, if not downright rude. I guess the French don't give up feeding and socializing for anything.

Sometimes, when I was by myself, driving around L.A., I'd panic, fearing the worst. I'd be in my RAV4, blasting Justin Timberlake's "Mirrors," the song Anaïs and I had made a split-screen video to. I'd see Anaïs and me dancing around—each in our own apartments, but dancing wildly like children without cares or inhibitions. We were experiencing everything in virtual reality, but the moments were times I would never forget. I was sometimes afraid that all our shared joy would be for nothing if our fairy tale ended.

My nervousness would disappear as soon as I'd see Anaïs on Skype again. Each time we talked, it became more and more obvious that we were bonded in some inexplicable way—a way that wasn't like what I had with my brothers. It felt like something much more. I never had a sister, but when Anaïs came into my life, I believed that this was what having a sister would feel like.

Despite my moments of anxiety, I very quickly realized that no matter the outcome of the test, we would be lifelong friends. It seemed like I had climbed mountains with her already.

At the moment, I just wanted to get to London. We weren't going to have the results until I got there—I know, a weird choice to wait until then. Most people weighing in thought we should confirm it first before spending all the time, money, and emotional investment. But, I had to meet my other hobbit-like half and get the results with her sitting next to me. Our friends were already convinced we were identical twins, because not only did we look so much alike, we had the same mannerisms. We both liked the same things, and our thought processes were kind of similar. She liked to say random, weird things and make strange jokes, just like me. The idea of having a French twin was pretty appealing, too. I had always wanted to go to France, and now I had a reason. Not that I particularly thought French people were cool—I thought they were a pretentious, smelly, cigarette-smoking people. But I especially wanted to go to the Riviera, where French people with their hairy armpits walked around topless on the gorgeous beaches. I also imagined cobblestone streets filled with mimes, bicycles, and baguettes . . . but first I had to get to London.

The day after I mailed my DNA packet, I had a really strange dream about Anaïs. In the dream, her friend Marie had just cooked us an amazing pasta dish without ever putting the pasta in hot water. Anaïs was walking down the street, signaling for me to follow her. Suddenly, she started to change, looking less and less like me as she walked away. All of our friends were looking at us out of big glass windows. The scene was kind of beachy, with old gas lampposts, but it was also combined with elements of my childhood neighborhood in Verona. I followed Anaïs for a while, until she stopped. When I finally caught up to her, she turned around and didn't look like me anymore. It was haunting. It was as if all the fears of mine throughout the day were playing out in my dreams/nightmares. My concern about whether or not I had a twin, or if I needed to pair a twin with a decent meal, was hitting me hard. The relief I felt when I woke up was palpable. Already, I had learned so much from Dr. Segal. Since my first visit, I had gone to see her several more times. I had so many questions for her. She showed me a few reunion tapes of other reared-apart twins she had studied over the years. Dr. Segal also showed me all of her work and research. She went over a couple of the studies she had conducted, including one she had coauthored in 2008 with a behavioral specialist named Yoon-Mi Hur from Chonnam National University in South Korea. The subjects were Korean twin sisters raised apart, one in South Korea and the other in the United States. Although their story was extremely similar to ours—if it turned out Anaïs and I were twins—one of the girls had been raised by her own birth family in South Korea, and the other by her adoptive family in the United States. The twins' biological parents already had two children, a four-year-old and a ten-month-old, and could only afford to keep one of the twins. The other baby was surrendered to foster care on the day of birth and adopted by an East Coast couple two months later. Both families stayed in touch via letters, facilitated by social workers in South Korea, so both sisters always knew they had a twin. The girls began direct contact with each other when they were twelve and met for the first time when they were seventeen.

Dr. Segal's study found some interesting similarities in the two girls. For example, both sisters hated fish, even though fish was a staple in South Korea; both were extremely musical, with one playing piano and the other violin; and they both had identical IQ scores, even though they had been raised in different cultures and with different educational exposure.

The scenario of one twin staying with the family and one being adopted was really upsetting. I couldn't imagine having to deal with that. What would I feel if I knew I was given away, but my twin was kept with our birth family? How would the family feel? Guilty? Also, how about the later emotions of the one who was not good enough, the one who was given up? But then again, what if I was the one kept with the family? Why should I be chosen to be kept with the family? And what about our mother? This was so much more haunting than thinking about my situation with Anaïs. In our case, we were equals, both given up by our birth mother. But, our equality ended when we went to our adoptive homes. I had feelings of guilt that I had the better deal. Anaïs was raised as an only child, but I grew up with two older brothers, and why was I so fortunate? I hadn't even met Anaïs, and I already wanted to tell her I would have switched positions with her in a heartbeat if it would have made her feel better.

From Dr. Segal's studies, I found out just how fascinating twins are, whether they are raised together or apart. Before I knew better, I always tended to think twins were just really creepy. It could have been the idea of having a blood relative that similar freaked me out, but identical twins especially were completely uncanny. In Dr. Segal's book *Entwined Lives: Twins and What They Tell Us About Human Behavior*, published by Dutton in May 1999, she talks about the genetic influences that affect every person's character. According to her, genetics play a role in sociability, IQ, athletic ability, career choice, job satisfaction, and personality.

In twins, Dr. Segal has the best possible subjects to explore genetics and human behavior. Some of her focuses are competition, cooperation, and bonding, traits I looked forward to exploring with Anaïs. The bonding that was already going on between us, two strangers really, was remarkable, and I was excited to learn more. Could Anaïs be just as strange as me? Would she like to eat cheese? Did her feet smell? I was already an anthropology nerd, so I was really into the concept of nature vs. nurture. If Anaïs and I could bond as strongly as we had over the Internet, what would it be like in person? In our text messaging, we could communicate using only emoticons for pages on end. What would we possibly be saying to each other after we met?

As for Dr. Segal's study of twins separated at birth, she had been on the cutting edge of many high-profile and important studies. Early in her career, she had participated in the landmark University of Minnesota Study of Twins Reared Apart, a comprehensive research project on genetic influences in humans. The study was initiated by Dr. Thomas Bouchard, a professor of psychology and director of the Minnesota Center for Twin and Family Research at the University of Minnesota. This was the most extensive research to show that nature (genetics) as well as nurture (environment) affects someone's personality and psychological traits. Until this study, the assumption was someone's upbringing and environment were the major components of his personality and behavior. It didn't discount the importance of role models and parenting, but it showed a person's behavior might just be genetically driven.

Dr. Bouchard had launched his study in 1979, when he learned of a set of identical twins, Jim Springer and Jim Lewis, who had been separated soon after birth and reunited thirty-nine years later. He read about the men's reunion in a newspaper and was intrigued by the astonishing number of similarities outlined in the story. Both men had been christened "James" by their parents; both had childhood dogs named Toy; both had married women named Linda, whom they divorced, and remarried women named Betty; one had named his first son James Allen, the other James Alan (the same first and middle names, albeit spelled differently); both had police training and worked part-time with law-enforcement agencies; both men were nail biters; and both had identical smoking and drinking habits, with both smoking Salem cigarettes and drinking Miller beer. The ability to study identical twins reared by different families enabled Dr. Bouchard to observe shared mannerisms that were likely genetic.

Dr. Bouchard and his "Jim Twins," as the men came to be known, attracted enormous attention and publicity. It was a time in American psychology when genetic influence was actually unpopular. Not many people explored the blend of genetic and environmental influences on behavior, but Dr. Bouchard's study of this one set of reared-apart twins created such interest that many reared-apart twins started contacting him. What began as just a small examination of a couple of pairs of identical twins grew into a full-blown study of more than 130 sets of twins, both identical and fraternal, who had been adopted and raised apart. In most of the cases, the subjects had not known they had a twin somewhere until much later in their lives.

When the study began, Dr. Segal was a graduate student at the University of Chicago, where she was also studying twins. She had found a pair of identical twins separated at birth in her research, and she referred them to Dr. Bouchard. In 1982, she joined Dr. Bouchard as a postdoctoral fellow, and eventually she became the assistant director of the Minnesota Study of Twins Reared Apart. She did everything from contacting twins, to analyzing data, to handling the twins' arrangements while they were in Minnesota. She described the experience as "heaven on earth," and credited Dr. Bouchard's success with the study to his brilliance, charm, and engaging personality.

The Minnesota Twin Project went on for twenty years, from 1979 to 1999. The data collected was mind-blowing. Dr. Segal said the information gathered was so extensive there is still a treasure trove of data not yet analyzed. Some of the commonalities the twins in the study shared with each other seemed impossible, except they were true. One really interesting pair was Oskar Stohr and Jack Yufe. They were born in the early 1930s in British Trinidad to a Romanian father and a German mother. When they were six months old, their parents split. The mother took Oskar back to Germany, where his grandmother raised him in the Catholic faith and where he participated in the Hitler Youth. Jack, who remained with his father in the Caribbean, was raised Jewish and spent part of his growing-up years on an Israeli kibbutz, and was a member of the Israeli Navy.

When the men met in their early twenties, the first time since infancy, they failed to find common ground or any reason to forge a relationship. They spoke different languages, German and Yiddish; they had no commonality in politics or religion; and they didn't particularly like each other. Although they wrote letters once in a while, the two didn't see each other again for twenty-five years, until Jack read something about the Minnesota study of twins and called to see if he and his brother could participate. From the moment the two men met at the airport, the uncanny similarities between them began to emerge. They were both wearing wire-rimmed glasses, their shirts both had two pockets and epaulets, and they both had mustaches.

Other fascinating things that came out during their testing were that both men were absentminded, liked spicy foods, dunked buttered toast in their coffee, drank sweet liquors, read magazines from back to front, wore rubber bands on their wrists, struggled with math but showed talent in sports, and fell asleep watching TV. The two most bizarre coincidences were that both men flushed the toilet before and after they used it, and they let out loud, fake sneezes when they were in an uncomfortable silence, such as in a crowded elevator.

I found twin similarities to be incredibly intriguing. I learned that the participants in the twin study were asked more than fifteen thousand questions and stayed on location in Minnesota for a week, undergoing hours upon hours of testing. Dr. Segal was going to do a battery of tests on Anaïs and me, just as soon as it was established by DNA that we were twins. The DNA would show if we were identical or fraternal. I was surprised to find that even parents were really poor judges of whether their same-sex twins were fraternal or identical, but that's exactly what Dr. Segal discovered: that you can't necessarily tell by appearance. Twins who look almost exactly alike may be fraternal and twins who don't resemble each other so closely may be identical.

Dr. Segal had a pair of twins in the Minnesota study that showed just how hard it was. The two girls, Kerrie and Amy, were adopted as infants by different families in different parts of Vermont. When Kerrie moved to a city in Vermont at the age of eighteen, she noticed that people started to call her Amy.

Seven years later, she was at a party and one of the male guests said he'd bet a million dollars she had a twin named Amy. He even offered to introduce them. Several phone calls later the women met and were amazed by their resemblance to each other. However, the interesting piece was that they were not identical twins, as confirmed by their DNA test; they were look-alike dizygotic twins, aka fraternal twins. This was the only occasion in the Minnesota study where fraternal twins found each other by being mistaken for the other one. To show how difficult it is in some instances to tell identical from fraternal, in the case of Kerrie and Amy, Dr. Segal's team did an informal assessment of the women and guessed that they were identical. They were wrong, but just this once.

Essentially, dizygotic twins come about when two eggs are fertilized by two different sperm. Identical twins, also known as "monozygotic twins," come from one egg fertilized by one sperm that divides up to fourteen days after conception. Identical twins, which are about one-third of the natural twin population, occur in approximately three of every thousand births. Whatever kind of twins we were, we were looking beyond that to the personality testing. We were both really looking forward to finding out what Dr. Segal thought our similarities and differences were.

IQ tests scared me. I didn't really understand how they worked or how they were scored, but I always thought of myself on the lower end of intelligence. I'd be dismally dumb, Anaïs's would be off-the-charts smart, and sure enough . . . I was, in fact, an idiot. Anaïs knew better how these things worked and assured me that most twins came back almost exactly the same. At that very moment, we were so dumbfounded at our similarities that it took all the attention away from the fear of being scored . . . a complete idiot. Thankfully, Anaïs was smart enough to use social media to find me, and I was smart enough to (finally) message her back! Otherwise, we would never have connected. Either that, or we were so "twin-connected" that we found ourselves crossing paths on social media only because our inner souls were always searching for one another. Perhaps we had always been searching for each other, and our stars finally aligned.

Dr. Segal gave the Internet a lot of credit for bringing reared-apart twins together. The twenty-year Minnesota study ended when the reared-apart twin pool seemed to be drying up, which led to the assumption that the majority of that population had been discovered. However, she said because of the Internet, twins were discovering each other like crazy. In fact, she had a pair of seventy-eight-year-old twins in London about to meet each other for the first time. They were the longest-separated reared-apart twins to find each other in research history. I was relieved that Anaïs and I didn't have to wait that long. We'd look awfully silly if we had met fifty years later—we'd be two seventy-eight-year-old Asian hobbity identical twins dancing to Justin Timberlake: not quite as cute and appealing as we were now. Maybe fifty years from now, we would not have had to fly to meet each other. We could use drones to transport us to each other's doorstep, and the DNA test would be a complete scan of our bodies, which by then would be advanced enough to tell how many cells we had in common and how many seconds we had been alive, so we could finally put to rest which of us was older!

Already, Dr. Segal was 99 percent convinced of our biological connection. She even called it a foregone conclusion. She said not only were we so similar, but we fit together perfectly and were amazingly comfortable with each other. It was a comfort level she had seen in other twins who were separated at birth. The only thing that was still giving her pause was that we had been handled by different adoption agencies in South Korea. It was a strange concept for everyone.

Dr. Segal said that she would be more surprised if it turned out we weren't twins. Anaïs and I felt the same way, although I did have moments when I simply couldn't believe it myself. But, Dr. Segal's "99 percent convinced" actually left me teetering on the ledge—what about the 1 percent chance still there that we weren't twins? The 1 percent overwhelmed me, because in 1 percent, I could lose my footing, lose myself, and lose my Anaïs. I liked being in control. When I knew with certainty, I could take a course of action. With 1 percent still out there, I didn't want anyone to know that I was 99 percent insecure. I wanted to be strong inside, to show that it didn't matter whether or not we were twins. I truly believed the idea that she would still mean something very special to me, but somewhere inside I was terrified.

That was until I got a call from Ben Sommers, my social worker at Spence-Chapin in New York City. Ben had been assigned to my case in February, when I had first called the agency about the possibility of being a twin. I learned that he was a Korean-American adoptee as well, and had even reunited with his birth family.

Ben was my main correspondent between the adoption agency in New York and the Social Welfare Society (SWS) in Seoul. He was also in contact with Holt International, Anaïs's adoption agency. Ben translated every bit of information we got from SWS about our birth families. He was incredibly support-ive. Knowing that he was an adoptee himself was comforting on a very deep level, since he understood what it was like to find blood relatives and be reunited with them for the very first time. He wasn't there to tell me how my experience would go, but to offer his own experience while guiding me through mine.

On April 30, I got a message from Ben, asking me to call him. He had important information, but he didn't say what. I immediately panicked. I had the feeling that happens after you have a doctor's appointment, and the doctor calls saying he has the results, and asking if you can come in. I mean, that only happens when they're telling you something very dire. Ben's call probably had something to do with my birth mother or some problem with our birth records. My heart rate was bumping from my butt to my throat.

When I called Ben back, he told me there was good news. My heart rose from out of my butt, back into its residing position in my chest. Apparently every Korean citizen has a Resident Registration Number, similar to our Social Security Number, and my birth mother's number matched that of Anaïs's. The chances of this being some sort of typo or mis-take were almost impossible, especially in light of our shared birthdays and physical similarities. But there was more. A social worker at the postadoption agency in Korea had been able to confirm that Anaïs and I had been born in the same birthing clinic in Busan. However, the person could not get any further information. The clinic had long since closed, and the doctor who had delivered babies there had passed away.

Ben said my birth mother had also been recontacted. The year before, when I had been in Korea, I knew there had been an attempt to contact her, and the result had been "no response." I thought that meant she hadn't answered their inquiry. But Ben seemed to think someone had talked to her, and she had denied having given birth to any children, ever. He said her response was the same this year as it had been last year. Again, she told them she couldn't be my mother, because she'd never had children. When they pressed her further, asking about twins, she still denied it. I asked Ben if it could be possible that they really did have the wrong woman, but he didn't seem to think so. So really, the only way we could find out what happened and why we were separated was with information from our birth mother, who was currently denying our existence.

I fell silent. I was frozen. What do I say? How do I respond? I was just completely overwhelmed. It wasn't bad news, yet it didn't feel good, either. I was making obligatory "uh-huhs" and "yeahs" on the phone to let Ben know that I was still there, that I hadn't hung up on him, but I'm not sure if I was even really listening. I could hear everything he was saying, I could hear his voice, and I was taking it in, but my body felt inflated. I could feel it breathing and pressing against the air.

When his words became clear again, Ben was suggesting that it would be a good idea for both Anaïs and me to write a letter to our birth mother and send it to SWS, along with a current photo, so they could keep them on file. He told me it could take a long time for a birth mother to reconcile the past. He said unfortunately sometimes mothers who have given up their children for adoption didn't feel the level of empowerment often needed for them to face something that they had long tried to bury. Korean society had a lot to do with it. He thought it was slowly beginning to loosen and the stigma around adoption was lifting. Once that fully happened, more and more birth mothers might feel comfortable enough to establish relationships with their birth children. He explained that every birth mother was different, and some could find that courage more quickly than others. So much depended on their support system, their level of disclosure about having put a child up for adoption, and their current situation.

The phone call with Ben ended with him telling me not to be too discouraged. "I do hope that you don't feel like this is the end. I know it's tough and frustrating to not get further in your inquiry, but there will be future opportunities to revisit this," he said empathetically. Once again, Ben was there for me, guiding me or giving me fair warnings about what could possibly go wrong. He told me that sometimes meeting a birth family was more awkward than joyful, that although there was a connection, the timing might not be right. With a letter to her on file, if she ever decided to come forward, she would find it waiting for her.

When I hung up, I dropped my head into my hands and

started crying. I felt so much pain for my birth mother. It pained me inside to think that she was living in denial and could never be honest with herself or her family about her family and her past. I felt pain for myself, too. I felt pain for Anaïs. My own parents were filled with crazy emotions about all this. They were really upset that Anaïs and I hadn't been available to adopt together. If they had known I had a twin, they would have happily adopted both of us. However, my mother acknowledged that if she had taken both of us, the Bordiers would not have had their delightful Anaïs, as they were meant to be her parents.

Mom was also extremely upset that we had been separated, because we had been denied a lifetime with our twin, time we would never get back. While Anaïs and I were celebrating that we had found each other, our parents were mourning the loss of our childhood together, regretting the situation on our behalf. It was a very parental reaction, because both sets of our parents had devoted themselves to our happiness and joy, and they felt we had been shortchanged. They were probably more desperate to know why we were separated than we were. That was the remaining mystery, one that we might never know the answer to.

Ben followed up our phone call with an e-mail that included the letter from the postadoption department of Spence-Chapin in Korea:

Regarding this case, we spoke with the birth
mother couple of times on the phone.
Unfortunately, her reaction was same as last year.

She still denied the fact that she sent her baby
for adoption. She also didn't admit that she
delivered twins.

As I informed earlier, her birth parents name is
same as Holt's. Furthermore, their birth clinic was
also same. Judging from these circumstances,
Samantha and Anaïs are twins.

However, we were not able to obtain any clue or
explanation from the birth mother. So we tried to
find the doctor of their birth clinic, but the clinic
was closed long time ago and the doctor already
passed away.

Therefore, we were not able to get any further
explanation about this twins case.

I'm so sorry that I can't give Samantha any
clear answer. However, there's no other way for us
to make it clear at this point.

The news was definitely remarkable. Even the agency was
confirming we were likely twins. Our birth mother not admit-
ting the past didn't change the solid evidence. All that was left
was the DNA results, which we would have in a couple of
weeks. I can't speak for Anaïs, but the fact that our birth mother
had again denied birthing us was completely overwhelming. I
wasn't angry; I was at peace with the fact that I had always been
loved. Still, it was emotionally devastating to hear.

I didn't know how to tell Anaïs. She had always had a
feeling of rejection and never wanted to explore our past. And
it was for this exact reason. I didn't want to confirm the pain

she had always feared. I wanted to dance and celebrate again, like the day I got Anaïs's message. But I couldn't, and I had so much left to do, including having to break the news to Anaïs in about twenty minutes.

The days leading up to our trip to London were intense. I was still having "what-ifs" running through my head, but I was so focused on organizing the documentary, it didn't really hit me that we were leaving soon. Maybe distracting myself with the film was my way of tempering my emotions, my own way of dealing with the stress of it all.

Anaïs and I also decided that we were going to write a book about our experience to complement the film. We wanted our book to get deeper into the topics of nature vs. nurture, adoption, sisterhood, and the power of social media. Both projects would be so much fun to do, and sharing our experience with the world could possibly even give others courage to seek and find something they had only dreamed about.

Anaïs and I did not need a DNA test to prove we were twins. As far as we were concerned, the test was simply to let us know if we were fraternal or identical. Learning about Anaïs had undeniably changed my perception of who I was. In one way, she was a stranger to me, as I was to her. Yet, the feeling of love and connectedness we had for each other could only be the love of family.

Our incredible twist of fate could lift one to rejoice that anything was possible, and that the biggest boundaries in life were the ones we set for ourselves. There are so many possibilities and so many crazy things that happen in a lifetime, and it is a gift to embrace them all. At the moment, our relationship was a "virtual reality," but how was it possible to feel so strongly about someone I had never properly met? Why was I able to lose all inhibitions and speak to her more frankly than any other person? It has been said that "the eyes are the windows to the soul," but did that count if the eyes were connected through an electronic device that I was able to hold in the palm of my hand? All I knew was I had an innate, unconditional love toward this relative stranger.

For now, I was counting the days until I would meet my sister. Every morning, I would wake up and look at my phone to see if she had texted me. I couldn't wait to just hang out with her—to see what connections formed, what thoughts and feelings arose, even in the inevitable silences. I played over and over again how our meeting would go. Turning our story into something we could share with the world was what we wanted to do in the book. The documentary was going to capture the immediate reactions and feelings of everybody as they unfolded live.

The weekend before London, I ran around L.A. to rent camera equipment, get production insurance, and finalize last-minute travel plans. When things start to feel like they are out of control, organizing helps me get my head back into the game and makes me feel productive. My family was coming from different places, my parents and Matt from New Jersey, and Andrew was coming from Oregon. He had finished a tour of duty in Iraq with the U.S. Army, and he was studying fisheries and wildlife biology at Oregon State University. I was flying from L.A. earlier, but that didn't keep me from fretting about the details of their arrival. I wanted everything to go absolutely perfectly.

The Sunday before we left was Mother's Day, so of course I had to work! It's a mandatory workday in the restaurant business, as it's the most popular day of the year to eat out. In Beverly Hills, a lot of mothers are a bit self-centered, so if their food doesn't come out right away or they can't get exactly what they want, then you're doomed. In my opinion, they should be thankful for having families that want to spend time with them. I am beyond grateful for my mother and what she has done for me. And I was especially grateful for the support and love she was giving me now, as I was potentially finding a blood relative, a sister! My parents have surrounded me with nothing but love from the moment they received their first photo of me in the mail. I was in their hearts from the beginning, maybe before they even began the adoption process.

Besides all the things I had to do to get ready for London, everyone was calling and texting me, and I felt like all I wanted to do was crawl into bed with a bag of Lay's baked sour cream and cheddar potato chips, watch some Science Channel, and take a big-ass nap. But I didn't have time for that. I was in full "go/work" mode. I wasn't nice to anyone, except Anaïs. When I would text her, she would inevitably make me happy. Being in a bad mood is so funny sometimes, except for the parties on the receiving end. I know it's ridiculous, but I get in this mode where if people say anything I remotely disagree with, I can't even look them in the eye for the rest of the day, and digging me out of that pissed-off hole can be challenging.

Luckily, I have the most amazing friends and family;

they know when to deal with me, and when to leave me alone. That week, they pretty much stayed back before we left on the trip. Maybe they were scared of me having a mental breakdown, chopping off all my hair, and trashing the apartment, in true Hollywood meltdown style, or maybe it was all in my head. But they just kept everything positive and let me go into an organizational rampage.

Ryan was filming almost every moment up until we left. If I was freaking out, he would just start filming and let me resolve everything myself. His job was to capture every important moment on camera, not to make me feel better. Sometimes, I appreciate someone just listening to me instead of telling me how I should be feeling. You cannot hide from the bad or hard things in life. Without the negative, there is no positive. There is such a balance in life, and sometimes things can get really difficult. What do I do to help myself? I organize everything! I vacuum and dust; I make my bed; I do small things to help me feel like I have at least a pinch of control. Besides, what use was there to get all wrapped up and have a "Samantha Meltdown" and try to control everything?

By the day I left, Monday, May 13, I had done almost all of my tasks. I had a few more to complete during the course of the morning. So I woke up early, took a shower, did a video blog at my producer's behest, got dressed, went to Burbank to drop off my production insurance check, picked up Kanoa, went to get lunch, brushed my teeth, put my toothbrush in my suitcase, and got everything into the car. Phew.

Now it was time for the trip to LAX, Los Angeles International Airport, and I was finally calm. I had Ryan, Kanoa, and Lisa with me, and it was time for me to just say: fuck it. Even if Anaïs and I were not twins, this would be a defining moment in my life. It was going to be the single most intense experience I would ever have. I was going to find, hopefully, my long-lost twin. Lindsay Lohan's character had made it through the experience in *The Parent Trap*, and I could, too. And if I couldn't? I didn't want to imagine. And there was no use in trying to. And if Anaïs and I turned out to not be twins . . . then that would be even more insane.

At the airport, I was rolling my ugly-ass polka dot suitcase toward the sliding glass doors, when I suddenly got fired up. I started dancing and jumping around. My heart was pounding in my chest, and I felt elated, extremely present in that very moment. I could even feel the air on my skin as the sweat started to form. I was going to meet my twin sister for the first time since we left the womb!

We checked our bags, exchanged some money, and headed to the duty-free shops, where I bought See's candy for our new-to-be friends in London, and red wine for Anaïs's parents. By the time we got to the gate, it was so crowded that we had to sit on the floor. I took out my iPod and started taking selfies of me, my ticket, Kanoa, Ryan making his video, everything. I couldn't stop. The moment was of excitement, fear, and accomplishment all in one.

When we were called to board, it was time. I quickly texted Anaïs to let her know we were on the plane and about to take off. What I really wanted her to know was that I hadn't changed my mind; I was still coming to see her. If I were Anaïs, I'd want that final text message right before takeoff. Otherwise,

I know I would be freaking out, worrying that she had changed her mind, and that she didn't really want to see me. At that point, I'd be so distraught at the disappointment and failure that I wouldn't know what to do. I couldn't let Anaïs start imagining the worst, so I let her know that everything was going as planned. Everyone getting on the flight sounded so British, which made sense but impressed me nevertheless. It made me giggle in the most immature, ignorant way possible. I stared out the window as beads of sweat started to form on my neck, armpits, and hands. My thoughts began to race. I was playing out the two scenarios in my head. The first would be if we weren't twins. In that case, I would enjoy my time in London exploring the vast city with a short but insane story to tell. If it turned out that we were twins, then I would spend the rest of my trip and the rest of my life exploring the realm of possibilities of finding my other half. Then the announcement came on. The cabin doors had closed and before I knew it, I could feel the plane rumbling underneath me. We were taking off. It was time, and there was no looking back. It reminded me of the time I went bungee jumping in New Zealand, standing on a ledge looking down 134 meters to the landing zone in what would be one of the most insane moments I'll ever experience, especially being afraid of heights. I could feel my heart pounding in my body and my breath billowing through. I was only looking forward and had nothing left to do but jump.

11

ANAÏS

london

The week before Sam arrived, I was freaking out. I couldn't have been happier that I had contacted her, and our plans to meet in person were getting closer, but I was plenty nervous. I still had my fashion show for my final project to put on, and that alone was overwhelming. Between Sam arriving, her parents and brothers coming, my parents coming, learning the results of the DNA test, and the fashion show, there was a lot going on. As crazy as it sounds, being this hectic was actually energizing.

May 13 was the most extraordinary day. Even when Sam's plane was still in the air, I was delirious. *Do I feel something? Do I feel something?* I would keep saying, barely able to focus on anything but where she might be in her flight. As each hour passed, I'd think, *Okay, now she is closer.* We were bonded by invisible strings. There was a lot of wind that day, too, so I hoped there weren't any delays. Sam finally texted to say her morning touchdown at London's Heathrow Airport was eventful, but I couldn't see her yet. The plan was well thought out in terms of where, when, and who was going to be with us when we met for the first time, but we had both agreed it wasn't going to be in such a public place as an airport. It was so exciting, though, knowing she was now on my side of the ocean, closer to me than ever.

I went to school in the morning as if it were any other day. The agenda was to attend morning classes, pick up my parents around noon, and meet Sam around three. I had invited my Korean friend Jennifer Lee to accompany me. I knew Sam had friends with her, and having someone with me would make our first meeting less scary. My parents had taken the Eurostar from Paris to London, arriving at Kings Cross around lunchtime, and Jennifer and I met them there to walk them over to their hotel.

After my parents put their luggage in the room, my dad headed to Piccadilly Arcade to visit his retail store. He liked checking in if he was in town. One thing about him, he was very hardworking and dedicated, and I appreciate that. Mum was going to come with me to meet Sam. I had been waiting for this moment ever since Kelsang had first sent me the You-Tube video, and my mother deserved to share it with me.

Mum, Jennifer, and I headed for the bus that would take us to Old Street, where Sam and the documentary crew were staying in a flat they had rented in Shoreditch. Old Street was in the trendy, young part of town about thirty minutes southeast of Finsbury Park, where I lived. Sam's parents and her two brothers would be staying at a small hotel in Islington, not too far away, but they weren't arriving until Thursday.

Sam and I agreed that it would be too scary to be just the two of us at our first meeting, so the flat already had lots of people there as supportive friends on both sides. Sam had James, Ryan, and Kanoa—part of the crew but friends as well; and Lisa, her flat mate; I had sent Marie, Lucas, and my friend Mátyás ahead of me, especially wanting Marie to scope Sam out, and I had Jen and Mum with me now.

On the bus, my mother was on a cloud and saying very little. I could see in her eyes she was somewhere else, like she was daydreaming. "I can't believe this is really happening," she kept repeating. I thought she would be stressed out or overly excited, but she wasn't. "This is fun," she said. "I can't even comprehend that we are on our way to meet your possible twin sister."

A few minutes into the ride, I got a text from Marie saying she was in place at the flat, and she had met Sam. I didn't want to ask Marie too many questions about what she thought, because I didn't want to have anybody else's impressions influencing my own. The one question I asked was if seeing Sam had caused her to be emotional enough to actually cry. "Almost," Marie informed me. She told me to hurry up and get there, as she was really excited and anxious.

We were late, of course. First, the bus was slow, and then we couldn't find the flat. Old Street reminded me of Brooklyn, New York, with a lot of former warehouses turned into residential lofts, so finding the right building wasn't easy. Finally,

James, a producer of the documentary, came looking for us. I had met him the night before. He had flown in ahead of the rest of the group, and he had come to my flat to do some on-camera interviews with me. It had been a lot of fun. He was really nice, and it had been my first chance to be in front of the camera and express feelings I was having about Sam's arrival. James had made me very comfortable with that.

I started to get really nervous as James led us into the building. Sam was so close, if I screamed her name, she would be able to hear me. My heart was pounding in anticipation, as if she might jump out from a doorway and startle me. James was beaming as he encouraged me on. When I'd turn around to see how Mum was doing, she'd just smile her huge smile. She was so happy for me. James stopped at a massive door that led to the flat. I imagined everyone lurking behind it, almost like they were waiting for me at a surprise party. I was so nervous that I decided to get behind my mother and Jennifer and let them go in first. James slowly pushed the door open, as my anxiety piqued, but there was no one on the other side. It was just a large hallway, where there were other doors that actually led to living quarters. False start!

Now, without a doubt, everyone would be behind the next door waiting. My mischievous side got the better of me, and I decided I would have Jennifer enter first and pretend she was me. She was Korean, but she really didn't look very much like me. Nobody would be expecting her, though, and while they would eventually catch on, I still thought it would be really funny. Plus, it would give me a few more seconds to compose myself, and I could spoil any tricks they may have had planned.

I knew Sam was as capable as I was of crafting something. Being pranksters was something we had in common.

James opened the second door, and I nudged Jennifer in. For three seconds, there was nothing but silence. "This is Jennifer," I finally heard James say, exposing my stunt double. What happened next was a blur. I might have pushed my mum in before me, but maybe she pushed me in. I knew Sam was in the room, but I couldn't hear her saying anything, and I still didn't know if she had a surprise entrance planned. I had fantasized so much about this moment for so many months, but I had also had fleeting moments of fear wondering if we would be disappointed in each other. What if we weren't that much alike after all? I usually dismissed those fears quickly. Sam and I Skyped every day, using our webcams, and we were most definitely alike. But would we hug?

Finally, I couldn't delay any longer. I entered the room, and there was Sam. She was sitting in the corner on a three-foot-high carved golden elephant, part of the eclectic décor of the apartment. Everyone in the room was staring at both of us, silently waiting for us to have a reaction. I wasn't even sure Sam was looking at me. She seemed like she was avoiding eye contact, instead looking at her friends. I wasn't really looking at her, either. Finally, she stood up. OMG, was she short. I wondered if she was thinking the same thing about me.

The whole experience was so awkward and scary. Neither of us knew what to do next, so we just stood in the middle of the room, staring at each other, like two tiny dogs sniffing each other out. I was staring at my clone, looking at myself in the mirror, but my reflection was not doing what I was doing.

At first, I couldn't hear anything, not that people weren't speaking, but I wasn't processing their voices. Then I heard Jennifer's voice. "Hug!" she was yelling. "Hug!" But neither Sam nor I moved. We were just paralyzed in observance of each other. Suddenly, I burst into uncontrollable giggles, and Sam started giggling, too.

Mum was just staring. She had tears in her eyes, and she looked stunned. In fact, I had never seen her this dazed. Usually in circumstances that were emotional, she was very expressive and animated. Now she appeared as paralyzed as Sam and me.

"No, you have to be twins," she kept repeating.

I moved closer to Sam, then poked her in the head. I had to see if she was real. When I felt her skin, it was confirmed, but I still couldn't look her in the eyes. I had always heard that if you look directly into your eyes in your reflection in the mirror, you might die, and Sam was my reflection. But it was weirder than that. When you looked in the mirror, you were seeing yourself in 2-D, and Sam was me in 3-D, a perspective of myself I had never seen before. She looked so much like me, I briefly thought I was in a near-death experience, when you leave your own body and see yourself dying. That was how out-of-body it was. I didn't want to stare too long, but I couldn't help myself.

By now, everyone was giggling. I don't know how much time passed, but eventually everybody became a little more composed and social. I already knew James, and I recognized Ryan, Kanoa, and Lisa from our Skype time. Now Ryan was behind the camera and Kanoa and Lisa were sitting on the

The Bordiers picking up Anaïs at
Charles de Gaulle Airport

Anaïs, 1988

Sam with the judge, gaining her citizenship

Sam, Verona, New Jersey, 1988

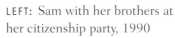

LEFT: Sam with her brothers at her citizenship party, 1990

BELOW LEFT: THE Futermans in J-E-T-S regalia!

Sam with Kevin Wu at the premiere of *21 & Over*

Sam's first trip to Korea, 2012

LEFT: Jacques, Patricia, and Anaïs Bordier in Korea, 1995

BELOW LEFT AND RIGHT: Anaïs in Korea, 1995

Anaïs's Central Saint Martins College of Arts and Design graduation

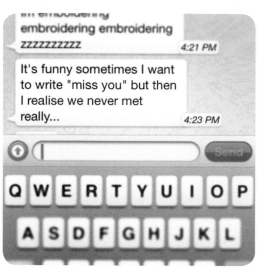

Screenshot of Anaïs and Sam's
WhatsApp conversation

Anaïs and Sam Skyping before
they met

BELOW: Anaïs and Sam on the day they first met

The documentary crew with friends and family at the Harry Potter studios

Sam, Anaïs, and Kelsang cutout
at the Tower, London

Birthday celebration with the Bordiers.
Vive la France!

ABOVE: Sam and Anaïs in Los Angeles

BELOW: Anaïs and Sam at Gyeongbokgung Palace

Anais and Sam at the Los Angeles Angels' game

LEFT: Anaïs and Sam at Holt International Children's Services

BELOW: Anaïs, Sam, and Anaïs's foster mother

BELOW: Anaïs, Sam, and Sam's foster mother

Anaïs and Sam on their
twenty-sixth birthday

Anaïs and Sam in Montmartre

The Futermans and Bordiers during Thanksgiving

couch, staring and smiling. Kanoa was even more gorgeous in person than he was on webcam. Ryan was pretty cute, too. I tried my best to act naturally in front of Ryan and his video camera, but it was pretty hard, in light of the fact that this was the most incredible thing that had ever happened in my life. The same with Sam's life, but she had been trained to be in front of the camera and seemed very comfortable. The ten people in the room with us really stayed in the background and allowed this to be our moment, but it still felt so public and awkward. We had buffered ourselves with a lot of people on purpose; the idea of being completely alone together was just too anxiety provoking. I was afraid that it might be awkward and we wouldn't hit it off—or worse, we would have nothing to say to each other. Throughout the introductions, Sam and I kept watching each other. So that's what my nostrils look like, I thought. Sam had such small feet, too. I knew my feet were small, but seeing them on Sam, they looked freakishly small. We even had the same hair length, although Sam's was parted farther to the side.

Everybody was starving, so after about a half hour, we decided to go to the Breakfast Club for pancakes. There were about six of these casual American-style cafés in London, but we went to the one on Hoxton Square, where Central Saint Martins students liked to eat and hang out. My friend Olya joined us there. I wanted to share my experience of meeting Sam with her, and she had been particularly curious.

The whole group stayed at the restaurant for a couple of hours. Sam and I were sometimes sitting next to each other, sometimes not, as everybody changed seats and moved around the table in order to optimize conversation. Although Sam and I tried not to be too obvious, we would often catch each other inventorying the other one's looks. I couldn't get enough of looking at her, still in disbelief. One thing for sure, Sam was pretty. I hoped I was as pretty as she! Both my friends and hers were really connecting, which added to the comfort level of the whole event.

After the laid-back afternoon at the Breakfast Club, my mother and most of my friends left for their hotels or flats. It had been tremendous fun, but Sam and I were exhausted and needed a nap before the second-most-important event of the day—Dr. Segal was scheduled to Skype us the results of the DNA test at ten p.m. London time. How strange that we agreed to take a nap together in the same bed. Actually, it wasn't even awkward. It felt almost natural, completely normal. It was our first moment alone together, and how much more intimate could it have been? I mean, it was weird to sleep next to someone I didn't know, but in this case, Sam was the first person I had ever slept next to, even if it had been in the womb. So there were no reasons at all for this to be weird. We hopped into Sam's bed and fell asleep straightaway, our unconscious minds processing the whole eventful day.

When we were both asleep, with no makeup, we looked so exactly the same that nobody could tell us apart. Under the covers, our clothes weren't visible, so there was nothing to distinguish us. We were probably moving in our sleep at the same time, and lying in the same positions. Maybe this was our way of resuming our story where it all started—twins in the womb. We were resuming our life together, waking up with no fear of being separated ever again.

At nine thirty p.m., Sam and I got up. Meeting a potential twin had been exhausting, but I was ready to receive the results. This was the end of the marathon, the moment we would know exactly where we stood, and I was going to stay awake.

My friend Jonathan, my *frère de coeur*, joined us just then, coming straight from his job in town. I really wanted him to be there with me for the big reveal. Ryan, Kanoa, and James were organizing the laptops and GoPros, getting the cameras ready—pointing one where Sam's and my face would be, the other at the laptop screen where Dr. Segal would be. As for Sam and me, we were drinking wine and eating some of the Thai takeaway brought in during our nap, but we were basically waiting . . . waiting . . . and waiting. Even the wine couldn't keep all fears out of my head. Again, the prevailing thought was that we were already too bonded to not be twins, but we vowed to stay close even if the news was not what we were expecting.

When it was ten, no one else was in the room but us. We were alone together at the table, wine in hand. The cameras were rolling, and then, technical problems! Dr. Segal wasn't popping up on the Skype screen! OMG, what was happening? No one knew yet that she had an old version of Skype, so while the tech people tried to figure it out, Sam and I drank more wine and giggled about nothing. Fifteen minutes later, after Dr. Segal logged off, installed her new version of Skype, and logged back on, we were once again ready to roll.

Finally, there was Dr. Segal, beaming at us from her office at Cal State–Fullerton. She was so happy and excited that I can safely speak for both Sam and me—we knew it was going to be good news!

"So, Samantha and Anaïs, are you ready for this information?" she asked. "It's a very life-changing thing, whether you are twins or not." She kept going and going, or so it seemed. Finally, she said what we had been waiting to hear . . . "Okay, both of you turn and hug your identical twin sister!"

It had been such an emotional roller coaster, and we were finally done. Samantha and I were identical twins! WE WERE IDENTICAL TWINS! We immediately hugged, but it wasn't a hug of pure affection, per se. It was a hug of relief, as we fell into each other's arms. It was what fantasies are made of. Even with all our emotional preparation, it was unbelievable.

Now it was time to tell our relatives, who were undoubtedly waiting anxiously. We called my parents first, as they were right here in London, and it was getting toward eleven p.m. now.

"We're not twins!" I announced, too gleefully for it to be anything but in jest. I told them right away I was just kidding.

"I am happy," Mum said, "but we are just going to sleep." Dad was the same. Luckily, I knew how to read their voices. They were speaking in a different tone and a different rhythm, talking more slowly with more space in between their words. This meant they were happy, just not emphatic!

We decided to call Sam's brothers before we contacted her parents. Matt was first. I could hear Sam telling him, "Hey, we're not twins. . . . No, we *are* twins." Next, we called Andrew, and then we had Sam's maternal grandmother on the phone. I faked Sam's voice with an American accent to tell her we were twins. "I am happy, because I just had a White Russian," she responded. She was already celebrating. "Good-bye, sweetie, or should I say, SWEETIES," she said before hanging up. OMG, I had a new grandmother!

We called Sam's dad, but he didn't answer. Rude! Then we called her mom, who also didn't pick up the phone. Double rude! When we finally got her mom, Jackie was really happy. She was so in shock, she even swore the second she found out. "Really? Holy sh*t!" But she was trying to get off the phone quickly so she could call Sam's dad. "Okay, good-bye, sweetie, or should I say SWEETIES." "Good-bye, sweetie, or should I say SWEETIES," by Sam's mother *and* grandmother—was it nature or nurture?!

The next day, Sam came with me to school. We had lots of fun switching places. After all, this was our first chance to do this! Around dinnertime, I took Sam to meet my dad for the first time. We went to their hotel, where I knew my parents were having dinner in the restaurant on the ground floor. Sam stayed close behind me, semi-hiding, as we approached their table. Dad stood up when he saw me, and Sam popped out from behind. He kissed her and hugged her, which was not his style. Although he is very loving, he is not a hugger. But, with Sam, it was instantaneous, showing just how happy he was. It was so funny. Sam and I didn't want to touch each other, but everybody else wanted to hug and touch us.

The next day was the fashion show, something I had put *mon coeur et l'âme*, "heart and soul," into for the past four years. I was very exited that Sam and my parents would be seeing it, as they were the most important people in my life, and the show was the most important moment of my university career. I wasn't going to be able to see much of them until it was over, though. I would never in my life be busier than in the four hours ahead of me.

Tickets for the show, which was being held at Central Saint Martins Platform Theatre, were very hard to come by. We were only allowed a small number of them, usually only a pair for parents. It was quite difficult to get extras, but I had gotten one for Sam. There was a funny twin story that went with Sam queuing outside with my parents. One of my French friends saw her and went to speak to her. She was asking her in French, "Hey, are you excited about the show? Wait, how come you are not backstage? Are you finished already?" She thought it was me.

The fact that Sam was here at the show made me happy, but in a way, it made me even more stressed. My collection was very personal, but what if my sister did not like it, or any of my work? I would be so disappointed. At the same time, she gave me confidence. I just didn't want to disappoint anybody.

The rehearsals for the show had reminded me of the plays I had done in theater classes in secondary school. They filled me with the excitement and stage fright I had felt then, right before stepping onto the stage and into the footlights. Maybe this was the feeling Sam had every time she was onstage. Through our different industries and activities, we were still doing the same kind of performance work, putting our artistic talents on display in front of a live audience. We

had chosen similar pathways, both creative, and both bringing us to the stage from different directions.

Academically, the show was so important that most of
our grade for our final year was based on it. Not only would
our fashion tutors be there to evaluate the work, professionals
from within the industry and reporters from all over the
world were always on hand for the spring graduate show. The
six pieces I was presenting were the result of my years spent
at Central Saint Martins. But all that work and effort would
be up and down the catwalk in one minute and thirty seconds, here and gone. I guess that's what fashion is: convince
people and make an impression straightaway, in the blink of
an eye, or it is gone forever.

For the building of my collection, I took inspiration from
the women in the 1940s who temporarily replaced men in the
munitions factories. I was trying for the twist between an
ultrafeminine silhouette and the less fitted, manlier profile of the
emancipated woman, which required a lot of padding. I also
mixed this with the work of the German artist Joseph Beuys,
who integrated life with art and found materials. I took special
interest in his work with felt, a material that also became popular
in the 1940s. In my pieces, I used battleship-gray felt mixed with
new-technology neoprene foam, which allowed me to create generous volumes without too much weight or constraints. My technique included embroidery to blend the contemporary-looking
neoprene fabrics with the natural-looking felt. By layering, over-
lapping, and draping my materials, I came up with my minimal-
ist, industrial style. Part of our assignment had been to select a
market level for our collection, and I chose luxury ready-to-wear.

In the hours leading up to the event, I was quite stressed out, running around like crazy trying to sort out the fittings and the last accessories, finishing the hems, ironing, labeling, preparing all the tights and shoes, and putting everything into the garment bags to give to the dressers. There had been fittings for the collection close to the show, and after the last one, all my garments were bagged and carefully organized on rails with numbers and then divided into their running order according to the professional models especially hired by the school to model them. A cameraman would be filming the show, and two photographers would be capturing it from two different angles.

Backstage was at once a nightmare and the most exciting place in the world. My collection would be the thirteenth to go on, but you couldn't hear or see anything happening onstage. You had models racing to get changed, while running around throwing garments back on the racks, and dressers running around after them to put your designs back into the bags. Meanwhile, I was running after the untied shoes, as I heard my name being called, because my models were lining up and ready to enter the catwalk, but someone had forgotten to finish tying the shoes or had mixed up their accessories. It was a lot of running, yelling, being yelled at, stressing, and holding my breath. Then, I turned my head, and the first model was already backstage again. That was fast! All six of my outfits were modeled in one and a half minutes. Three years spent on campus in London and an additional year of internships and placements were done. My mark for my diploma had just been decided.

In a couple of hours, the show was over, and all forty of the final-year students had shown their collections. The pressure dropped suddenly after an extremely intense year. Backstage was euphoric. I was as light as a cloud, all my worries—about the button not being the right diameter on that coat, or the hems being two centimeters too short, or the stitching color not the exact gray, or the waistline a bit wavy—all those worries were gone. I had achieved my goal. I should have been tired, and I was so exhausted from it all, but the stress was gone. It felt nice.

After we emerged from backstage, we were all running to our parents, friends, fashion tutors, and other students. Some people were crying, because we knew our years here were almost over, and we would all be going our own ways after being together in the studios, working from nine a.m. to ten p.m., six days out of seven. But even so, everyone seemed happy. I felt like I had no barriers anymore, and I went to my sister and hugged her. I grabbed her by the neck and starting kissing her on the cheek. This was the first time I had really embraced her with full emotional love. The people who mattered the most were here with me. I was at the beginning of a new life with my sister, and at the end of my long years of education. I was emancipated, ready to move into my adulthood with my twin sister by my side.

The last few days had been a whirlwind. First, I had met Sam and learned we were identical twins, then I had put on my collection at Central Saint Martins, and now I was about to meet the Futermans. In French we say, *Jamais deux sans trois*, "never two without three." I had completed two, and the third was about to happen.

After dinner, Sam and I went to the hotel where her parents would be staying. I was two-thirds relaxed waiting to meet them. I guess that's the same kind of feeling you would experience with your family-in-law. They don't know you, but you want them to accept you into their hearts and like you straightaway. I just had to act as normally as I could. Would they like me? What if they did not like me? What if I did not get along with Sam's brothers? If they didn't like me, what would Sam think about me? Would she not want me as a sister anymore? The questions flooded in again. Would they consider me as family? Would they like my parents, too? What if our parents did not get along? What if they did not like London after traveling so far to get here? Would I feel a connection with them as quickly as I had with Sam? I was also wondering if my anxiety would show on camera. I didn't want anyone to see my questions surfacing on my face.

Sam's parents were not answering their cell phone long after their plane had landed. I could read Sam's stress without her saying anything. We should all have been happy for what was about to happen, but in a way, it was stressful. Sam wanted them to be there. Perhaps she needed the hug and comfort of her parents, especially as I had been with my parents throughout this, and I think Sam really missed hers.

Finally, the Futermans came up the street from the Tube station—Jackie first, then Judd, then Matt. They looked really nice, although exhausted, as I watched them through the floor-to-ceiling windows of the hotel. Sam made me run out, pretending I was her, but I was still scared. Would they hug me? Would they be standoffish, thinking I was some kind of clone? I fooled them for only a second, when they stood completely frozen. Then, when they knew it was me, they just hugged me, and Sam joined us right away. I had never gotten or given so many hugs in a single day. I felt like we were a family, even after only a few minutes.

Right then and there, I had no doubts I could trust the Futermans. I could see Sam had been raised in a very loving family. Matt was the only brother there yet, but his deep love for his sister was apparent. I wish everyone could experience the degree of happiness I felt that day in front of the hotel. That pure happiness, joy, and love could never be replaced. My thoughts went straight to my parents, and I could not wait for the two families to finally be together the next day. I had been hit by indescribable happiness, and it started changing me in all the best ways possible. I had no idea where Sam and I and the Futermans and the Bordiers would go, but we were definitely heading there together.

12

SAM

coming face-to-face with . . . myself

It was time to face it: Anaïs and I had been in a long-distance relationship. We were so long-distance, the only way to even see each other was by plane. I knew the relationship was going to be worth it. We'd just have a visiting schedule, when it turned out we were twins. What made all of this even more exciting was that this was my first trip to Europe.

When I woke up on the plane, we were over Ireland, only one hour from London. My tray table was open and I had butter chicken waiting for me. I don't know how, but I always manage to wake up in time for food. The chicken was definitely the tastiest option, although it was very airline and not dairy-free. I stared out the window in a daze, half-hearing the sounds of the plane around me, that soft rumble that echoes throughout your head. I could feel the air flow above my seat, putt, putt, putting down my hair. I was in disbelief that I had made it this far. Then the very British pilot came onto the PA system and announced that we were nearing Heathrow International Airport. It was time to prepare for landing and for meeting Anaïs.

Soon, I would be standing in a room, staring at a person who could quite possibly know me better than I knew myself. She could be someone who understood me better than my friends of ten years. Or she could be awful. I always tried to make light of it in my head, so I'd picture her six feet tall and a total bitch. Obviously, the six feet tall wasn't the case, but the other part . . . ?

After customs, Kanoa, Lisa, Ryan, and I took a van to the apartment we were renting in the Shoreditch neighborhood of London, which seemed to be incredibly far, but my anxiety was probably making it feel farther. The distance was definitely building a suspense in my body, but I tried to keep calm and in the moment by spotting all the trees, making jokes, and taking in the scenery. In what seemed like forever, we were finally there. Was Anaïs in the apartment already? What was about to happen?

When I heard footsteps coming down the stairs of the apartment and saw the door crack open, my heart jumped to my throat. Could it be Anaïs? What if this was the moment? Was the camera rolling? As carefully orchestrated as this day was, I still had no idea what time my sister was going to show up. I wanted to make sure we caught this moment on film, or perhaps that was my excuse to distract myself from the stress I was feeling. Phew, it was only James. It was really nice to be staring at a familiar face, but thankfully not too familiar. I wasn't quite ready for that yet.

We got everything upstairs and explored the apartment. The furniture was a collection of pieces picked up here and there, futons and folding chairs, crushed velvet couches of different colors, mismatched end tables, and many throw pillows in Indian patterns. There were two working bathrooms, plenty of light, and a big open kitchen equipped with everything. My favorite piece of décor was a funky three-foot-tall carved golden elephant next to the couch, which could serve as a stool or an end table.

As we were settling in, Anaïs's friends Marie, Lucas, and Mátyás arrived. Of course, my first instinct was to play a joke on them. I didn't like to show my emotional insecurities, and humor was a good cover. I immediately felt comfortable with them, perhaps because they seemed comfortable with me as well. Anaïs's friend Marie was so sweet. Of all Anaïs's friends, I "knew" her the best. At one point, as we were all hanging out, she started crying. Anaïs's arrival was imminent and the air was thick with emotion.

I knew she was getting close. I could tell by the little birdy noises Marie's phone made when she was texting with her. "THEY'RE HERE!" somebody yelled. I didn't know where to go. I was freaking out inside. I was moving around and couldn't sit still. Kanoa and James told me I was being weird, and Ryan just kept filming. I hid under the table . . . I sat on the couch . . . I sat on the golden elephant. And then it was time . . . she was coming. My heart was pounding throughout my entire body. I could feel it. I could feel her close. James went downstairs to get her. Holy sh*t. This was it. . . .

The echoes were getting louder and closer and my heart

was beating faster and harder. I put my hands on my face, debating whether to cover my eyes as though to prepare myself for an eclipse or keep my vision free of any obstacles. Just then, I saw a body move in the doorway. Oh God, it's her. No, wait . . . it was James . . . by himself. He couldn't find her! I was relieved. Phew. Then Marie's phone buzzed again with more birdy noises. James left the room again, and I heard a door close followed by a familiar laugh. Holy shit. That was my laugh. I sat just staring at the door, waiting to see who was about to enter. And then, I started to squeal as an Asian girl came quickly running through the door. Ahh, oh, right, it wasn't Anaïs. It was her friend Jennifer. I burst into laughter and gave her a massive hug. I had seen her on Instagram, but I didn't know that she was coming with Anaïs. As I turned around again, the sweetest face popped into the doorway and walked hesitantly into the room. Her face was mine, but it was bright red, and her hair was a mess. I froze. And then, I had the longest and most uncomfortable laughing fit I've ever had in my life. I couldn't stop. My brain wasn't working. My body was just pumping blood and adrenaline all the way through. I was hot, sweating, freezing, and amped up all at the same time. It was me . . . it was me . . . she was me!

Seeing her face for the very first time was remarkable. I never thought that I looked like that. It wasn't me, but it was my entirety staring back. It felt like a dream where you know that the person in it is someone who you've seen your entire life, like your mom, for instance. But for some reason, she looks like someone else, someone you have never met before.

"Turn and hug your identical twin sister," I would later

hear Dr. Nancy Segal say. Anaïs and I were identical twins! I had known it when I had seen Anaïs's picture, but when I heard the words from the expert, I was overcome with joy and relief. Our next step with Dr. Segal would be all the testing. She was even going to see if we were "mirror-image twins," twins whose physical features mirror those of the other one.

The next day, I met Anaïs at her apartment. It was a really cool place. It seemed very "college," or as they say in England, "uni," Brit-speak for "university." From the street outside, I could see a mannequin in just a skirt in the window. The skirt was one of Anaïs's designs, as she had showed it to me on Skype. Inside the apartment, there was a big table where she and Marie did their designs. My sister's bedroom was beautiful, bright, and fresh, with a huge white-framed bed topped with a stylish down comforter.

I was going to accompany Anaïs to Central Saint Martins to see where she spent her time and to meet all the important people in her life. We decided to have some fun and switch outfits to see if her friends would know the difference. It was my idea, but Anaïs, with her sweet/evil smile, complied. To be honest, we felt weird in each other's clothing. Our walks had to change when we changed shoes. Carrying her purse was strange, as I don't carry purses, and Anaïs had to walk like me in order to support my backpack. The funniest part was that we both put our hands in our pockets exactly the same way.

The university was impressive. The Central Saint Martins building is a massive brick structure with beautiful fountains in front. I could tell by the gorgeous costumes displayed in glass cases in the entry hall that this school was top rate, and that Anaïs must be especially talented to go here. Seeing the reactions of her friends to our switching places was priceless. Her friend Jewon was our first target. Anaïs had prepped me on exactly what to say, so I jumped out and, using my best French accent, said, "Jewon, my seester eez here!" He stopped and stared as though an alien had arrived before him. We all had a laugh.

All of Anaïs's classmates were incredibly enthusiastic about meeting me. Anaïs had a lot to do in her studio, so I just hung around watching as she worked. She had fittings and was prepping for the next day, her big fashion show. At one point, she assigned me to lacing up the boots for her models. Like a good assistant, I laced every shoe.

That night, Anaïs and I walked over to the hotel where Jacques and Patricia were staying. They were having dinner in the restaurant, and we were meeting them there to say hello. I was nervous that her father wouldn't like me, because not only was I American but I was also making a documentary about his daughter and me, which he might find exploitive. The Bordiers were reserved and were not sure they wanted their lives on display. But I really wanted Jacques to like me. Patricia and I had formed a nice bond at the restaurant, and I was hoping I'd find the same with Jacques. He had been so skeptical from the beginning about Anaïs and me being twins, and I wasn't sure how he would feel about me.

When we found them in the restaurant, his expression was nothing I had feared it would be. His eyes went wide and he couldn't conceal a smile. I was so relieved. His apparent love for both of us was so touching.

The next day was huge. Anaïs's fashion show was in the morning, and my parents were arriving in the evening. The first thing I did was hang out with my sister at school for a bit before meeting up with her parents in front of the theater where the fashion show was being held. I had never been to a fashion show before. This one was absolutely astonishing. The show took place in a black box studio set up with risers, a runway on the ground, and video cameras on the side. The audience was filled with all sorts of characters: a mix of fashion students, professors, family, reporters, fashion scouts, and friends. You could see the professors grading the pieces as models strode the catwalk. The outfits were breathtaking and creative. One of Anaïs's friends had constructed shoes with plastic water bottles for soles, so as the models walked, they would make a unique sound in order to complement the collection. I had never thought of sound being something so integral to a design. I could tell how important this fashion show was by how tense and serious everyone was. These collections were the work of the up-and-coming designers of our generation, and knowing that my sister was one of them was incredible. Anaïs's stunning designs were applauded throughout the room, which was not always the case with the other designers in the show. I thought her collection was the best of any of them, and seeing her clothing flowing so beautifully on a real live model made me proud. Anaïs's blood runs through my veins, so hopefully some of her creativity runs in them as well.

After the show, we beat my parents to Tommy Miah's Raj Hotel, where they would be staying. When Mom, Dad, and Matt got out of the tube station, we were waiting in the lobby, and Anaïs ran out before me. I had told her to pat my dad on the belly, like I always do, and say, "Hi, Steve!" She did. My dad's smile was so wide that he looked Asian, too! He couldn't stop staring at Anaïs. He had the look of a proud father the day his baby is born—one of pride, surprise, and pure joy. In a way, it was true. In that moment, he was meeting his new baby. It was clear that both of my parents were overwhelmed with happiness.

We sat in the lobby of the Tommy Raj, which was also a Bangladeshi restaurant, and talked. Anaïs was shy around Matt, although they seemed to bond right away. They were already giggling and joking around, and after only a few short moments the awkwardness left the air and they just began to enjoy each other's company. My father was continuously asking questions. Where do you live? What is it like? How do you like London? He was sitting with his elbows on the table, staring at her like a schoolboy. It brought me so much joy to watch. I imagined this was what he would be like as a grandfather seeing his grandchild for the first time.

The next day, we all went on a bus tour of London. This was the first time our families were together. We rode a double-decker and saw the big sights until right before lunchtime, when Andrew arrived and met us at a fish-and-chips pub. Andrew pointed at Anaïs and me and said, "That's Sam, and that's Anaïs." He got it right. He sat down at the table near Matt and me, a safe distance from Anaïs. He was a little weirded out at first by how much Anaïs looked like me. He was giggling, and I think it was because he was a bit uncomfortable, although relieved to find out that we were twins.

Andrew had been the biggest skeptic in my family, and the one who had kept reminding me not to get my hopes up. But once the DNA test confirmed what the rest of us had been sure of all along, he was thrilled for everybody.

Our big lunch together with all the families was so much fun. Matt, Andrew, Anaïs, and I, sitting together as the four "kids" for the first time, were acting like it. We were quite playful, annoying, goofy, and having a great time. I threw a pea in Andrew's drink, and then Anaïs threw a pea in right after mine. She then slipped in her evil smile, and we all had a good laugh. I was happy she was beginning to experiment with having brothers. It would have been mayhem for our parents in our childhood, had we been all together. Seeing Anaïs with Matt and Andrew was surreal. She had siblings now for the very first time. I loved it.

That night, we had a private dinner with just families, no cameras, at a Korean restaurant, of course. Anaïs's parents were far more laid-back without the cameras and had a lot more to say. Filming made them uncomfortable, which is completely understandable. Not that they weren't impressed with the entire production and the production team, but the Bordiers are more private than the Futermans and unaccustomed to simply ignoring the cameras. Our parents loved talking about Anaïs and me as kids. Everybody shared pictures and presents, too. Anaïs's mom presented our family with gifts from the Bordiers' shop. I received an orange alligator-skin wallet, and my mother got a beautiful red leather bracelet.

After the meal, the parents went back to their respective hotels, and the rest of us went back to the flat to get ready to go to what turned out to be an INSANE party with all of Anaïs's friends. It was at her friend Olya's apartment, and it was packed from wall to wall with super-artsy kids from Central Saint Martins. Her best friend, Jonathan, was there, but he looked so completely different that we didn't even recognize him at first. He had been at our DNA test result reveal, and he had looked like a lovely young French businessman that night. But now, he was wearing a big puffy jacket with a fitted cap and had the persona of a young American rapper from the Bronx. Once we figured out who he was, we were all shocked. Maybe it was his American twin? The rest of her friends were from all over the world and delightful to meet. Her friend Olya was a firecracker from Ukraine. Everyone seemed to know Anaïs. I felt so proud to be her sister.

The next morning, we all woke up early, so we could go see the Harry Potter studios, one of the absolute highlights of the trip. Everyone met at the train station, where we would catch the train to Watford Junction, twenty miles northwest of London. Andrew was particularly excited about the studio tour, as a massive "Pothead" (the term for one obsessed with Harry Potter). He even has a tattoo on his leg that says, "RIP Dobby," probably the thing that I am most proud of about my big brother. We had a blast that day. I have been on many sets in my life, but these were special. My sister was totally obsessed, too, and I imagined us being the Weasley twins, running around and playing jokes on everyone at Hogwarts.

We were back in London by late afternoon in time for the Bordiers to check out of their hotel and catch their train back to Paris. It was amazing to have two new "parents." They hadn't

raised me, but they were a brand-new relationship to explore—
one that was created just for me. I imagined it was the same for
Anaïs and my own parents, something akin to having in-laws.
And they all got along so well. Our parents had already been
swapping pictures and e-mailing each other. With the love the
Bordiers showed me, how could I not love them back? Plus,
they had raised my sister and made her the person she is today.

Later that night, the young people all went to a club.
Kelsang met us there. This was the first time I had met our
matchmaker in person, although we had already been
acquainted on Skype and through pictures. He really meant
a lot to me. Without Kelsang, who knows when my sister
might have seen me, if ever? We all danced and celebrated
into the wee hours of the morning.

The next day was dedicated to more classic tourist attrac-
tions. Our first stop was the Tower of London. My favorite part
of this tour was watching Anaïs aggressively grab a piece of
chain mail from a little boy who was hogging it. It was in a
hands-on display, and the boy had played with it too long, in
Anaïs's opinion. She wanted to feel it, too, and she grabbed it
from his hands. I called her out on it, and we all started crack-
ing up. Sometimes it was very clear that my sister was (as in,
used to be) an only child. Now she has my brothers and me to
call her out. She had better get used to it.

Andrew left the next day. I was sad to see him go so
soon. I didn't know when I'd see him again. He had come to
London having only one sister, and he left having two. By the
end of his time in London, he and Anaïs were really hitting it
off. There was a farewell dinner for my parents and Matt that

night at an Indian restaurant, as they were leaving the following morning.

Once my family was all gone, Anaïs opened up about feeling abandoned by our birth mother. It was both sad to hear her feelings and comforting to know she trusted me with them. She confided that when she was a child, she often felt as though she had been abandoned. I had never been ripped apart by those kinds of feelings. The adoption never made me sad. I never thought of myself as being abandoned.

Maybe having brothers helped. I hadn't had time to think about what happened after my birth. I was too focused on keeping Matt and Andrew out of my room and from "torturing" me, but that "torture" was really just a display of love, which engulfed me my entire childhood. Anaïs didn't have the same brotherly distractions. She didn't have siblings to love her like that. She had her imaginary friend, Anne, who couldn't answer back. She felt as though her birth family hadn't wanted her and was afraid to find them lest they reject her again. She also worried about what would happen when her parents passed away. "I would have no one," she told me. She said she didn't want to search for our birth mother. She would rather keep alive in her mind the slight possibility and fantasy that she had been sent away for something better.

I didn't believe that we were given up for something better. The truth of the matter was, we had no idea why this happened to us. We could assume and think that it could have been this or that, but there is only one person, potentially two, who could tell us the truth. The circumstances must have been rough for the woman who gave us birth, and perhaps her intentions weren't positive. Even if they weren't, who is to say she's the same person now that she was back then? If she's anything like us, which I imagine she probably is, she is strong and has the ability to adapt to whatever circumstances come her way. And whatever the circumstances were at the time, she made her choice. Anaïs and I were meant to be split apart, and I didn't hate our birth mother for that.

Anaïs and I didn't have a lot of time left together before I headed back to L.A. Our last day consisted of a very special French dinner with both sets of our friends and an adventure up and around the London Eye, the huge Ferris wheel on the Thames. Even though Anaïs and I are pretty scared of heights, we decided to go for it. From the top, we could see the entire city. It was worth conquering our fear for—it turned out to be not that scary, once we were inside the pod. Our trip had begun with the fear of meeting each other, and we had dispelled it. Now we were ending this trip on a high note—literally. As human beings, we develop so much anxiety around intense situations, yet with someone we love, any fear is conquerable. I came to London having no idea whether or not Anaïs and I were related, and I left feeling like I had known her my entire life.

13

ANAÏS

california, here i come!

Right after the fashion show, there were two weeks when I could fit in a visit with Sam in Los Angeles. I had to be back in London in mid-July to pack up the flat. From there, I would go to Paris for three days for a wedding and a job interview at Gerard Darel, a well-established Paris fashion house known for its "simple, chic, ultra-feminine style." I had seen a posting for an internship and had applied, even though I wanted a full-time job. I was thrilled when I was invited to interview and hopeful that the internship would lead to something more permanent. From Paris, I was heading back to London for my graduation ceremony. Right now, I was just feeling really relieved. My studies were finished, the fashion show had gone extremely well, and Sam and I were madly in "twin sister" love.

The reviews of the fashion show had been unequivocal raves. It had gotten significant press coverage in fashion markets around the world, as it was considered the showcase of up-and-coming talent in the industry. The *Grazia Daily* said, "London's deserved reputation for nurturing more 'big new things' per square mile (or season!) than any other fashion hub in the world was again proven last night with the Central Saint Martins MA graduate show." *Elle UK* said, "Seductive palettes of pink, explosive neons, and sedate, sculptural silhouettes were the order of the evening at a Central Saint Martins graduate fashion show that was as eclectic as it was accomplished—eclectic in the best way." I couldn't help but be proud to have been part of it. But nothing could trump how happy I was to have met Sam and to have bonded with her so profoundly.

I really hoped that we could spend some time alone on this trip. In London, she had been with her family, her friends, and the documentary crew, and I had been with my family and friends, too. But all the extra people detracted from our chance to be intimate as sisters. We were already extremely close, especially considering that we had never even heard of each other a few months earlier. The Internet, Skype, and smartphones allowed us to fall asleep in each other's virtual arms, which was better than nothing. But because we had been denied a childhood together, I wanted to have Sam to myself. When there were too many people around, I sometimes felt like we were a sideshow, with everyone fluctuating between outright gawking and playful peeking, wondering how we were going to act. They wanted to witness our first embrace, our first misunderstanding, and our first argument, maybe our first fight. It was inevitable—even identical twins have fights. But, I didn't want every one of our "firsts" to be spectator events. In

L.A., I was hoping there would be opportunities for just the two of us to have some fun.

Seeing Sam on her own turf was going to be interesting. London had been a fairly neutral city for our first reunion: both of our families had to travel to get there, British English was kind of a foreign language for everybody, and both our groups had equal footing when it came to food—French and American food is better than British! Now, though, I would be able to see Sam on her territory and provide her with an appropriate backdrop. I would soon see the restaurant where she worked and the bedroom from which she texted me while in her bed and under the covers. I would be experiencing her everyday life, which meant seeing her friends, her workplace, her chilling places, and her daily behavior. Would she have the same closeness with her friends as I do with mine? What did she do with them? How did she meet them? Would they behave in a sophisticated, grown-up way with one another, or would they be playful, with the fun kind of immaturity that only close friends feel safe doing?

My flight from London to California was direct, but it still took twelve hours. I left London Heathrow Airport at seven p.m. and landed at ten p.m. in Los Angeles, so even though it looked like three hours, the sun was already up in London, and it had just set here. Landing at night gave me incredible views of the city. From the sky, the city lights, which ended abruptly at the darkness of the Pacific Ocean, reminded me a lot of the Côte d'Azur near Cannes in the South of France. Here, though, there were many more square miles of twinkling, and the lights looked very organized, like in a grid. Now that we were in our approach to the airport, I was finally able to feel the relief that comes with a real vacation. I was getting the feeling down in my belly that I always get when I am about to touch the ground. You have reached your final destination, and you want to start running . . . especially when you know there is an identical twin waiting for you in the terminal!

Sam and her roommate, Lisa, both came to get me at the airport. Sam, who had come straight from work, brought us sushi from her restaurant, which we ate in the car. Thankfully, Lisa was the driver, so we didn't have to worry about getting in an accident, as Sam and I were very animated to see each other on our second reunion. Ryan was there, too, filming away. Sam had let me know before I got here that she and Ryan had started dating. I had kind of suspected it by their flirtatious behavior during our early Skype calls and in London. I was happy for her, but it was weird to see my double flirting with someone else.

The cars in the United States were so big! I was already small enough, and I felt even smaller here, like in a distorted perspective. The roads were huge, too. I had been to the United States twice before, once when I was fifteen for a three-week exchange program in Norfolk, Virginia, and the second time just one year earlier. I had saved money from an internship with John Galliano in Paris, and I wanted to discover New York City. I also spent a week in Chicago to visit my friend Maxence.

I was quickly remembering what had impressed me so much the first two times—the driving! Although Americans tend to think of driving as an undesirable necessity, I love it. In the United States, even though you spent a lot of time driving, you could go anywhere. The world was huge and open. France had been built up for so many hundreds of years that every space was either occupied or cultivated, so it didn't feel like this. In America, it felt as if the backgrounds kept changing and surprising me. It is such an appealing place for wanderlust. I have no idea of the distance in front of me, but who cares? I am on the road.

It felt so strange to be standing on another side of the planet with Sam. We had always occupied the same planet, but we had not been in the same orbit until London. This was one of the fun parts of having a twin with a completely different experience than yours. I could explore L.A. and New York/New Jersey, her worlds, in her company, and she could be with me in my worlds, London and Paris. We were each other's tour guides to some of the greatest cities in the world.

The day after I arrived, I woke up in Los Angeles. Sam's apartment had a little balcony with an amazing view. Almost to make sure I knew where I was, the world-famous HOLLYWOOD sign was visible from the balcony. Yes, Anaïs, you are in Hollywood! The weather in Los Angeles was perfect, warm but not humid, the sun shining through and the feel of the heat on my skin.

The architecture of Los Angeles is unique. From on the hill outside the city, it looked like Disneyland-Paris. The whole city looked like a back lot of a cinema studio, although it was real. Everything is quite exotic, new, and modern, and built quite quickly. One day, I went driving around Beverly Hills with Kanoa. It was so interesting to see the big mansions with all the different styles of architecture mixed together. You could see a house with a Florentine top, and the bottom of the house would be built like a Parisian Hotel and mixed with Venetian details. It felt like I could read the social history of the first owners on the buildings themselves, telling me what part of Europe the families had come from originally.

We went to many of Sam's favorite places to eat, some cafés, some brunch places, the restaurant where she worked. There was every kind of food in the world in Los Angeles, and it was all so good. It seemed like it had been grown under the sun, especially when compared to the food in London, which was a bit heavy and starchy. It seemed like everything in L.A. was about health and the benefits for your body. I knew I was far from home when I ate things I had absolutely never heard of, let alone could pronounce. Sometimes, I'd have to ask someone, "Is this edible for real?" Lots of things looked like they were made of plastic to look realistic, like those platters of plastic food on display in London restaurant windows to be the example of what you could order. You'd think it was real food except the colors were too bright, and it was often a little dusty.

The sun and the heat of Southern California definitely put me in a different mood, too, like I was charging my batteries. There, people are outdoors all the time and it feels free. My sightlines were so extended that I feel like I could look far, far away. In a packed city like Paris, you see buildings and obstacles everywhere, making you feel a bit imprisoned in a way.

The lifestyle in L.A. is also so very different from most

European cities. It is more spacious, and so people need more time to go from one place to the other, which in turn makes time feel like it is extended. I also feel a healthier distance from other people's problems, away from their anxieties. Imagine a jam-packed place in London—Oxford Circus at four on a Saturday afternoon, for example, where everything goes so fast, and you bump into people, and by touching them, you catch their stress. L.A. isn't like that. I could suddenly imagine Sam when she was driving during a Skype call—this scene was her backdrop, or this was where she was making a turn, or this was the red light she said was going on way too long. These points may not have been exactly the locations where Sam had been, but by being in her city and community, it was easier for my imagination to tweak what I had previously pictured.

Sam made sure we covered all the tourist spots, which I adored. We visited Venice Beach, Hollywood Boulevard, and Disneyland. I went to see my first baseball game between the Los Angeles Angels and the Saint Louis Cardinals on the Fourth of July. It was fabulous. Sam and I bought complementing baseball caps, mine blue with a white A, and hers red with a blue A. We drank beer, ate hot dogs and cotton candy, and watched the fireworks that happened after the game on account of the Fourth of July, and not because of the Angels' unbelievable win. Down five runs to two in the bottom of the ninth, they scored three runs and won!

We went to the beaches of Southern California, of course. In Malibu, where we ran on the beach and made a bonfire, I met a lot of Sam's friends. Her friend Michael accidentally stepped into the fire pit, which was hard to see because of the layer of sand we had put on top of the hot coals. I felt so sorry for him, and for Sam, who was shouldering a lot of the blame. It is strange—when I look at Sam, I can feel what she is going through at the moment, without her speaking, in this case her agony about Michael. It comes from our body language, which is similar. It is like the secret language of twins. There's an expression in French—*se mettre dans la peau*, "to put oneself in somebody else's shoes"—that is this exact feeling. Your body reacts the same way the other person's does, so you know how she feels. It was hard for me to see Sam so distressed about Michael. I was unhappy, too, because I knew I would have blamed myself the same way. It was also hard for me to find the arguments to make her feel better, because I knew that no one else's argument would have made me feel better. But, on the other hand, when I saw Sam stubbornly stuck on blaming herself, I had an opportunity to analyze my own behavior. I could step back and say, "Wow, that is what I do," so next time, I could do it differently. For example, I could learn to be less hard on myself and let things go by watching Sam not do that, even though I would have done what Sam did if it happened to me first! Great therapy!

On some matters, I know Sam and I are different. But, when Sam is my mirror, I can see how I behave, and I can learn from that and try to change or do things another way. She's my unwitting psychoanalyst as I try to solve my own problems. So, through poor Michael's unfortunate injury and Sam feeling responsible, I had quite an enlightenment.

Venice Beach, another Pacific coast town we visited, was very interesting. The beach was large compared to the

Côte d'Azur, and so was the Pacific compared to the Mediter-ranean. Space in California had a different vanishing point. Compared to the palm trees we had in the South of France, the palm trees here looked stretched out, so high and so thin. In California, you had space to grow taller and faster, and you still had space around you, so it looked like everything grew tall and fast without ever taking up too much room. During our visit, we ate at a great restaurant that served a Hawaiian dish called *poke* (POH-kay), bite-sized pieces of seasoned raw fish, extremely similar to Japanese sashimi. I loved it.

Observing the "double lives" of the people of Los Angeles was so much fun. It seemed everyone was an aspiring actor. Valets, bus staff, hostesses, cooks, and waiters were all reading and learning lines for auditions. Nobody was hiding it—they were in the hospitality industry only until they didn't have to be anymore. It made for a very artistic mood and feeling. There were lots of people in workout clothes, too, either coming from or going to a fitness center. That wasn't really odd, either, because I knew looking fit and tanned was integral to a Holly-wood career. Besides, lots of the athletic clothing featured designer labels, making it a true Southern California fashion statement.

Fashion and acting really do have a strong relationship. Models are short-term actors, and actors are short-term mod-els. Without fashion and costume, cinema would be dull, and without theater and film, fashion would be substantially short an audience. Both industries push the edge of daring and creativity, so even though Sam and I had chosen different career paths, our choices were related. One of us liked to be in front of the camera, and the other behind it. Here in Hollywood, it was inspiring to see people living their passion.

I loved the transparency of Sam's double life. It was great to follow her throughout the day to discover her routine. She wakes up and goes to an early morning yoga class. Afterward, she does a lot of work on the documentary. Then it's lunchtime, and at least while I was there, she eats something very healthy. After lunch into the early afternoon, she prepares for auditions. If she has them scheduled, she heads out to do her thing, hoping to land a role. Otherwise, she works ambitiously on her two projects—organizing the documentary and putting her thoughts on the computer for the book. Then, if she has a shift at work, she heads to her job at a restaurant in Beverly Hills. It's a very attractive French-themed brasserie with a lot of framed posters of old French advertisements. The menu has a few traditional French dishes interspersed with Japanese cuisine—very delicious. Sam is such a hard worker. It was quite a crazy schedule to follow, and it was inspiring to see her running around like that. This book and the documentary mean so much to her. She is like a superhero, living a double life to achieve good things for others. I could see Sam's eyes glowing when she talked about sharing our story on film and in print.

While I was in Los Angeles, I had lots to do to get my own career going, now that I had finished my studies. From Sam's flat, I was sending CVs and looking for job ads on the Internet. Even though I had the interview in place with Gerard Darel, I had to keep searching and submitting CVs until I had something secured. Getting a good job in fashion was really tough, and I was looking at everything. My hope was to stay in London, or even go abroad, but I certainly wouldn't object to Paris. Trying to find a match for myself was really hard, but job-hunting in the company of Sam gave me the most amazing feeling. It was like we were sharing our experiences and things that really mattered together. We were really connected. We could branch away from each other, too, and it would still not break our bond. Every day, being together was more and more normal, not in a boring way, but in the best way possible. We were living together and acknowledging that our lives were now intertwined. We would grow old and share memories together. We were starting to build our own stories now, too. I no longer had to check my phone or her Facebook every morning to make sure she was real. We were living things together now, be they touristy fun things or everyday errands. It was not only about discovering each other anymore—it was sharing.

I enjoyed watching Sam prepare lines for auditions. It was fun to see her rehearse and watch her build her characters. Now, every time I look at her tapes and sketches on the Internet and see her in films, I see her very differently. She is the character. I know it's called "being an actor," but I am still amazed how she acts and how she has to move differently, being someone else suddenly. It was funny to discover what was happening behind the cameras of the TV shows I usually watched from my laptop in Europe. One day, we watched Sam's friend Kanoa on a set. He was part of the production team, and I could see how long it took to make even a small scene. So much patience was required, as even the shortest skit had to be done and redone up to four or five times. The actors had to be prepared to repeat and repeat, until there was satisfaction that the take was the best possible.

This is also very similar to the fashion industry in a way. Everyone has to work very hard under enormous pressure on a short run. You prepare for such a long time for a very short artistic appearance; then your product is unleashed and becomes property of the industry. It was great that Sam and I could understand each other in the stress of our work. Both of our pursuits are very intense and exhausting, but we do them with passion, and we both take it personally when our efforts are rejected.

I spent a lot of quality time with Sam's friends. When she was working, I would spend time with them on my own. It was strange how quickly I bonded with them. I guess Sam's and my physically identical resemblance was reassuring, even though it could also be disturbing. Past that awkwardness, I felt like I had known these people for ages. The similarity of our friends was a reflection of our own similarities, of course. We thought similarly, and therefore we developed friendships with like-minded people who shared our personalities.

Now that I was in Los Angeles, I could also do my testing with Dr. Nancy Segal at the Cal State–Fullerton campus. The whole twins-separated-at-birth experience was so interesting, especially the whole nurture vs. nature question. When I was a kid, I felt everything about my personality was shaped more from my education and my environment than my genetics. Now my perspective was changing. I was amazed to discover so many common points with Sam, from our body language to our personalities. I am not saying that everything is genetic, but I was very surprised to see how much of who we are is anchored deep within our genetic makeup.

Sam and I had a few hours of tests, which were quite humorous to do. Many of my tests were in French, so as not to give me a disadvantage. There were life history interviews, IQ tests, special cognitive ability tests, personality inventories, self-esteem scales, job satisfaction questionnaires, and medical life histories. I could not wait to see what our studies showed, although we hadn't finished all of the testing. It felt amazing to know that Sam and I were part of something that could help people understand more about the development of human personalities.

While I was in Los Angeles, Sam and I discussed going to Korea together. Sam was interested in attending a gathering sponsored by the International Korean Adoptees Association (IKAA) that would take place in Seoul from July 29 to August 4. She had heard about it from a friend of hers who was going, Dan Matthews. Dan was a Korean adoptee who had been raised in Southern California. He was very involved in the adoption community, and when Sam had met him for the first time a few months earlier, he had mentioned the IKAA gathering in Seoul. He strongly encouraged my sister to look into it, saying it would be a great experience. He said that the two of us would have the chance to bond with other adoptees and just hang out in Korea. Although there were other, smaller gatherings in other cities with Korean adoptee populations on an annual basis, Seoul only happened every three years. It was a special opportunity to bring adoptees back to their homeland.

Sam was very keen on the idea, but I was a little more hesitant. It was all a little rushed, and it was a huge decision.

Also, Sam was so stressed about the gathering and all the details, I was not sure I wanted to go. I may have been scared about going and finding things I did not want unveiled. Some things are better hidden, as long as you are happy. Sam had been to Korea the year before, and she had an idea of what I would probably go through emotionally. I liked the idea of hearing the stories of other Korean adoptees, but I didn't necessarily want to discover things about myself, too. It wasn't the past that worried me; it was the feelings buried deeper inside.

We were also writing to our birth mother, as had been suggested by Ben Sommers, Sam's social worker at Spence-Chapin. I felt very anxious about this. Sam and I were sitting on the couch in her living room and trying to say something to a woman who we didn't know. We guessed she knew who we were, but it was so scary to choose what to say. We were constantly changing the subject or writing things that were not connected, as we had trouble focusing on the main point at the same time. When one of us finally focused, the other one would make a joke, and vice versa. Suddenly, I got very emotional. It was weird how out of the blue this can happen, a rush of feelings surfacing when you don't want them to, but not being able to do anything about it. It was so comforting to be near Sam, because I knew I could weep or shout or anything, and she would understand. I trusted her, and her alone, to reason with me about my emotions and validate them.

That letter took ages to get written. Sam's mum had sent us some photos of our trip to London and a published book filled with letters from birth mothers to their biological children. The letters had been sent with the kids when they were adopted and had been assembled for a book, *I Wish You a Beautiful Life: Letters from the Korean Mothers of Ae Ran Won to Their Children*. Some of the letters were so touching. I never thought or imagined there could be so many reasons for a kid to be adopted, and I guess it had been easier for me to simplify my own story by saying, "I am angry, you abandoned me, end of the story."

Still, writing to that woman was strange. I felt like I was cheating on my parents. My parents are the people who raised me and helped me grow up. Some kids don't look like their parents even when they are their biological children. I am speaking of them physically, but I am also speaking of their personalities. We have so many genes of our ancestors within us, and there are so many different combinations possible within all this lottery of genes and alleles.

I had watched a documentary on twins from the National Geographic channel where they were showing how some characteristics that were within you could also be deactivated or activated by your environment, which explained why Sam and I were half so identical and half two very distinct persons. In finishing our letter to the woman who gave us our genes, our structure, we let her know that whoever she was and whatever the reasons were, we were thankful she gave birth to us. That was all that mattered. Sam and I had found each other, and we had our lives to spend together now. We were not angry. When she felt ready, we could meet her, and we would still like to know what happened someday. I felt relieved once we wrote that letter.

It was best to do it with Sam. Writing to her and marking her as the starting point of our life was like going back together to the moment we were conceived. I was slowly getting used to our story becoming more and more real and taking shape.

Finally, Sam and I made our decision to book a trip to Korea for the conference. I felt so happy with Sam, and was thankful she convinced me to make the IKAA trip. I felt like she was being the older sister this time, even though I usually thought it was me. It felt good for someone else to lead the way and even better to know we would see each other again soon. The L.A. trip had helped us discover more about each other, including the differences in our lives, which made everything that much more exciting. We still had so much to learn from each other. Our story was still going on, and I never wanted it to stop. I was leaving L.A., but I missed Sam already.

14

SAM

korea

I hate losing time. Already there isn't enough of it in the day, which is why traveling can be daunting. The hours and hours on the plane getting to the destination seem wasted, especially when you are waiting to see your sister.

July 26 was going to be a huge travel day, about thirteen hours in the air to get from Los Angeles International Airport to Incheon International Airport in Seoul. I was meeting Anaïs in Korea, the place where we had first been stripped from our birth family, the common factor for all internationally adopted Koreans. This was the last place I had contact with my sister before our separation. Anaïs and I were coming back to explore our history and experience it alongside the five hundred other adoptees who were attending the IKAA conference.

Before leaving my apartment, I did what I always do—I woke everyone in my family, wherever in the country they might be, and told them that I was going somewhere. My brother

Andrew especially hates it. I always call him enough times to wake him from his deep, bearlike slumber and say, "I'm going to _____." He usually replies, "That's cool, Stinky," in a groggy, half-impressed, half-cavalier voice. After Andrew, I call my grandmother and my parents. You never know what might happen when you get on a flight, so you have to make sure to tell your loved ones that you love them.

James, Ryan, and I were traveling together. At the airport, we found out we were on the same flight as Dan Matthews, the friend who had turned me on to this trip. He was a musician, and he worked for an Asian-American entertainment company that had a huge YouTube presence. His musical talents were even going to be on display at the Hybrid Club Vera in Seoul, as he had been selected to take part in the closing concert, which, in his words, was the most epic and fun night of the conference.

Dan and I had met for the first time over brunch a few months earlier, right before I met my sister for the first time. He hadn't known it when we first met, but unbelievably, he was also an identical twin separated at birth. He discovered it right after my trip to London to meet Anaïs. When I got back, I hung out with him a second time and showed him the pictures of Anaïs and me together. They totally blew him away. He said he had started a birth search of his own to put together the pieces of his own bloodline. He hoped to be finding out a few details quite soon.

A few weeks later, at the very moment Anaïs and I were picking out souvenirs from a shop on the Venice Beach boardwalk, Dan sent me an e-mail with the subject line "Sam . . . I think I have a twin, too." His message read: "Hey, Sam, read below. I'm not even fucking kidding, but I was just told that I might have a twin as well. We need to chat soon. Dan."

Wwwwhhhhhhatttt?! The person who had told me about the conference, my Korean adoptee confidant, was a twin, too?! It was insane, like a Dr. Phil–worthy coincidence. According to what Dan had learned, his birth parents hadn't been able to afford to take care of both him and his twin brother, so he had been given up for adoption. His twin still lived with the birth family, and Dan was going to meet all of them for the first time when we were in Korea.

I was so honored that Dan was able to share such intimate information with me that I was literally moved to tears. But I also tried to imagine his twin brother's position. How do you process that information when your mother gives it to you? Guess what?! You have a twin brother who I gave away, and he will be here in two weeks to meet you for the very first time! Yay! Although I had been through something strikingly similar just a few months earlier, both Anaïs and I had been given away, so we were on more equal ground. I was stunned by Dan's story.

In the airport, Dan was filming, too, which made for a subtle battle of the film crews. Luckily for Dan and me, their territorial issues were very much secondary to the events unfolding in our lives. I had already met my twin, so I had my experience to share with him if it could be of any comfort. "This is crazy, Dan," I cautioned him. "Once you step foot on the plane, it becomes real. After this trip, your life will never be the same." Anaïs and I had been lucky to learn quickly how to just breathe and let life take us where it would. I wanted Dan to feel the happiness and joy in his new adventure in life, not dwell on all the potentially negative aspects of his situation. For a second, I saw myself in him. "Don't be scared," I told him. "Life will never present challenges to you that you cannot handle." He started to smile as he heard my advice, and by the time he was rocking back and forth and spastically scratching his chin with a nervous energy, I knew he'd be just fine.

Incheon International Airport, Seoul's gateway to the world, is unbelievably organized and very high-tech. Anaïs had landed before us, but Oliver, a friend of a friend, had picked her up and was taking her around Seoul, and she was meeting us at the hotel. My friend Sue was picking me up. She had been my homeland tour guide the year before, and with her motherly energy, my mom, she, and I had established a very strong bond. She made me proud to be Korean by show-ing me the strength and determination of the Korean people, the people whose blood runs through my veins. Although Korea may not have meant much to me in my childhood, it did now. After seeing how large a role nature plays in our lives, as per my ever-growing relationship with my sister, it meant even more to stand proud and say, I am Korean. Plus, Sue always fed me the most AMAZING Korean food, and every-one knows food is the way to my Seoul—I mean soul.

I had truly never imagined that I would be back in Korea so soon. Yet here I was, and there was Sue, emerging from the crowd of Koreans in the terminal. Sue isn't a genetic relation, of course, but I consider her family.

On our trip from the airport to the hotel, Sue and I

talked about the entire past year. She had seen Anaïs's and my story on the news and had even showed me the video clip from a Korean national news program. It had pulled some of the footage on our Kickstarter trailer and pictures on our social media platforms. It was really both bizarre and thrilling to see that so much care and effort had been taken to tell our story, especially by people who had never met us, let alone talked to us. In fact, my lack of privacy was terrifying, but I quickly got over it, since I had made the choice to publicize the private part of my life. Press is a funny thing. Although it is quite invasive, it allows us to reach many people in what is a very positive way for us. In return for going public, we received messages via all our social media outlets—Kickstarter, Facebook, Twitter, and more—from adoptees who had been moved by our story. Some have decided to start their own birth searches just because of us. Sue even begrudgingly granted Ryan permission to film the two of us together, for the sake of the story.

Sue was no ordinary tour guide. She gave tours throughout the year, but the roots tours, like the one I had been on the year before, were the most dear to her. In fact, she specifically requested to be the Korean leader of that tour group every year. She took so much pride in showing adoptees their homeland. Besides being a guide, she also served as a translator for reunions between adoptees and their birth families and/or foster families. It took an incredibly strong human being to loan herself as the main support in such intense situations. Without her, the families would never be able to communicate. She devoted her life to making others happy. Of course, she is a twin, too. Sue's identical twin sister lives in Oregon. They hadn't been separated, but her sister had met a man from the States and moved there to be with him. Incredible how my life kept putting me in touch with twins.

Sue took us to our hotel right near Myeong-dong, the busy, hip shopping district in Seoul. It was not exactly the Times Square of the city, but sometimes it felt like it. Our hotel was Hotel Biz and was most definitely not the Ritz. We reached it only after turning down three or four alleys off the main road. Right outside the entrance was a heaping pile of cat poo. Believe me, in the Korean summer heat, it wasn't pleasant. The concierge inside was remarkably hospitable, telling us where our rooms were and what hours breakfast was served. We put our bags in our tiny rooms with rock-hard beds. The wallpaper in the room was patterned with landmarks of London. How funny is that? Of the thousands of hotels in Korea, we stay in one with London-themed wallpaper. My eye was immediately drawn to the image of the London Eye, reminding me how much I had experienced in just the past five months.

Korea in the summer is brutally hot and humid, with temperatures climbing to what feels like a billion degrees. By the end of the day, you are salty, sticky, and sitting in a pool of your own sweat. I was already drenched by the time we got the bags to the room, so I took a quick shower and waited for Anaïs. When she finally got there, we hugged and jumped up and down a hundred times. I loved seeing her. She felt like . . . my sister. Even though we were in touch daily online, that wasn't even close to being with her in person.

Being apart didn't feel wrong, per se. But when we were

together, it was like a fairy tale, a honeymoon, so right that it was almost too good to be true. Our bond has been hard to explain. There were so many things in the past that we still didn't know about each other, yet there was almost no need to discuss them. We had a much deeper understanding of each other that completely surpassed having experienced everyday communication for a consistent twenty-five years. In life, there exists sympathy and empathy. I have both of those with Anaïs, as I am certainly able to relate to, identify with, and have compassion for the feelings she is going through. But what I have with her is beyond that. I have literally felt in my body what she is feeling. I know exactly where in her throat she gets choked up when she gets upset and the blood rushes to her face. I know how hot it actually feels. It's not telekinesis that we share, but the ability to recognize and fully experience what the other is going through. Don't get me wrong—it's not all the time and obviously the situations differ, but the raw feelings of emotion that are evoked inside my twin can be felt in the exact same places in my own body.

Our hug fest ended when I said I was starving, so we headed to the Myeong-dong market, where the prevailing population of shoppers seemed to be young Korean couples. Everything seemed brand-new, colorful, and vibrant, with street vendors selling every kind of merchandise and food in the world. We met Sue at a Korean BBQ that she recommended, where we indulged in steak and beer while she got to know my sister.

The next morning, we headed over to the Lotte Hotel, the venue hosting the conference. It was a beautiful, upscale hotel staffed by exceptionally beautiful and hospitable people. It was only a ten-minute walk from the Hotel Biz, but in the Korean heat, I felt like I was trekking across the Gobi Desert. On the way, it started pouring and in no time, my shoes were ruined, Anaïs's shoes were ruined, the equipment was in danger, and the rain kept coming. We stopped into a convenience store to grab some inexpensive umbrellas, rain boots, and ponchos. Some advice to those who might find themselves in this kind of predicament in the future—don't wear a poncho in the sweltering heat of Korea when it rains, because your own stench gets caught under the plastic and you smell for the rest of the day. We could all smell Ryan mixed with plastic for days afterward, and we didn't let him live it down, and thus we coined him as the smelly friend. (There is always one.)

After we had registered and signed up for a few seminars, we took one of Seoul's inexpensive cabs to Gyeongbokgung Palace, a massive tourist attraction that gets extremely crowded, especially on Sunday afternoons. The beauty of the place was that when you were facing it, you could see only the mountains in the background, so you had no human artifacts to detract from what it must have been like hundreds of years earlier. Then, when you turned around to face the city, you see an ancient palace wall backlit by massive Samsung buildings and water fountains in Gwanghwamun Square. It is a lovely reminder of how far and how quickly the country and city has built itself up, a true representation of old and new. I had been to the palace the year before, but I wanted to show it to my sister. I wanted to imagine us running around the grounds in a past life together. I guess a girl's dream of being a princess never goes away.

That night, Kanoa and Tomas arrived in Seoul. Tomas had seen my stress over the documentary production, and he offered to pay for Kanoa and him to join us and help out. His support was so incredible that my gratitude was beyond words. Kanoa was not only my best friend, but my sister had a teenager-like crush on him, with his handsome hapa face, so his presence made her all the happier, too. The four of us were quite hangry, our way of saying angry from being hungry, so we found a random Korean restaurant, the only one that seemed to be open. No one in the establishment spoke English, and the food was so spicy that Anaïs and I, who have a pretty high tolerance to spicy, couldn't even finish. The only way we could communicate with our server was by playing charades.

The next day, the IKAA conference got under way. It was sponsored by Samsung, so we could expect a highly professional, very carefully planned agenda, beginning with the opening ceremonies. When we arrived at the Hotel Lotte, there in the lobby was Dan being followed by his film crew. We had a pretty good laugh about how both Korean adoptees from L.A. had film crews following them around. I was like a living stereotype—I was an actor, which meant I was a waitress; I was Asian, which meant I was a terrible driver; and I was from L.A., which meant that my life was a reality show. At least I broke the stereotype by being bad at math (and I would soon have the IQ test to prove it).

The conference's opening ceremonies included a prerecorded speech by the president of Korea, Park Geun-hye. So much care had been taken to make this conference special, and to have someone as important as the president of Korea welcoming us home was so moving. It reinforced the thought of how much love went into the process of adoption, even though at many times, the conversation was about the negative. All the important people from the adoption community were there, too, including representatives from all the adoption agencies. I was so engulfed in the ceremony that I had no idea Anaïs had begun to cry until I glanced over at her.

The tears weren't the happy kind. I could feel something more going on. I didn't want her to be sad, even if she was just overwhelmed and being emotional. We were in Korea together for the first time since our separation. Anaïs hadn't been all that sure that she wanted to come in the first place, but here we were. The planning to get here had caused me a great amount of stress, and Anaïs had seen a lot of it during her visit to California. She was upset that I was stressing myself out and told me the trip wasn't worth it to her unless it was going to make me happy. She also thought it was a bit rushed. I assured her that my stress was only proof of how much I wanted to get there. And here we were, battling to take care of each other, but inside knowing how much we wanted to be in Korea together.

After the ceremony, we headed to the cocktail hour, where, of course, we met a bunch of other adoptees. Some had already heard about our story and had lots of the same questions we had been hearing for the past year: When did you find out about each other? When did you meet? Are you similar? How are you different? They were all noninvasive questions and although it was fun to share our story, it could get exhausting repeating ourselves a billion times. But, while sharing our story, we got to hear incredible stories from some of them in return.

We met a middle-aged Danish-Korean man who had been adopted as a baby with his twin. When the two conducted their birth search, they found out that there was a bit more to their story. They were triplets. The birth family had kept one boy and given the other two up for adoption. The cost of keeping so many children in the home was a real financial hardship for many Korean people, especially at the time this man had been born. I'm not sure how "lucky" twins are considered to be in Korea, maybe just the opposite. To me, I get the feeling it is not a happy thing. If you're a twin born in the States, it seems it is always a gift, a two-for-one deal, perhaps. But in Korea it was beginning to seem as though almost all the adopted twins had been separated, except in the case of my good friend Sue.

After the cocktail hour, we all got ready to go out and experience another important part of Korean culture—the nightlife. Koreans are known to excel in drinking and kara-oke, and the Koreans on this trip were no exception. It was also Ryan's birthday, and I really cared about him, so I wanted to be sure we got a nice celebration in. I wasn't able to offer much because of the hectic schedule, and I felt crappy about it the entire time, so I was glad to be able to get some partying in on his behalf here. We pre-gamed in Dan's room, and then headed out to what seemed like a sports bar in the heart of Myeong-dong. Everyone had just enough to drink and with the heat, it got to our heads fast. Eventually, Dan and I got the

entire bar to sing "Happy Birthday" to Ryan. It wasn't much—
I had wanted to give him so much more—but I hoped at least
he got a birthday wish in.

The next day was really huge. We were going to see my
foster mother and visit the Social Welfare Society (SWS), the
adoption agency where I had been taken after my birth. The
trip was already a bit stressful. I was getting frustrated with my
producer, James, who for some reason was depending on me to
have the itinerary, addresses, and such. I thought it was his duty
to handle all of that so I could focus on being with my sister. I
was in no way prepared to keep track of all those details, especially while going through such an intense experience and especially on that day. Sure enough, at breakfast, we were all
scrambling to figure out the best way to get to SWS. The heat
making everyone sticky and agitated didn't help. I think Anaïs
could sense my anxiety level, which caused her to withdraw.
For her, we were taking this trip to have fun; the last thing she
wanted was for everyone to be stressed out about stuff.

SWS was near the Gangnam area of Seoul, a twenty-
minute van-style cab ride away. I was looking forward to seeing SooJoo, my same social worker from the previous year, and
I wanted to meet Shinhye, the head of postadoption services.
But most important, I could not wait to see my foster mother
again. I never imagined that seeing her so soon would be in
the realm of possibility. My foster mother was the cutest lady
ever, and this time, she was bringing her whole family.

The SWS building hadn't changed—it was small, old,
and cramped. We took the elevator upstairs, and there in the
office was SooJoo, looking just as beautiful as I remembered

her, tall and thin with fantastic porcelain skin. She was still exuding her cheerful, kind energy, too. Soon, Shinhye came into the room and introduced herself to everyone. We talked about our story and about Ben Sommers, my social worker from Spence-Chapin, and caught up a bit about the events that had transpired over the past few months. It was really exciting to be able to sit and look through my birth records with my sister sitting next to me. We were able to take a good look at the physical page in front of us and really see what was written down. We kept looking at all the names and the facts, asking every question that came to our mind, trying to analyze and compare. Unfortunately, through no fault of her own, Shinhye's responses were unsatisfying. We wanted answers to fill in our history, but we also understood that it was quite possible that what was written down wasn't necessarily the truth. In our case, Anaïs's and my records were so wildly different that we understood a lot of it could have been completely made up by intake workers.

Then it was time for my foster mother to arrive. Within a millisecond of hearing her walking down the hallway, the blood rushed to my face from excitement. But when we saw each other, my adrenaline spiked. She came running into the room with her arms spread out and hugged both me and Anaïs. Like everyone else, she thought Anaïs was me at first. I was filled with pure joy. I was with my sister and with my foster mom, my first caretaker. She had brought her second daughter and her adorable granddaughters with her. They brought us gifts: necklaces, earrings, and K-pop posters and CDs. I brought them gifts, as well. I had gone to Kitson, a very "L.A." store, the day before leaving, and I'd bought my foster mom two vases from L.A. and nail polish and sunglass cases for the girls.

It was still strange to sit with someone you can't fully communicate with. I cared so much about my foster mom, conveyed in our smiles and hugs, but I had no idea how to actually say anything to her in words. Communication was happening in a time lag, the words in the conversation and the reactions delayed. The first time I had met her, she held my hand and talked directly to me, pouring her heart out, it seemed, and although I understood the general feeling, I couldn't understand the words. Then I would hear the social worker's English translation in my ear. The funny thing was that social workers don't necessarily translate completely accurately. For example, in a written letter, my foster mother wrote that she hoped I would find a nice white man, but the translation read she hoped I would find a nice man. Our first meeting had been quite intense and very emotional, but now that I knew my foster mom, this meeting felt like a true reunion and was much more joyous. Everyone was thrilled to be together, despite any language barriers. I promised myself I would learn Korean, mostly motivated by my desire to speak with her. I love her, and one day, we will talk without translators.

Anaïs seemed pretty happy and comfortable to be witnessing the reunion, seeing that someone who really didn't even know you cared so much about you that she had to meet you. I hoped this would calm any anticipation she had about meeting her own foster mother in the next few days. I hoped she saw that she was surrounded by love from the day she was born, whether or not she originally thought of our early days in that way.

For lunch, the adoption agency treated us to the amazing bulgogi. My foster mother, seated next to me, started spoon-feeding me like a baby. It was so funny! I have a pet peeve about being fed like this, but in this instance, it wasn't weird at all. I doubted she did it because she once fed me like this, although I'd like to think that that connection still remains today. I think of it more as a symbolic connection, that she was nurturing me again after twenty-six years of being apart.

My foster mother told me that when I get married she wants to come, and the next time I come back to Korea, that I must stay with her at her house, and she will cook for me. My God, that sounds amazing, so much fun to me. I would love to see where and how she lives. It's like I have a Korean mom, and at every turn, my family is expanding. Too soon after lunch, it was time for my good-bye hug, and I didn't want to let go. Although I knew it wouldn't be the last time I saw her, I didn't know when I would hug her again. I loved being there with her. She calmed me and made me happy, like any mother should.

The next morning began on quite a stressful note. At breakfast, my sister revealed to me that she was unhappy. She had been talking to me about it a little on the way to the Lotte Hotel, but when the crew joined us at the table twenty minutes later, I sensed that she hadn't said everything she needed to say. With one glance, I noticed that she was about to burst into tears and we quickly went to the bathroom, as I didn't want her to cry in front of anyone or to make her uncomfortable. We needed a private moment and a private conversation, with no cameras and for no ears but mine. We had made a pact with ourselves to be honest on camera about all of our emotions because it was for a greater good, but in this moment, we didn't care about the pact—I only cared about my sister's feelings and wanted her to be happy. She was more important than any documentary or project.

I'm glad that I pulled Anaïs away, since the production of the documentary was the source of her discomfort. She didn't understand why we had to stop and do an interview the moment after anything happened to either one of us. In most instances, she was unsure how she felt and she certainly didn't want to make it up on the spot, especially if it was going to be shared with the rest of the world. She told me that although I felt comfortable expressing myself on camera, she preferred expressing herself by drawing or sketching a cartoon. I told her that was totally okay. It was my objective to tell the story creatively, how we wanted it, what we wanted to say. This was not just facts, it was us! More than anything, I wanted her to be comfortable. "If you are feeling crazy and cannot pinpoint an emotion, then that is what you are feeling," I reassured her. When she told me she was so unhappy, I felt awful. I wanted her to be okay. This documentary was for her as much as it was for me. I wanted to show her our country and give her an experience that she would remember and be grateful for. My intention had never been to bring her to Korea and stress her out. But she wasn't comfortable. The Hotel Biz wasn't inviting or relaxing, we were both completely out of our element, she always had a camera stuck in her face on what was to be a trip of great importance, and to top it off, the next day was her reunion with her own foster mother. It seemed as though the circumstances had really begun to weigh down on her, and her anxiety had spiked.

The next day, the first of August, was the day we were meeting Anaïs's foster mother, so it was going to be my sister's most intense day yet, and she was getting nervous, especially about the filming. I sat down privately with Ryan to explain that Anaïs was upset with the way we were documenting everything, so we had to be a bit more aware of her feelings from here on out. From what I could decipher, Anaïs was finding the experience intrusive and complained of a lack of privacy in certain situations—particularly those that were emotional and overwhelming. I am an actress and found comfort in being in front of the camera, but Anaïs is not. Ryan didn't want to change our approach, because he thought he knew exactly what the documentary needed. Although I trusted him, the safety and comfort of my sister, who was my family, took precedence in that moment. I warned him that he risked having her shut down entirely, and he reluctantly agreed to take a more gentle approach to filming.

I crept back into our room to see how Anaïs was doing. She was changing her clothes a few times, figuring out what she wanted to wear. As she was getting her gifts for her foster mother together, she started asking if I thought they were sufficient. They were beautiful teas and chocolates from France, and I assured her they were perfect and her foster mother would appreciate them.

We were going to be meeting her at Holt Children's Services, the adoption agency that had placed my sister with her French family so many years ago. Holt was located a cab ride away in the heart of downtown Seoul, so we decided to eat lunch in Namdaemun Market, an outdoor market, on our way to the agency. We had cold noodles—*naengmyun*—Anaïs's and my favorite shared dish. On a hot day, these noodles have the most cooling effect. They are noodles made from buckwheat, so they are chewy and rubbery, and the broth is a mixture of cold beef stock, vinegar, cucumber, and a variety of other things. After lunch, Anaïs found a shop that sold mass quantities of salty dried seaweed snacks, which made her ecstatic. There was no such shop in Paris! She bought way more than she could possibly carry, but she was happy. She was like a kid in a . . . dried seaweed store?

Then it was time for Anaïs to meet her foster mother at Holt. Despite her nerves, I hoped that this was what she wanted. I didn't want to force her to do something she wasn't ready for. I had been through it before, so I hoped she found some relief in my experience. Maybe I was being selfish, wanting to be there for her, because it made me feel good. I couldn't help second-guessing my motives, because if they were causing her to be unhappy, I was unhappy. I wanted to be doing these things for her. I imagined this was what a mother felt like when she hoped she was doing the right thing by her child when she made decisions. In the cab downtown, Anaïs ended up falling asleep, which was adorable and quite typical for both of us. When things get stressful, we nap.

Seoul is an amazing city, a complete mix of different time periods. One block can be from one century, and the next block can be totally modern. Some of the streets are crowded with older buildings, where everything looks quite brown, and the next street has beautiful, massive contemporary buildings most likely built by Samsung or Hyundai. Holt was in a smaller building, a little run-down with a big green sign saying HOLT POST ADOPTION SERVICES. When we walked in the door, a most kind older gentleman stopped us to tell us to take off our shoes and put on slippers. My heart started to beat hard, and I knew my sister's was, too. It was all becoming real. What if her foster mom was there already? What if she showed up right behind us? What would she look like? Would my sister be okay? Would she be ready?

Upstairs in the main office, we asked for Franck, the social worker handling all of the correspondence relating to Anaïs's adoption. He was the one in constant contact with Ben at Spence-Chapin, as the two tried to put the pieces together for Anaïs and me. Like Ben, Franck was an adoptee as well, except he was adopted to France, which, I was sure made my sister feel all the safer.

Franck did not match the image I had in my head. He was shorter with longer hair and bold jewelry. I hadn't expected him to be so cool and casual. The craziest part about him was that he was speaking English to the crew and me, French to Anaïs, and Korean to the other social workers. It completely blew my mind, and I think my sister was impressed, too. Finally, someone was speaking French. Anaïs had been so out of her element, surrounded by Americans all the time and in a country she had never been to before. But now she could breathe, feel like herself, and speak in her native tongue.

Franck brought us to the room where we would be meeting Anaïs's foster mother. It was nice, a bit more comfortable than the one at SWS, with light green walls and big comfy couches. Anaïs sat down with Franck to look over her records. She had seen most of them before, but there were a few pictures that were new to her. They were photos of her on the day she was born. I guessed that I must have looked like that, too. For a hot second, I wondered whether or not my picture was taken right next to her, or if we had already been separated. Was I there? Were we split up right after being born? Was one of us put down in the wrong bed? But I snapped back into the room and told myself this wasn't about me, it was about my sister. This was her experience. So there I was, watching my sister and Franck review her records in French, and every once in a while politely turn to me to tell me something in English.

There were discrepancies in Anaïs's records, as we had discovered even the few days after we had made contact. It is partly frustrating that I may not ever know the truth about my past, yet comforting in a very dark way to think that someone spent the time officially typing up these records to give the adoptees a feeling of importance. None of it had anything to do with the social workers that were currently working with us, so there was no reason to have animosity toward these people.

Finally, it was time—Anaïs's foster mother had arrived. My sister stood up and patted her clothes. I imagined she was feeling what I had felt the year before, wanting to be calm and able to handle what was about to happen. For me, the second the door opened, even just a crack, my stomach dropped into my butt and my nerves went crazy. Then, once I saw the face of the woman who first took care of me, my body went calm, the anticipation was over. I was with her again, the person who had given me so much when she would receive so little in return. Like my foster mother, Anaïs's foster mother was a hero. And here she was!

From the instant I saw her, I was awestruck by the similar energies she and Anaïs generated. Like Anaïs, she carried herself in a calm, shy, reserved way. Could it be that our personalities had begun to develop even in the few days, weeks, and months after we are born? How possible was it that the very base of our personalities had been solidified by these two women? I knew genetics played an important part in our lives, but there was an energy that I shared with my foster mother, my first nurturer. When she had come into the room at the Spence-Chapin the day before, she had screamed and hugged us super-tight, even playfully slapping me on the arm. She was touchy-feely, and she had been like that even the first time I had met her.

But Anaïs's foster mother was different. She was shy, happy, and warming up to the room much more slowly. When she was standing next to Anaïs, they were staring at each other as if they were communicating. How could it be that our foster mothers reflected so much of what we saw in ourselves? To me, it was becoming clear that every person in my life had affected me in some way, even the people whom I may not remember. These women were caring for us as our brains were quickly developing and our bodies were growing. Of course we would be similar to them! They had been the base and strength of our development as children.

When we all sat down together, my mind exploded. Three languages were going on. Franck was translating from Korean to French, and on occasion someone would turn to me and speak in English. I felt awkward. I felt like I was Anaïs sitting there and watching herself have a reunion. I sat staring in awe. Although I could not understand the languages, nor understand at which point they were speaking French and when they were speaking Korean, I still understood the connections. The only language I understood was the body language, and it was saying so much. It was like trying to translate a Spanish soap opera. I was observing and thinking to myself, Okay . . . Anaïs's foster mother is pleased to be sitting in her company. Anaïs said she's happy to meet her. Her foster mother is upset. . . . No, wait . . . she's happy. . . . She's astonished that one of the children she cared for thought enough about her to come back to meet her . . . and now Anaïs and Franck are telling her how good foie gras tastes. . . . Damn, I'm good. I imagine that most foster mothers do not get a chance to meet their grown foster children. Even if my translation of this conversation is not spot-on, I think Anaïs was incredibly grateful for the experience.

After talking for a while in every language possible, Anaïs's foster mother invited us to dinner at a Korean BBQ place around the corner from Holt. She was thrilled to be showing off her turf. She ordered everything for us and sat us down on the floor. The best part was, she started feeding my sister like a baby! She also did the same to me and even to Ryan and Kanoa. She was so motherly that she had to take care of all of us.

I don't think I've ever seen Anaïs as happy as she was at dinner. She couldn't contain her smile. Her foster mother was telling her how she was as a baby. I leaned over to her and told her that my sister was an incredibly talented fashion designer, knowing Anaïs would never brag about herself. I wanted and hoped that Anaïs would be that happy for the rest of her life. I loved seeing her like that.

Despite our protests, Anaïs's foster mother insisted on paying for dinner, and that was that. We walked outside to the bus stop after she refused to take a cab. "Please," we kept saying. "You took such good care of Anaïs as a baby, and it's our turn to take care of you now." She wouldn't have it. No way—her Korean pride took over. She hugged my sister and literally bolted down the street, full speed, running as fast as she could toward the bus, all the while shaking her hand good-bye in the air. The crew and I were in such shock. We all stared at each other in awe. Then I looked over at my sister, and she was in a complete fit of laughter. Pure joy.

Back inside the Holt building, Anaïs and I wanted to see the little babies upstairs in the nursery. They were incredibly cute. We were allowed to hold them and play with them. For the first time, I was so happy to hold a baby. I wanted to take care of them all and never let one go. My sister, too, was cradling a baby in her arms. I could tell that one day, she will be an amazing mother.

When we got back to our hotel room later that day, Anaïs and I finally shared a moment alone. She very quietly turned to me and thanked me.

"For what?" I asked her.

"For bringing me here and making me meet my foster mother," she replied. "I wasn't sure if I wanted to do it, and I'm glad you pushed me to."

I was so relieved. I had wanted her to have an amazing experience in Korea. When I had visited the previous year, for the first time I felt so proud to say that I was Korean, and my reunion with my foster mother had been an exceptional experience, knowing I was taken care of since the day I was born. My sister was even willing to be interviewed for the documentary, and for the first time, she really opened up, expressing how she truly felt. It was one of the first times that she revealed the sadness of her adoption as a baby. Even though I had never felt this kind of profound remorse, at least now we had each other.

The next day, we visited the N Seoul Tower, the highest point in the city. It was beautiful up there, and from the glass observation deck, you had a 360-degree view of Seoul and beyond. The tower was next to a centuries-old traditional pagoda with ornate, colorful wood, stone, and tile work, so side by side, the modern tower and the ancient shrine. It reminded me of my sister and me. We were in Korea discovering the old, where we had come from, yet we were here celebrating the new, our brand-new relationship. Such metaphor!

Etched in the top of the glass in the windows of the observation deck were the names and distances of world cities and other points of interest that were in that direction. So, gazing out over Seoul, I could look past the horizon and dream of being in those cities while seeing how far I'd come. Anaïs and I walked around the room looking at the view from every different angle, as Anaïs snapped pictures of the "Paris" and "London" directions, and I was taking mine toward "New York" and "Los Angeles." Another tradition of the tower was the locks and keys. With permanent marker, you write your name on a lock and hang it on a railing, then throw away the key. It was so corny and really for lovers, but I wanted to do it with my sister. I loved the idea of a love locked until eternity, never able to be broken.

As the last nights of our visit approached, my sister and I began to primp ourselves. I imagined that is what it would have been like in high school getting ready for all the parties, if we had been raised together in the States. We were attending a very formal gala hosted by Samsung. As we were putting on our outfits, my sister started to get really frustrated. The joy of meeting her foster mother was beginning to fade, and her anxiety was creeping back. Perhaps, it was anticipating the end of the trip and when we would likely see each other next. But she was wildly uncomfortable, she hated the hotel room, and she couldn't get her dress zipped up all the way. She kept saying that she was fat and ugly. It made me incredibly sad to see her like that. I kept telling her she looked pretty, but I couldn't get her out of that headspace. She was deeply convinced at that very moment that her appearance was appalling, and I didn't want to point out that calling herself fat and ugly was, umm, inadvertently calling me the same—rude.

We arrived at the gala a bit on the later side, which meant we missed a couple of speeches, but not the entertainment. One act featured traditional Korean dancers, and another was a K-pop group. It was so cheesy, but necessary. No Korea visit would be complete without seeing a K-pop performance. K-pop is such a strange phenomenon, so tacky, with the men wearing a ton of makeup, and the girls going wild for them. Go figure.

The gala was great, with amazing food and wine. Anaïs

seemed really happy to finally be eating European-style food again. She even turned to me with a big smile and said, "This is the perfect amount of silverware," which made us all laugh. I loved that she was enjoying herself. I was beginning to acknowledge just how invested I was in her happiness, and I didn't want her self-image to get in the way of her joy.

The next night we were attending a "black-and-white" concert, followed by the late-night dance party at Hybrid Club Vera. Anaïs and I had bought matching dresses—hers white, mine black. There was some downtime before the epic show at the Hybrid Club Vera, so Anaïs and I went there early to meet up with Dan Matthews. He had invited me to join Bobby Choi, his guitarist, and him for one song, which was such an honor. Singing, however, was something that had always been a little touchy for me. As a young performer, I hadn't been the best singer. For some reason, I wouldn't be able to hear the notes right, so every time I started singing, the wrong tones would come out. It was incredibly embarrassing, and the other kids would snicker and giggle, but I didn't let it get to me. I worked as hard as I could to improve, often practicing two hours a day in my room, until my brothers and parents were . . . ready to kill me. Eventually, I became decent, but that didn't mean I still didn't get nervous, especially in front of my friends. It wasn't as frightening, but I always get a little bit shy right before I sing my first note.

I practiced with Bobby first, as Dan hadn't arrived yet. After a little bit, Dan came in, and guess who was with him? His twin brother! It was such a trip. I knew Anaïs and I looked exactly alike and had been through this entire thing just a few months prior, but it was so crazy to see them together. They had the exact same mannerisms, and the exact same face. Their sister was with them as well. I was staring—rude! I was thinking, Holy shit, this is the craziest thing! Anaïs was standing right next to me at the same exact time they walked in, and for the first time, I was observing what everyone else had been seeing when they had been looking at her and me for the past three months.

I loved knowing there was someone else in the world who had also just found his identical twin. It was comforting to know that Anaïs and I were not alone. I just couldn't imagine how Dan felt. I never had the courage to ask him about it, as it was probably painful.

The rehearsal went well. While I was onstage practicing, Anaïs left to have coffee with a friend from Paris who lived in Korea. When she got back, she was all stressed out, almost in a panic. She was trying to get her microphone pack on, but the leg strap was bothering her, and she felt nauseous and hot and wanted to lie down. But it wasn't just that. I could see her stress building, like atoms multiplying about to spontaneously combust.

Soon, the show started, and the club was getting crowded. I was backstage with Dan and Bobby, getting ready for our turn, when Ryan told me that Anaïs was freaking out and throwing up in the bathroom. I found her there kneeling over the toilet, crying. She said she was overwhelmed—everything was becoming super-real, we were leaving Korea tomorrow, and she didn't know the next time she would see me. I tried to console her, but I didn't know what to do. And, to be honest, it was the first time that I couldn't understand what she was feeling. I never had anxiety to this extent. I just held her, because I was afraid if I said anything, it would make it worse, and all I wanted to do was to make her feel better.

It was time to get onstage, so I asked Anaïs if she wanted to join me, but she said she would watch from backstage. Part of me feared that I had forced her into this trip that she hadn't wanted to make. I had told her so many times that I cared more about her than the documentary and everything else. What if she was just going along for the ride because she didn't want to disappoint me, but that she was getting overwhelmed with anxiety?

The performance went extremely well, although I wasn't really present onstage. I didn't care about anything but my sister, and if she was okay. I ran off to find her immediately after we finished, and when she said she was feeling better, we went out into the audience and grabbed a drink. As the music and night escalated, we started dancing, releasing all sorts of pent-up anxiety. Thankfully, Anaïs was beginning to feel more alive. Soon enough, after a few cocktails and time together, we were both laughing and jumping around like little girls. It was fun to de-stress together. There was no question that the comfort we offered each other made hard situations far more bearable. The next morning, I opened my eyes to see my sister lying next to me—always a joy. Anaïs was going home today, so after we got up, we headed toward the metro station, where she was catching the train to the airport. Time was slowing as we were saying our good-byes. I felt like I was in a scene from *Love in the Afternoon*, with Audrey Hepburn and Gary Cooper at the train station in the final seconds before the train departs. We just stood staring at each other for what seemed like forever. We had already spent so many years apart, and this was the first time we didn't have an exact date to see each other again. I gave her the tightest hug I could, trying to transmit how much I cared about her through my embrace. Eventually, she took the elevator into the station. I knew she had a massive flight ahead of her, and she was probably stressed out about it. I hoped she would be okay on the flight. I didn't know if her anxiety would come on the plane or not. But I thought she was more than relieved to be going back home, where she could speak her own language, be with her friends, and feel like herself without a camera in her face. She was heading back to her life in France, something I still hadn't experienced. I imagined her going back to eating croissants for breakfast and riding a bicycle past the Eiffel Tower. It's funny—she was my sister, but we were still strangers in so many ways.

15

ANAÏS

korea

I wasn't absolutely certain I wanted to go to the International
Korean Adoptees Association convention in Seoul. Sam had
mentioned it after she met Dan Matthews, but I had never been
a huge fan of adoptee gatherings. I had attended a few in France
with my parents when I was younger, but as an adult, I had
been to only one program, a screening of a Korean documentary hosted by Racines Coréennes (Korean Roots), which I
attended with my Korean friend Anaïs. The documentary was
incredibly happy and sad, as the girl in the film meets with her
birth family at the airport in Seoul (how could I control my
tears when I saw that?) but then she does not get all the answers
she was looking for (how could I not feel her frustration?). I
enjoyed the prescreening gathering and we met other Korean
adoptees, some of whom were a bit older than I, but it felt good
to be with people who understood my experience and seemed
very happy in their lives. Ultimately, though, I was scared to go

to those gatherings too many times, as I feared they might turn into something like AA meetings, and the people were just here to sort out their problems.

As for going to Korea with Sam, I still had the same fears as I had always had. I was scared to have questions I had not yet been able to even ask myself, and then not find enough answers. I also feared getting either frustrated by the lack of information or discovering information that I did not want to have. Basically, I was scared. I had found Sam, and that was satisfying enough for me. I didn't need anything else.

We finally agreed to do the trip. The networking angle was appealing: "The vision of the IKAA Gathering 2013 is for the leading global network of adult Korean adoptees to reach out to adult adoptees worldwide, and to provide comprehensive social, professional, and cultural networking opportunities to the international adoptee community, including interactions with Korean society," the brochure said. The weeklong program had a lot of fun-looking things going on. I remember being in Sam's flat, and her being all stressed out and tearing out her hair (in French, *s'arracher les cheveux*). She was saying Korea would be great for the documentary, but in the meantime I mostly wanted her to feel happy and ready to enjoy herself rather than being all neurotic and stressed. Knowing we'd be together for the experience was a comfort, because with Sam, I have no fear. I was just worried about the balance between stress and joy.

Even though I would have Sam, I wished my parents were coming with me. My sister had made her first trip to Korea with her mother, and I would have loved to do the same thing with my mum and dad. I had been to Korea as a seven-year-old, but not as an adult. I am not scared of traveling alone—on the contrary—but this time, I would be living the film *Lost in Translation*, a complete stranger in a country that, on some level, I thought I should understand. That is the worst, when you are so far from your own attachments that you feel like you are drifting away and apart from any group and that you don't belong anywhere. There was great importance in meeting my foster mother and visiting the adoption agency, and I would have loved to share those things with one or both of my parents. I had checked with them before I booked the trip to be sure they didn't mind me going without them, and they had given me their approval, although they thought it was a little rushed. Even being with Marie or Kelsang would have helped. Sam would have people she already knew, as she was very close to the documentary crew. But I had only her.

I knew two people going on the trip, although they were only acquaintances. I had met them briefly at the Racines Coréennes documentary screening. Hélène was the president of the club, and Charles was the treasurer. The entire roster of the more than five hundred people going to the IKAA Seoul event had about a dozen French adoptees, including Hélène, Charles, and me. It was nice to know some Frenchness would be part of the party. I don't know how weird it might sound to say that we would all be back where we had come from, but I did feel community with other French-Korean adoptees, and home for me was the small French team that would be at the gathering.

The weeks leading to the trip went amazingly well. The

week of July 14, I had my interview at Gerard Darel. The head of leather goods liked me enough to ask me to draw a project for her and send it the following week. My graduation ceremony for Central Saint Martins was July 17, and I sent the project a few days after. The day before leaving for Korea, I noticed a missed call and a voice mail from a human resources person at Gerard Darel. It was unfortunately too late to call back.

The day I left for Seoul was also the day I was officially giving up my share of the flat on Stroud Green Road in Finsbury Park, so I had to pack everything and clean my room in the morning. When that was done, I packed the rest of my suitcase and opened my voice mail one last time, where I heard the message from Gerard Darel telling me I had been hired. Even though I was now running late, I was jumping with joy as I raced to Heathrow to get my flight to my birth country. When I arrived at the airport, the lady at the British Airways check-in desk told me I had been upgraded, and that I was now flying business class. I hadn't been this lucky since Kelsang discovered Sam. I still deplore the fact that I could not find a single place to buy a lottery ticket in the whole airport!

It didn't matter. I looked forward to meeting Sam in Korea. It was funny—I quite enjoyed the feeling of arriving in a distant city somewhere on Earth, and with a preplanned meeting point, I would find my sister. It felt like I could go anywhere, and we would always find a way toward each other. I love flying, my favorite parts being when you start going into the sky and when you see the ground and you are about to land at the other end of the planet. This time was to meet my twin sister again, and there was nothing more exciting than this. All throughout getting ready and during the flight, I was thinking of what she might be doing at the same time—packing, being late, running to the airport, etc. The excitement of traveling took away my fears. I felt really emotional as the pilot made his announcement soon after touching down in Korea. "We wish you a pleasant stay, and for those who are coming back, welcome home." *Home*, he said. Wow. I was both modes of passenger—the one coming for a visit, and the one coming home.

I was fortunate to have Oliver, a second-year student at Central Saint Martins and a friend of friends, pick me up at the airport. He was Korean, and he was back in Korea for a visit with his family and was kind enough to collect me in his mum's car. It was a good thing, too. I had the wrong hotel name, and my sister had given me the wrong address, so with his help, we could figure it all out.

Right near our hotel was the Myeong-dong market, which was a fascinating collection of stores, stalls, street food, restaurants, touristy stuff, and everyday goods along blocks and blocks of the city. I was fascinated by the nail polish stands, with so many colors. The market was a girl's paradise, and I could now understand how Korean girls could be so girly compared to me. Seaweed, my favorite, was everywhere, too! I wanted to eat all the time, as the seductive smell of greasy street food got more and more irresistible every time we passed a stand without getting something.

The conference opened with a most moving broadcast from the president of Korea, Park Geun-hye. Even though it had been prerecorded, she was acknowledging the fact that so many kids had left the country by being adopted internationally. It moved me to tears that the president of my birth country would take the time to honor us, almost. It also felt so good to know our fellow Koreans knew we existed. Just the simple gesture of letting the adopted community know that Korean people knew we were there made me so emotional.

The beauty of the trip was that there were blocks of time for sightseeing or visiting our own adoption agencies in between the organized lectures and events. The imperial Gyeongbokgung Palace was wonderful, even though it was absolutely pouring the day we were there. In fact, there were a lot of downpours throughout the week. When the rains stopped, everything felt like a steam bath, but when it came down like cats and dogs, it gave the country a unique feeling, like it was shrouded in something mysterious.

The palace, more than seven hundred years old, once had 7,700 rooms. However, much of it was destroyed by the Japanese during their occupation of Korea in the early 1900s, and the ongoing restoration was going slowly. One of the main gates, Gwangwhamun, was recently returned to its original design and had just reopened in the last few years. That was where the changing of the guard took place. I loved seeing tourist things like that. These weren't the Beefeaters in front of Buckingham Palace, in their tall Beefeater bearskin hats riding their elegantly dressed horses. These guards wore long robes/dresses in bright primary colors with primary colored pinafores and hats in the style of the Royal Canadian Mounted Police. They carried enormous banners and tall traditional weapons of the sword and spear family. Something I love above all else is drumming, and the drumming during the changing of the guard was spectacular. I love drums so much that I go absolutely crazy and want to dance when I hear them. Sam loves to dance, too. Can you imagine if we had started going wild? Even the stone-faced guards would probably have smiled.

The trip had stressful times, too. Sam had been through exactly what I was going through one year earlier, but I needed to slow down. I was in the middle of a huge city, I did not speak the language, and I was disoriented. The crew was all so worried about the documentary and speeding around, whereas I needed time to digest all I was seeing, watching, and hearing, and most important, I needed to realize what was happening. I was in my birth country, after all, and I needed to take a step back to look at things and feel clear and reassured about what was going to happen. Sometimes, Sam seemed as hung up about filming as the rest of them, and I would find myself alone and frustrated when this happened. Sam would be there for me, but there was no bringing her off her desire to make *Twinsters* the best film possible, despite my frustration to the point of tears. I'd just do my best and focus on the positive, like seeing Sam and her foster mother.

I was so moved by how much my sister's foster mother cared about her. In a way, I think it panicked me, seeing how affectionate they were. I was scared I would not have the same experience, that my foster mother would not be that cheerful or happy to see me. Maybe it was the fear of being disappointed and being abandoned again if the meeting went wrong. What if she mistook me for someone else she had cared for, or did not like me, or . . .

So many things were happening at the same time that

my brain was burning out. My sister was unhappy with some things about the documentary and the crew, which was horrible. I had a huge fear of disappointing her if I sometimes did not want to participate in all the filming. Sometimes, I was annoyed at the intrusiveness, but other times, it might be as simple as my microphone was itchy. I needed to process the events, but my feelings and my body were reacting more quickly than my brain could analyze anything.

Having Tomas and Kanoa with us was amazing, as they really were like two friends, but it was still frustrating to know we could not just hang out as friends do. Instead, we'd be yelling at each other about the documentary. To be honest, having Sam so involved with the documentary sometimes made me feel a bit lonely. However, I understood her passion to do it right.

On the day I was going to meet my foster mother, my emotions were everywhere. I was scared about being filmed, as I don't like to give away my feelings, especially when someone is recording them to edit afterward. I was also scared that something would go wrong, like my reaction to her would be wrong, or the expectation was I would act like her, so I would have to act like her to make everyone happy. Or, what if I did not feel anything special about her? Would that make me a monster? Would I actually feel anything for her at all? Sam would be there, and the crew would be there filming, of course. But would they be judging me according to my behavior? Could I have a French reaction to the situation? Would the Americans tell me how to do it? It was so stressful. I was excited, but terrified that if it did go wrong, I would feel abandoned all over again. The night before, when Sam had not been in the room, I had had a panic attack that I could not control. I felt lonely and mostly abandoned, like a wet kitten mewling in the rain. I was petrified of what might happen.

I was even stressing about the physical act of giving my foster mother her gifts. I wanted to thank the woman who had taken care of me, but I did not remember her at all. It was funny to imagine someone who knew me before my first memories, who knew about taking care of me, whereas I had no clue at all. I was excited to know how she would look, how she would look at me.

At Holt Adoption Services, it was great to have my case worker, Franck, on my team, someone I could rely upon. He is Korean, adopted as well, and speaks French. The amazing side of that trip was that you felt protected within this community of adoptees. You feel like you have five hundred brothers and sisters, who understand some things other nonadopted people might not necessarily feel.

Since Sam had been here the previous year, new laws had been put in place and now some information in birth records is hidden. When Sam had been at Spence-Chapin the year before, she could get the name of her foster mother, whereas with me, my request had to first go through the Holt agency, where they would contact the foster mother to get permission to give me her name, number, etc. Luckily, she had agreed to meet me, certain she remembered me.

It's not as if this was my first time seeing my adoption records. They were the exact same papers we had in Paris. Still, something about them brought up a lot of raw emotion.

Sam and I already knew the discrepancies between hers and mine. Now that we had confirmed that we were twins, it was even weirder to try to figure out why. Even the histories of our parents were different. It pissed me off to know it was likely all a huge lie, written in black-and-white.

Even the news stories about the *Twinsters* documentary were in my file. I wasn't just a baby who had been moved out of the country, and my case was closed. I was still an evolving person, so that was actually refreshing. I felt like I knew exactly who I was at the moment. I knew what was in my life, and it didn't bother me what wasn't there. It was an *Okay, I don't know more, and I am okay with it* sense of identity.

After the review of my records, I was as ready as I would ever be for my reunion. When I saw my foster mother enter the room, I was in disbelief at how she had not changed a bit. I had looked at her photo so many times in the last twenty-five years, and here she was! It was hard to describe. I even thought we looked similar, my foster mother and I.

She had gotten to Holt way early, so anxious she was to see me. It was so funny to see how languages worked differently in this moment. She would talk and talk, which sounded to me like she had just said so much, whereas when it was suddenly translated, it turned out to be something really short! I hoped I was getting the whole story!

My foster mother was a stranger, yet I was so relieved to see her and to see that she remembered me. I liked her immediately and felt an invisible bond with her already. I was so fascinated by her, I couldn't stop looking at her. Her presence alone was making me feel protected in a way. She had many stories for us, like how she had started as a foster mother not long before she started taking care of me. I had been her third baby. Apparently, I used to cry a lot when I was left alone, but her son, who was a child then, helped her take care of me.

She was probably the person I interacted with the most in the days and weeks after I was born. I agreed with Sam; such a person has to have an influence on you the rest of your life. You could definitely tell whose foster mum she was, just by our bond. Sam is bonded to her foster mother, too. I was discovering someone had loved me for ages, although she had never been able to tell me before, and I never knew. My foster mother hoped I could meet her husband, who was sick that day, but unfortunately, today was our only chance to see each other. Knowing that, she invited us for dinner straightaway at a restaurant nearby. It was delicious. She fed me and my friends, literally, as in putting small bits of food in our mouths.

There was no way I could put in words my gratitude for this amazing woman. Her heart was big enough to take care of a baby that she knew would leave someday. My life had been put in the palm of her hand, and seeing her again, I knew I trusted her completely and forever.

Foster mothers of Korea are selfless, generous, wonderful people. Meeting mine changed my point of view about my adoption. For a long time, I had felt very bitter about having been abandoned, and I thought my life started the day I arrived in France. Now I wasn't so sad about Korea abandoning me. I realized people cared so much about Sam and me from the day we were born. That they loved us from the beginning of our lives and still remembered helped me ease my bitterness, and a part of the deep anger, which had been lingering even before the trip to Korea. People had loved Sam and me until the very moment we had been put into the Futerman and Bordier families, and those families would love us from that moment on.

I did not want to know more about our birth parents, and, in a way, I am quite happy we did not find anything. I could see it meant a lot to Sam, but I am too scared to find out something I don't think I want to hear. But Sam and I are two, so mostly for Sam, I asked Holt to start the birth search, as Sam had done with Spence-Chapin. But I was not so keen on doing this now. With the new law, one has to fill out papers to grant you access to all your information and get in touch with your birth parents or foster mothers, etc. I guess it also felt like cheating on my parents, and I was scared to hurt them.

I still imagine crazy scenarios about what happened at our birth and our birth parents' story, especially after learning more about the history of the country and the different economic and social crises, too. At the North Korean defector lecture and the mini–documentary film festival, we learned that a lot of North Koreans fled to Busan by boat, and I was thinking that maybe we are from North Korean descent. It does not matter. It is not really looking back but more imagining and daydreaming. We have heard so many stories that anything is possible. If nothing else, the North Korean defector opened my eyes to how complicated my country of origin is. I now knew I had to read more about Korea and what happened to it rather than settle for the few pages in our French history books that covered the Korean War. I felt like I was learning about my own history.

We had a chance to visit the nurseries at the SWS and Holt International, which was an unbelievable experience. I had always wondered if I wanted children. When I was a kid, I always knew I was adopted and thought it was a wonderful and generous gift of life coming from adoptive parents. There are so many kids in the world without parents who need love and care that for me, adopting felt like something I had to do once I grew old. It started as a feeling of duty, to show by good example. I imagined myself like an ambassador of adoption with children who had been saved and cherished, rather than been left to be raised as orphans.

Later, I had the "adoption conversation" with a friend of mine, and we discussed how being adopted gave you a need to search for somebody similar looking to you, somebody with a close physical appearance so that you would identify with that person and know who you were. After thinking this through for a long time, I decided that I also really wanted to have my own kids, from my body, and feel that physical attachment.

The babies at SWS were so cute . . . and fat! They looked like they were very well taken care of, for sure! We were looking at them through a glass window and saw them sleeping quietly and peacefully in their cribs.

At Holt, the babies were not behind glass and were playing and eating their dinner. The oldest was probably two years old, tops. With a nurse's authorization, I held a little boy, and he smiled back at me before making a very strange and distorted face! Then he began smiling again. From the smell and the contentedness on his face, I correctly reasoned he had just peed on me.

Seeing the babies at each of our orphanages like this, happy and healthy, made me stop to wonder about my earliest days. I hoped that Sam and I had been treated that well, and even had we not been, it was such a relief to see how the babies were treated here.

Currently, Korea is phasing out international adoptions. There are strong campaigns, some featuring celebrities, pushing for Korea to take care of its own and allow children to remain in the country of their heritage. I am very sad about this, as I do want to adopt a baby from Korea as well as have my own biological children. One upside of the policy is that it shows progress is happening, as the stigma of being an adoptee lessens and the secrecy surrounding adoptions eases. However, not all of the babies find homes. I have heard that babies or children found without any paperwork or birth certificates cannot be adopted, which means there are many orphans in Korea. Some mothers who fear being identified if they are forced to do the paperwork place their babies in "baby boxes" in churches from where the children are more than likely destined for orphanages. It was always really hard to think of any child abandoned.

The final nights of the conference involved the Samsung gala and a dance party at the Hybrid Club Vera, and although each of us adoptees felt differently about the circumstances that had brought us all back to our homeland, this night was in honor of us. Unfortunately, my body was reacting to the emotional upheaval I had been through in the last ten days. I was not recognizing these new feelings. What I had felt before seemed like it was not right anymore.

Sam was very patient with me. When I finally got myself together, we made our way to the very impressive dinner. Everyone was elegantly dressed in suits or dresses. The food was a French menu, which, of course, delighted me. The event the next evening was what I had been most looking forward to. The entire group of adoptees went off-site to the Hybrid Club Vera for some live performances. Dan Matthews, Sam's musician friend from L.A., was performing, and Sam was going to sing with him.

While Sam was practicing, I went out for coffee with a friend I knew from France. She was Korean and was now living back in Seoul. She had always talked about wanting to get back to her roots in Korea, but now that she was here, she was having culture conflicts, realizing how French she was, even though she was Korean. For whatever reason, this brought up a real storm of emotion in me. Who was I? I was born in Korea, and here I was in Korea, but I was French, and the only place I had ever known was France. On top of it all, I now had an American twin sister, and here we were, together as visitors in our homeland, still not knowing anything else about our family. The emotions stirring inside of me were not going to be able to be controlled.

When I got back to the Hybrid Club Vera, Sam had no idea what was going on with me. The last thing I wanted to do was disrupt her shining moment, but I was completely overcome by my feelings. I found myself racing to the ladies' room to try to compose myself. I was sweaty, nauseous, and extremely anxious, not sure if I could pull it together. Thankfully, Ryan found me and seemed to sense what was going on. He sweetly took me to Sam, who invited me to watch the show from back-stage. Slowly, my panic subsided, as I lost myself watching my sister's performance from the wings.

The show was utterly amazing. Sam and Dan were so professional and such great artists, and they were so well received. Dan's energy was boundless, probably as a result of his meeting his twin for the first time. I felt that way after my first contact with Sam. It was an energy like I had never felt before. After Sam's bow, she and I went to the main floor in front of the stage and danced the night away.

So much about my week in Seoul had been rewarding beyond my expectations. Besides meeting Sam's and my foster mums, I loved hearing crash adoption stories from my fellow travelers. I learned more about how they had handled their feelings and how they had experienced adoption in many countries—Denmark, Sweden, Belgium, and so many more. Some adoptees had grown up in countries that had virtually no Asian communities. I imagined it must be harder to have been raised in a country without any Asian people around.

Sam and my generation of adoptees in Korea was prob-ably the biggest and was represented by many nations. We all had funny stories and anecdotes to tell. We did not have to become the best of friends forever after this trip, but it always felt good to be able to share our experience with other people, obviously going through the same things and equally happy to share.

The gathering felt really good, like a field trip with over-nights for adults. We had nights out with all the Korean adoptees, and during these times, you felt like you belonged somewhere you knew. We were not random fish lost in the ocean. We were a whole cool group of fishes, and we were all having fun together. Before I came, I had been worried that it could tip into too much drama, but everything that was happening was exciting and filled with emotions, though not the kind that made people uncomfortable.

I must say, I still had times when I felt lost in translation, and those times were tough. When I'd feel particularly vulnerable, I liked spending time with the French contingent. You'd always be able to find us—we were the group smoking cigarettes outside in the corner. For the most part, as long as I was standing near my sister, I was happy. Sometimes, I wanted to have her for myself and keep her away from the crew, mostly because I could see her anger and frustration when there were problems in logistics or opposing opinions. But whatever was happening, I was still happy and reassured to be with her, discovering new things and starting a new life with new memories.

I often wondered where Sam had spent her first three weeks after she was born since her foster mother had said she had started taking care of her when she was three weeks old. At Holt, they had a theory that the mother wanted to keep one baby, but only one. They thought she gave me up first, right after birth, then came to terms with not being able to keep Sam, either, and brought her back to a different adoption agency later. Our records said we were given up for adoption the next day after the birth, so we might never know what transpired next. We were born together, me first and then Sam, and then we were separated.

I have many theories how we came to be, like we are robots, or clones sent from outer space, but apart from that, the story could be anything from the simplest to the most complicated dramatic story ever. I guess I used to need to know why I had been abandoned. Now, Sam is here, and nothing else matters anymore. We found our way back. We lived the same story once, and now we can go ahead and live happy lives together. We don't really need to look backward. That is their story, not ours.

16

SAM

birthday trip to paris

In retrospect, there were parts of our trip to Korea that weren't fun. At some points, I wasn't sure if anyone was actually having any fun. But Anaïs and I had a life-changing nine days together and had learned a lot about each other and ourselves. I was seeing my birth country with my identical twin sister. We struggled through a lot of it, but we had come out the other side closer than ever. Now we were going to be spending our birthday in Paris together, and that was where I was putting my focus. I couldn't be apart from Anaïs too long, and I couldn't imagine spending our first birthday since finding each other over Skype or social media.

The plan was for me to fly to London, spend the night with Marie, and hop a Eurostar to Paris the following morning, a train ride of only two and a half hours. Whoever would have thought that something this lucky was possible: spending a birthday with a twin for the first time in twenty-six years. Even luckier was the fact that Jacques paid for my flight. I was going to hang out and tour France.

My flight was Sunday, November 17, two days before our birthday. Tomas and Kanoa were coming with me, which was a treat for both Anaïs and me. My two friends had been incredible throughout our trip to Korea, and our birthday party in Paris was going to be far more relaxed. Getting our bags from Heathrow to the Finsbury Park Tube station wasn't fun, but at least I had two handsome men to help me. It was so good to see Marie when we arrived at her flat! And to my delight, Kelsang arrived at the apartment right as she was serving her three Asian-American guests Chinese chicken with black bean sauce. I truly adore Kelsang. Without him, and his finding me on the YouTube video, none of this would have been possible. It was so nice to see him, too!

All through the evening, I was texting or Skyping with Anaïs. It was so weird to be so close to her, yet still so far away. That night, I stayed in Anaïs's old room, which was strange and funny. Marie said it was like having my sister back in the apartment. She was coming with us to Paris, partly to be with Anaïs and me for our birthday party, partly to spend time with her family.

What could be more fantastic than boarding a train to Paris on my birthday?

Anaïs had told me to expect her mom at Gare du Nord, so was I ever shocked to see an adorable little French version of myself in a cute fur-lined coat at the end of the platform in Paris. She looked so pretty and happy and French. She was in her element and at her best.

Apparently, Neuilly-sur-Seine is a pretty ritzy part of town. Should I ask again how much luckier could I get? At the apartment, the three Americans all settled in. I hoped Anaïs wouldn't get too stressed with so many people setting up camp in a one-bedroom apartment, but she seemed thrilled to have us. She took us on a short walk in her neighborhood, and while out, I searched the scenery for some healthy green juice, my favorite L.A. veggie beverage. Well, there was no green juice, so the two stops were the bread store for some croissants and pastries, and the "health food" store for a coconut water, which pretty much tasted like water and a splash of earth.

The Bordiers didn't live far from my sister, but we still drove. It was so crazy to see Anaïs's tiny royal-blue Mercedes. In L.A. my RAV4 looked average-sized. Here, it would look gargantuan. It was so funny watching my sister drive. Even though her car was semiautomatic, it drove like a manual car, so she had to change gears. It was so enlightening to see Anaïs in her own environment. Up until now, I had only been able to imagine the Bordiers' apartment, but soon I'd know exactly how it looked. It was comforting, yet I also enjoyed the mystery of letting my imagination run wild. Maybe that was why my sister never wanted to know about our birth mother. She wanted to have a beautifully painted picture of what she looked like and what happened, because sometimes reality can be disappointing.

Jacques and Patricia, as always, were so kind and sweet. Sometimes I get nervous that I'm going to be too outrageous for them, with my wry, rude sense of humor. But all my fear of disapproval goes out the window when I see the joy in Patricia's eyes. When someone gives you that much positive and genuine happy energy, it's pretty difficult not to reciprocate.

To get to the Bordiers' apartment, four of us had to squeeze into the smallest elevator I had ever been in. When we emerged, I was curious as to whether Eko, their American Cocker, would confuse me with Anaïs, but animals are not fooled. She could smell the difference, but she was sweet to me, nonetheless. The apartment was beautiful, with incredible lighting, elegant wood and glass bookshelves, and insanely comfortable leather chairs and sofas. The glass dining table was covered with what I could only assume were our birthday presents. I don't remember if I had ever seen a display of gifts like this one. There was a beautiful bouquet of flowers in the middle of the table, and then the gifts were perfectly mirrored on each side.

The kid in me wanted to jump on the table and shake every single package and rip it open without care, but the timing was wrong. We first needed to take seats in the living room part of the apartment for a toast. On the TV stand were pictures of Anaïs throughout her life. It was so strange to see myself in all those photos, in a life I hadn't lived. I guess it could have made me wonder about what my life could have been had I been adopted by the Bordiers, but I don't really think about our situation in those terms. This was Anaïs's childhood, and these moments were the defining factors in who she was. They were little glimpses into the pieces of her puzzle. They were not lost years of my own life, but the moments that had helped Anaïs flourish and grow into an amazing young woman. Anaïs and I were the first to exchange gifts with each other. I had bought her a dress and a shirt. Our styles were quite different, and although I thought I would look awkward in the outfits I selected, I knew that she could make them work and look as classy as ever. Buying clothes for your identical twin is pretty easy—you just try something on, and if it fits you, it fits her. I also got her some small cosmetic products from a brand I love, but I chose a shade lighter for Anaïs, as her skin is a dab lighter and pinker.

Anaïs had bought me a French sailor shirt, white with blue stripes. She was trying to make me French! What would I open next, a beret? Yes, a beret—how did I know? She had also bought me a luxurious candle from Paris, personalized with our names engraved on the back.

After all the gifts were opened and the photos were taken, it was birthday dinner time and my chance to experience Korean food in France. To be honest, I was skeptical. L.A. had the most amazing Korean BBQ, but of course, this was France! The traffic getting to the restaurant was insane, but the sights were more insane. One minute out the window, there was the Arc de Triomphe! The next minute out the other window, there was the Eiffel Tower! It was unbelievable. I had always fantasized that I was underneath the tower with a baguette and a bike having the kiss of my lifetime, romantic mush that I am. Strong and stubborn was just a cover.

When we arrived at the restaurant, one of the hostesses, a middle-aged Korean lady, began to stare. Anaïs smiled and introduced me. She seemed to enjoy telling people the news. To be honest, I loved revealing it, too, and seeing the reaction on people's faces. It is like a little secret and we are the keepers of the key, with the power to reveal it at the moment of our choosing.

Throughout the first six months of Anaïs's and my journey, I had concentrated on all of our similarities, but now I was beginning to notice the differences. I was starting to see insecurities in my sister. She had not grown up with brothers who had constantly teased and tortured her, and she seemed to have a little bit of low self-esteem. Every time someone said something even slightly negative about her, she would mull it over to decide whether or not it was true. If my brother called me fat, I would make sure to booby-trap his room, or embarrass him the next time a girl came over, but I wouldn't believe him. That's a rule in families, right? No matter what others say or do, you love and stick by them without taking them too seriously. Through "in-house" training, I had developed thick skin and learned how to walk away from insults. But what about Anaïs? She didn't have the torturous days and nights of big brothers. So I guess we developed a different sense of confidence and resilience. Even the creative outlets we chose as adults seem to reflect this. I chose a more outwardly creative field, and Anaïs's was much more inward. I put my energy out, and Anaïs pulls hers in.

Jacques was the patriarch of the birthday dinner. He is so knowledgeable about languages, and he greeted the Korean hostesses in Korean as he gave them a slight bow from the waist. Patricia was sweet and warm, too, and, fortunately, familiar with the fusion-style fare this restaurant served. I've been to many Korean restaurants. In both L.A. and Korea, there is an extensive range of entrée choices that are eaten family-style. Everyone double dips his or her spoon into the shared meal. Here, there were very few choices and everyone ordered his own.

Another thing I had never experienced before was the pairing of Korean food with a bottle of rosé wine. I would never have paired a rosé with marinated beef, but, oddly, it worked! To be at this special restaurant with Anaïs, eating Korean food on the day we shared our first birthday in twenty-six years, will be one day that I will always remember.

I woke up in the morning next to my sister. Funny, twenty-six years apart and I was so comfortable sharing a bed with her. It was like balance restored. Usually, I must be fairly intimate with someone before I let him share my bed. And I pretend that it's fine so as not to insult my suitor, but toss and turn and never get a good night's sleep. With Anaïs, I slept like a log. We always sleep in the same pattern when we share a bed: Anaïs on the right and me on the left. I wouldn't be able to sleep if I ended up on the right. When we were in bed together, it made me picture us as babies, poking each other's noses in the womb, me on the left side and her on the right. Dr. Segal had said some reared-apart twins might be more similar in some ways than those raised together because they weren't fighting for separate identities. They were letting nature take its course. I was seeing that she was right.

Anaïs had to work the next day, but she gave us an entire itinerary. She planned for us to visit the Eiffel Tower, and then head toward Notre Dame by walking along the Seine. From there, we would go to Saint Germain and the Rive Gauche. She suggested we have lunch at Saint-Sulpice, a trendy square

near Saint Germain, and then walk over toward Hôtel de Ville
for some shopping, with a final stop at the Centre Georges
Pompidou, the contemporary art museum. There was a lot to
accomplish in only one day, but we were ready.

We were kind of dragging by the time we met Anaïs and
her six friends at the end of the day. She had made dinner reservations for us, and we were going to meet her at the restaurant. Only when we sat down in the window and were drinking
a glass of wine did we realize that we were in the wrong place.
We looked across the street and saw another restaurant with
the same name. When we arrived at the right restaurant, Anaïs
was with Marie; two Korean French adoptees, one whom I had
spent time with at the IKAA conference in Korea; and a couple
of other good friends of hers from Paris. I loved knowing that
because of Anaïs, I now had so many friends and family around
the world. The next day our first stop was the Louvre. The two
things that struck me most when I was trying to see the *Mona
Lisa* were how pushy the Chinese tourists were and how many
security cameras lined the ceiling. My sister loves art. She could
spend days looking at paintings. She said she spent so much
time at the Louvre as a child painting and drawing that it was
old hat to her. Can you imagine? Someone who has had too
much Louvre?! I like art and painting, but I prefer TV and
film. If I'm in a bad mood, I can sit down, watch something,
turn off my mind, and feel better. I need more interaction,
more of my senses participating to be satisfied. I guess that
was the introvert/extrovert manifesting itself in Anaïs and me.
Dr. Segal's study had shown that I was more extroverted than
my sister. (No surprise there!) Of the Big Five Personality

Traits—openness, agreeableness, conscientiousness, neuroticism, and extroversion—this last trait was where we differed
the most.

After lunch with Anaïs, we went to her parents' shop. It
was in such a beautiful part of town. High-end boutiques and
beautiful Christmas lights lined the narrow cobblestone street.
Patricia was happy to see us, but she was very busy. She kept
glancing over to me and smiling while talking to her customers,
and I could tell she was beaming on the inside. When she did
have a moment, she excitedly introduced me to the rest of the
staff, who, by their enthusiasm, had been hearing a lot about me.

Our next stop was Anaïs's office in the headquarters of
Gerard Darel. The building was on Rue Réaumur, right in
the heart of Paris's fashion district. Anaïs introduced me to
her boss, who was as awestruck and amazed as everyone else
who had first known only one of us, then met the other. I
loved seeing Anaïs's workplace. I had only seen her office in
selfies, with rows of pocketbooks in the background. Now, I
could see exactly where she sat while she designed leather
accessories and pocketbooks for the label.

Our big birthday bash was taking place the following
night at a bar, where Marie had reserved the back part for us.
As the guests started to arrive, there was way too much kissing on the cheeks, the way the French do, for my liking. I
hate when people touch my face, especially strangers. But I
had to be a good sport for my sister. As the evening wore on,
her friends started to pour in, people from every part of her
life—her internship, her childhood, her college, her work . . .
It was amazing. Even two friends of mine from Boston Uni-

versity came. One was in Paris on business and the other was there to visit her.

I got a good kick out of how many of our guests couldn't tell the difference between Anaïs and me. They'd stop and stare at me, and I'd make eye contact long enough for it to be awkward and then point to Anaïs. One of Anaïs's friends gave us baby toys to mark our "first" birthday together.

Then I saw Marie carrying our birthday cake—one half was the American flag, and the other half was the French flag, and on top sat a beautiful cupcake, representing our first birthday. I couldn't have asked for anything more. I was in Paris for my birthday, standing opposite my identical twin sister. When it was time to blow out the candle, I didn't make a wish—I forgot. I was just so excited to be there in that moment. I hoped Anaïs had remembered to wish, though. If so, she got double the chances. Whatever she wanted, I wanted.

I still hadn't seen the famous light show at the Eiffel Tower that happens every night on the hour. So we had a bowl of French onion soup in a restaurant with a view of it, and it was the best onion soup I've ever had.

When we got back to Anaïs's apartment, we were hanging out watching a few YouTube videos when Anaïs pulled up "How It Feels to Be Adopted . . . I Am Sam." Ugh, I didn't want to watch that cheesy thing.

"No," Anaïs said quite seriously. "Can you imagine what I was feeling when I saw this?" She wanted me to experience the video as she had nine months ago when Kelsang had first shown it to her. "I was in shock. But I kept watching it, over and over," she told me. She was right. . . . What the hell?!

What if it had been the other way around, if I had seen Anaïs/ myself on the video stating that I was adopted, and I had just found out that I had been born on the same day and in the same city as this stranger/look-alike? There would have been no easing into it. The moment Anaïs had seen it for the first time, she knew we were twins. Her past, the past that she had never wanted to uncover, had to have been barreling toward her in a massive tsunami of fear, happiness, and probably any other human emotion we are capable of. Holy shit, it is hard to imagine.

Lunch at the Bordiers' was delicious. Patricia had prepared sauerkraut with sausages and ham, an Alsatian dish known as *choucroute garnie*. Earlier that morning, Anaïs had asked me if I liked sauerkraut, and I asked if we were having hot dogs. She had told me, in a very French voice, "*Non*, you don't eat sauerkraut with hot dogs!" My experience with sauerkraut has always been on a foot-long frank wrapped in sliced white bread with neon-yellow mustard drizzled over the top. Delicious, but I guess slightly subpar to the French palate. To be honest, Patricia's sauerkraut was excellent, but the dish *was* sauerkraut and hot dogs. Not really, but it was sauerkraut topped with two types of sausages from the hot dog family, and some additional bacon and ham steaks, so I wasn't totally off. It was kind of like an upside-down, open-faced hot dog! But anyway, it was superb. In America, we don't steam our foot-longs in white wine and juniper berries, and our mustard is bright enough to see in the dark and can probably survive the apocalypse.

When we were finished with lunch, we took a nap, only to be awoken by Patricia saying, "foie gras." Believe me, there was no better way to wake me than to whisper those words in my ear. OMG, if I believed in heaven, this was pretty much what it would look like—my sister by my side, Beaujolais, and foie gras. I mean, Anaïs wouldn't have to be there in heaven at the exact same moment as me. . . . She could come later, but I'd hope that she'd be there with me . . . am I right?

While packing back at Anaïs's, I couldn't figure out how to fit all the gifts. I rearranged and reorganized everything again and again, trying to fit them all in. There just wasn't space for everything. I decided to leave a few things with my sister to bring when she came to New York for Thanksgiving. Thank goodness for my twin and her extra luggage space!

After I was done packing, we were going to lie in bed and watch some TV, but we both just wanted to chat. We talked about everything—boys and bed bugs, and hair growth, and sex. We were like two girls at a sleepover right before going to bed. I loved being able to gossip and share and gush about men and crushes. I love having a sister.

Naturally we stayed up much later than we should have, but we talked until I fell asleep, and I mean literally fell asleep. It was midsentence. . . .

November 25 was a travel day. Anaïs got in the shower first, as she tends to take a bit more time to get ready. Yet, as I was just finishing up getting dressed, I looked up and there was my sister, standing in her underwear, offering me a piece of *saucisson*. What the hell? She was "first shower." Why wasn't she ready!?

We had just finished scrambling by the time Jacques arrived to take us to the train station. He gave us both a hug and helped get my stuff into the car. He said it was a shame we had just missed Justin Timberlake's "Mirrors" on his car radio.

At the train station, Anaïs helped me bring my bags upstairs to the Eurostar departure area. It was time. I didn't want to leave her. I knew I'd see her in a few days, but still I had had so much fun, especially the night before when we had talked the hours away. That had been my favorite part. The fairy tale of being in Paris was nothing to the fairy tale of having a best friend to share all your deepest thoughts and secrets with. That was the real gift.

17

ANAÏS

thanksgiving in new york

The three months between getting home from Korea and going to New York to visit Sam and her family went very slowly. Work was incredibly busy, as the design house I worked for had much to do to get its collection ready for the 2014/2015 season. My job was a leather goods designer in the accessories department. I did my technical drawings by hand rather than using the computer, because I love to draw. I also loved my job. It was teamwork. I worked with the production, marketing, and sourcing teams directly. We traveled to the factories and leather fairs in Northern Africa and Italy, to see new trends and buy the materials according to what was current. At the fairs, we would look at different types of leathers, hardware pieces, and new materials, as we tried to enhance our creativity. Everybody pretty much spoke Italian. I could understand it, but I couldn't speak it that well, so I was determined to learn.

We were working from morning till night, but I loved

that my boss Diane brought me along, giving me both confidence and experience all at the same time. I was not an intern anymore, and I appreciated that. Diane gave me a chance to be creative and trusted me in my work. I think I grew a few years in confidence in a few months.

Thanksgiving in America did not coincide with any holiday in France. The only two holidays we celebrate in November are All Saints' Day on November 1, and Armistice Day on November 11. In order to minimize how many days off work I would be taking, I decided to take a red-eye from Charles de Gaulle, which would still have me arriving at the Futermans' in time for the big feast. My parents were leaving one day earlier, because my father had business appointments in New York, so I would be traveling alone.

I really had no idea what to expect at an American Thanksgiving. The only thing we French knew about the holiday was that it had to do with the first European settlers in North America celebrating a harvest with Native American Indians, or something along those lines. For the French, most of our information about what Thanksgiving meant came from scenes in American movies. Even the nonanimated Spider-Man movie with Tobey Maguire had a Thanksgiving dinner scene. Hollywood versions always had plenty of gluttony, scatological humor, and dysfunction. There is often an underlying theme of a family member bringing in a new love interest to meet the family, and in that warm, comfortable place, everything that could go wrong did, as protected family secrets were unveiled.

I was curious if Sam would have some strange uncle

with an embarrassing habit, a taboo past, or an inappropriate sense of humor. Sam hadn't warned me about anybody, but according to the movies, there is always somebody who gets drunk and says too much. If there is no such character at Sam's Thanksgiving, I was sure she and I could step in and fill the role. We loved acting insane together. We could even switch places and take it from there.

My parents were scheduled to arrive first. Jackie and Judd had invited my parents to stay at the house in Verona, too, saying there were plenty of beds for everybody in one room or another. My parents, not wanting to impose, declined, so they were staying in a hotel within five miles of the Futermans' house. They were very social people, but very private at the same time. As much as they were looking forward to being with loads of Futermans, they also knew it would be best for them to have a hotel room, where they would be able to sleep well and relax, maybe even process their impressions of the people and places they had seen after the very busy days the Futermans had planned for us.

Since May, only Sam and I had managed to get together, so it was really important to me that our parents share time, and their flight itinerary allowed them to do just that. This was an opportunity for the two couples to get to know each other better away from the discerning eyes of their girls.

I tend to think of my parents as old-fashioned, even though they are actually the coolest people in the world to my friends. If my mom translates a word from French into English, but she pronounces it wrong or uses it incorrectly, I might get all annoyed, for no reason other than she is my mother. In my father's case, he might tell a well-intentioned story about something I did when I was small, but if it embarrasses me, I want to scream at him to stop. In this case, I was feeling protective of them—as they always are of me—and didn't want to feel embarrassed on their behalf.

Without me around, my parents could be themselves when they first hung out with the Futermans. It really mattered to me that they started feeling closer to each other. They were four people who had twin daughters together. They hadn't raised twin daughters together, but they shared them now. I knew my mum and Jackie had been Skyping regularly, and my dad seemed to really like Judd, too. My parents didn't have huge extended families, like Sam's family did. My mum's only brother was a priest, so no children or wife there. My dad had lost contact with a couple of his siblings in the last few years, so his extended family was getting smaller rather than larger. Now, with the Futermans, our family was growing again. I thought it would be great if my mum could find a "sister" in Jackie, and my dad a "brother" in Judd. All four of them were wholly likeable, warm, intelligent people. If they needed to find common ground, well, that was easy!

My parents were older when they adopted me, and I have no siblings so Mom, in particular, worried that I would end up all alone with no close family once she and Dad weren't around anymore. Now, she took comfort that I would always have Sam and her family.

My mum and Jackie had started to get close already. They shared stories about Sam and me as children, looking for similarities. The soup story was the best. According to Jackie, when Sam was little, she loved chicken noodle or chicken rice soup. It had to be Healthy Choice or Progresso or another canned soup, not homemade. Jackie said before she gave it to Sam, she would have to pick out every single shred of carrot, or Sam wouldn't eat it. If she saw so much as a teeny, tiny orange speck, she'd be upset. My mum had the very same story about me. No fancy homemade soup, but canned soup with every single piece of carrot removed.

Sam and her dad picked me up at the airport. By the time we got to Verona, I was quite sleep-deprived, but I would never be in a scene like this again, my first American Thanksgiving, just like in the movies, so I was going to make the most of it! It was crazy how I bonded with and trusted Sam's uncles, aunts, and cousins immediately. It was great to be in a position to observe their relationships, to see my sister interacting with the people she loved the most.

We didn't even mean to trick Sam's grandmother, but when she came up to hug me, thinking I was Sam, we couldn't help ourselves. Other relatives greeted me thinking I was Sam, too, until Sam would come up behind me, and the switch would be revealed. It was too much fun. I didn't need proof that Sam's family liked and accepted my family and me, but it felt good to see everyone in the same place discovering more about each other and spending time together, creating memories all together now.

Sam's house was so incredibly cool. When I entered it for the first time, I felt as if I was really and truly part of the family, seeing their intimacy displayed in every room. It was a testament to their love, habits, and passions. The house itself was welcoming, cozy, warm, and people/pet friendly, absolutely full of photos and treasures from the Futermans' lifetime here. The furniture looked like it was supposed to be there, and nothing was fussy, formal, or delicate, so there was no reason to be paranoid about doing something wrong.

I could tell immediately why Sam loved growing up there. I imagined what her room must have looked like when she was a child, filled with toys and friends who had come over after school. I envisioned her playing with her brothers in any of the rooms on the three floors, from the master bedroom with high-peaked windows on the attic level to the enclosed porch at the front of the house on the ground floor. I could picture her arguing in the kitchen with them, and Jackie and Judd teaching them how to behave and not to hit each other. I imagined her and her family sitting together in front of the fireplace or Sam running around with her dogs in the yard. I imagined the whole family watching a baseball game together on television on a Sunday afternoon. It was incredible to know she had been doing all those things while I was on the other side of the planet.

It looked like she must have had a very happy childhood with a big family and a lot of joy. The family parrot, Pelinore, loved to be in the porch room, probably because of all the windows. I had never known a family with a parrot, and I was fascinated by it. He was such a pretty bird, but I had never seen one in someone's home. He was aggressive and funny at the same time. The Futermans had gotten him when Sam was little, but Sam found him to be quite annoying. Jackie would tease her that "no, the parrot is not going to be made into parrot soup for the Thanksgiving holiday." I was curious if the parrot could tell the difference between Sam and me. If he was not able to see the difference, the dead giveaway would be my French accent. I think he thought I was Sam, though. She didn't like him and let him know it, so he was hating me from the beginning and trying to snap me with his beak. The family's two dogs, Maggie, a King Charles Cavalier, and Seamus, a Wheaten Terrier, were a bit friendlier. Seeing Sam with her family in her world made me understand her even more. Watching her interact with her brothers, cousins, and friends was fascinating. I could fill in some of the blank spaces in my head about her, about the times previous to the memories we were building now.

There was so much tradition involved with the Thanksgiving feast, with all the different dishes of food, the fancy plates, and the more formal table settings. There really was something to eat for everybody, and nobody seemed to be without a "must-have" side dish on the menu. To me, it seemed like an incredible amount of work to prepare so many different things, but it was also evident that after years of getting this meal ready for so many people, it was probably done by rote. Nobody seemed confused about his role, or what he was supposed to be setting, chopping, serving, stirring, or pouring. It was so much fun!

The food was totally "American." In France, we hardly eat turkey. For Christmas, my mother makes capons with chestnuts. Some of the Thanksgiving food I loved, and some of it I didn't really care for. Not that there was anything wrong with it, but it just didn't appeal to me. One thing I liked was the sweet potatoes with marshmallows baked on top. I had never had anything like it, and who could imagine that such a combination could work?! According to Jackie, it was a distinctly Southern recipe in its origins, but it was featured everywhere at Thanksgiving. The turkey soup Judd made was also outstanding! Sam promised me we'd be seeing a lot of it. She even mentioned it was a breakfast staple in the days after Thanksgiving. Not an American staple, just a Futerman staple. We would even have it for breakfast on the morning before our flight back to Paris.

The meal lasted for four hours and, just like in the movies, everyone was stuffed to a state of delirium. However, for the young people at the gathering—Sam, Matt, Andrew, and their cousins Jonathan and Jess—there wasn't a chance to sit around complaining about the excessive eating and drinking. It was time for touch football in the street, another American tradition faithfully honored by the Futermans. I'm not very athletic in contact sports, because in the past I was sidelined by an injury to the face. I used the opportunity to take my first good look around Sam's neighborhood.

Her street was lovely, huge stately trees everywhere. Each house on the block was unique and well loved, with yards in both the front and back. Some houses were separated from the neighbors' by some sort of fence, but many yards ran right into each other, fronted by the sidewalk, then the curb, then the street. The houses were wooden, just like you see in films. It was weird to see such an exclusively residential street.

Growing up in Paris, I had grocery stores, *boulangeries*, pharmacies, patisseries, and small produce markets everywhere within a block or two, so nobody ever really needed to drive anywhere to get the essentials. As peaceful as Sam's neighborhood was, it was still only twenty miles from Manhattan. In fact, the busy roads that commuters used to get to New York were just a few blocks away, yet here on her street, there was a feeling of small-town American charm.

Just as the game of touch football was ending, necessitated by darkness, my sister caught the winning touchdown, a highly dramatic moment that delighted us both, despite the fact that I didn't know anything about American football. She and her teammates whooped in glory, while the losing team, quite despaired, swallowed their pride and prepared to go back to the house for dessert.

Back at the house, my parents were holding their own beautifully. I was quite proud of them, actually. I am fairly shy when I first meet people, but in my case I had Sam with me, so there wasn't a chance I'd be at a loss for conversation. But here Mum and Dad looked relaxed and comfortable. Sam's dad or Andrew had been picking them up in the mornings, either to bring them back to the house or to begin whatever adventure was planned, and they wouldn't return until late. Plus, Sam's relatives were so warm and outgoing, it would have been almost impossible to not feel welcome.

For dessert, we moved away from the Thanksgiving theme and toward Sam's and my birthday. There were two birthday cakes for us—an ice-cream cake and the other homemade by Matt's girlfriend. This was only the second time I had spent time with Matt and Andrew. It was great to get to know them more. I was already WhatsApping Matt, and he liked to send me funny pictures. Andrew and I regularly talked on Facebook. It was crazy that I went from being an only child to suddenly having two brothers. I had automatically known that I could trust them from our first embrace in London. Sam had always had two big brothers to protect her, and now I did, too. In Sam's childhood bedroom, she showed me where she used to stand in front of her mirror to put on makeup. She drew a cow-spot print with her finger where she had painted on her wardrobe door. She was telling me stories from growing up, while acting them out around the room. I could imagine her at different stages of her life—shouting at the top of the stairs to her bigger brothers, running down the stairs being late for school, and tiptoeing back to her room on a late night. I was trying to match in my head the different parts of our lives. When she had been asleep here, I'd have been on a bench at school. When she was having dinner, I'd have been asleep and dreaming. When she had been drawing on a weekend, I would have been horseback riding. I would imagine Jackie telling them to come down for dinner. It was like looking at a past, like a mystery part of a life bonded with mine.

Finally, it was time to turn in. I was totally exhausted, as I had only slept five hours in the last twenty-four. As is our new custom, Sam and I crept into bed together. Hanging out under the covers, we once again talked about everything, from boys to friends and their gossip to family to Sam's neighborhood, her neighbors, and her memories of this home.

I only had two full days in Verona. The Futermans had thoughtfully and generously planned many exciting things for us, most of them unique to New York, such as the Christmas

Spectacular at Radio City Music Hall. Jackie had put her heart and soul into making this trip special.

It was uncanny how our parents shared similarities—birthdays, previous jobs, and many other things that were really close. Now that I was here, I would imagine Jackie cooking breakfast for the three kids as they came running down the stairs. I could picture her being very patient and asking one of the kids to calm down, or all of them to stop shouting at each other. She has a calmness and kindness that shows on her face. She has compassionate eyes and a soft, comforting laugh and voice. Samantha's dad makes me laugh so hard. He was the nice and happy dad, always making jokes to entertain his kids and family, while being the most serious person about work and important matters. He seems like a protective dad, too, trying to give space to his children, but at the same time checking them from the corners of his eyes. He did things to make sure everything would go in a way to make them happy. He has a great knack for telling stories, taking his time to tell them right.

The day after Thanksgiving, we headed to New York City. I had been there the year before, but this was much more special, because I was with my new extended family. I loved walking by Sam's high school in Manhattan. It was the place where she started building her career, where she learned how to sing and dance and act, where her dreams were starting to come true. I imagined her in *Fame*, hoping and dreaming to be famous one day and dancing her way up to it. All the places we visited, however briefly, each represented a major step in her life, helping her to become who she is today. It was like unraveling a mystery, like a quest or an investigation—matching links and numbers to be able to draw the picture of her life so far. I was entering the Futerman family's secret garden, and the admittance meant so much to me.

The morning I left, I was feeling full of familial intimacy and new memories. I would have liked the holiday to last longer and forever, to have time to run around with Sam, visiting some of her other childhood places. It made me so happy to see both our families getting along together and interacting warmly with each other. This was a strong family story, still pushing out the boundaries. It was like a wedding, where everyone hopes both the families will get along. In this case, it was even more important to me as our families could not just be cordial to each other—they had to genuinely love each other! For me, it meant more than anything. Before this, our parents had been e-mailing every other day, but seeing them chatting, enjoying themselves, and feeling comfortable at the Futermans' could not make me feel happier.

Now that I had gotten to bond with Sam's brothers, too, I wanted to know even more details about them, their jobs, what they liked and didn't like, their girlfriends, and what their plans were for the future. Getting to know them in their home was the best way to start!

The Bordiers and the Futermans, together in Verona, New Jersey, was an experience almost beyond words. We were two parallel realities becoming one, two lines in a drawing intersecting exactly where they should. The lines have always been there, but they don't become meaningful until they meet at an inevitable point in time and space. For me, I knew Sam.

She existed, and the people who cared about her cared about me. Still, I needed to see it and experience it physically, like a rite of passage. It was similar to my first physical encounter with Sam. I sort of knew how much I meant to her, and how much I loved her already. But it had been a "virtual" connection first, not completed by human touch. When she and I met, I was in shock. First of all, I didn't know I was that short! But it took me a few hours to acknowledge that she was real, even though I had gotten confirmation when I first poked her head. I still had to learn how to move around her, how to act around her. I needed to realize that she was not going to react like she was in a mirror, as the truth is she was not my reflection. No matter how identical we looked, we were two separate persons in the same space-time dimension.

On this trip, the amount of love I have for Sam and her family really got imprinted on me like never before. I didn't feel as much sadness anymore when it came time to leave them, but rather happiness knowing they'd be here anytime. What made me the saddest was wondering when the next meeting would be. All together or separately, I just wanted to learn more about each member of Sam's family, to know more about each important person in her life!

It is hard to express, but I think that because I have now experienced Sam and her family with all my senses, my love has become infinite. In this reality, even though we have only known each other for what might seem to some a short while, and to others it might look absolutely insane, nothing can take our love away.

18

SAM

twinsgiving

Thanksgiving 2013 was going to be the most memorable family holiday of my life. Not only was Thanksgiving my favorite holiday, but Anaïs and her parents were coming to the United States to be with my extended family. All of it was happening in Verona, New Jersey. Anaïs had never been to my childhood home, and although our parents had spent time with each other in London, having the Bordiers at my house with all my relatives was going to be incredible. It was like starting something brand-new. The holidays would never be the same from that year forward. The Bordiers were already my family, and now I got to have them with the rest of my family all in one place at one time.

Since my move to L.A., I only made it east maybe once or twice a year, and I missed it. If I could spend September to December in New York, and January to August in L.A., I'd be happy. I have always considered the East Coast to be my real home, even though L.A. was becoming my more familiar place, where I found creative stimulation and growth as a person and artist.

The Thanksgiving of 2013 was one year after the biggest North Atlantic storm in recorded history, Hurricane Sandy. My house had been spared, although a tree had fallen in Dad's fishpond. This Thanksgiving would be remarkable for all the right reasons. Not many people can say, "My French family, including my newly found identical twin sister and her parents, will be celebrating their first American Thanksgiving with us." The French may have great food, but they don't have the famous turkey soup my father makes! I homed in on French words for various aspects of the upcoming feast: turkey (*la dinde*), corn (*le maïs*), cranberry (*la canneberge*), gravy (*la sauce au jus de viande*), and stuffing (*la farce*). For dessert, pumpkin pie—*la tarte à la citrouille*. Since I didn't know how to pronounce any of the French words, I'd just have to let the food speak for itself.

After my mom and Matt picked me up at Newark Liberty International Airport, and we settled into our local diner in Bloomfield, New Jersey, for matzoh ball soup and salad, I was still a little loopy from the flight and the time difference, but I was happy to be back and eating comfort food with my big bro and mom. It was funny, spending time with my sister and her parents had stirred up a longing for my own parents. These were the people who gave us happiness, opportunity, and boundless love. When I got to the house, Mom gave me two very important gifts—a sweatshirt and a T-shirt with the New York Jets logo. Our family is passionate about the Jets. Despite their less than enviable seasons in recent history, they are the best football team in the land, according to my father. So far this year, they had four wins and six losses . . . not looking good, which meant my dad would be grumpy until baseball season.

The next day, I went to New York City to meet friends, getting back to Verona in time for dinner. My mom picked me up from the bus stop, just like when I was a kid. It never failed to amaze me how much she did for me.

Wednesday, the day before Thanksgiving, I woke up knowing Anaïs's parents were arriving. Dad came home early to make more turkey soup, as I had already eaten more than my share. He was also picking up the Bordiers at their hotel in New York City, where they had stayed one night, and bringing them to their hotel near our house.

For many years, I had noticed that fathers sometimes get shortchanged when it comes to "the bond" with the children in the family. Even in birth searches, adoptees are always on a mission to find their birth mother. This really doesn't give the birth father much credit in our existence. I thought about Anaïs's and my birth father a lot. Who was he? I wondered if he thought about Anaïs and me ever, or if he even knew that we existed. Why didn't anyone speak of the birth fathers? They were half of the equation, right? And who is to say that a father's love isn't as profound as a mother's? Although I had not experienced the bond between a biological mother and child, I notice that sometimes people speak as though there is a greater love from mother to child than father to child. The blood in my veins and the DNA in my genes comes from both my birth mother and my birth father. In my own family, I know my father loves me and my brothers as much as our mother does. Just watching him enjoy every minute of making his next batch of turkey soup reminded me why I loved him so much.

It was great to see Jacques and Patricia again, even though it had only been a few days since my return from Paris. There was something different about having them here in the United States. It was important to me that they got to see where their daughter's twin sister had been raised and nurtured, and I was proud of my town, even with its surfeit of pizza parlors and nail salons.

In fact, a pizza parlor/Italian restaurant was exactly where we were headed after exchanging our hugs and kisses. We packed into the car and drove to Forte Pizzeria & Ristorante, my favorite pizza restaurant in the world. There's a pizzeria on one side and a proper dining room on the other, but we always eat in the pizzeria. We're not fancy. I ordered pasta fagioli and eggplant parmesan with a side of spaghetti. I think the Bordiers were a little taken aback by Forte's brash atmosphere, extraordinary portion sizes, and no wine available. Eateries aren't like that in Paris. Jacques seemed simultaneously impressed and disgusted, but the food was delicious. After dinner, the Bordiers came back to the house for tea and a chat before returning to their hotel.

The next day was Thanksgiving and Anaïs was arriving! At John F. Kennedy Airport, Dad and I watched the arrival board, calculating how long it took for certain planeloads to get through customs, so we could better judge when to expect our traveler. For example, a Japan Airlines plane had landed at nine forty-five, and at ten fifteen, a significant number of Japanese people were entering the terminal, so about a half hour from gate to clearance. It was a great game to pass the time.

Finally, she came around the bend with a big suitcase and a massive Elle bag, which was decorated with numerous K-pop stickers. They might have found their way onto her bag in Korea, stuck there by an annoying twin sister—who's to say? In our embrace, I caught a whiff of her favorite French perfume, Chanel. How bougie of her. When I get off a plane I smell like snacks, whiskey, and stale farts. My sister, on the other hand, is so elegant, even after an all-night transatlantic flight!

Back in Verona, Anaïs was bombarded by my relatives. My immediate family hadn't seen her since London, so my mother was overjoyed to see her again. My grandmother was pulling up to the house just as we were, and she had never met her. It must have been hard for Anaïs to meet so many people who were that excited to be near her, like she was a rock star in a crowd of fans. My relatives wanted to know everything about her entire life, and Anaïs accepted her celebrity graciously. I told her to run up to my grandmother and hug her, pretending she was me. Sure enough, my grandmother was fooled. Next, my cousin Jill and her husband, Tom, arrived at the house. Tom gave Anaïs a massive hug and kiss on the cheek, assuming it was me. Even though my sister didn't know who they were, she went with it. Tom was shocked when he realized his mistake. A few seconds later, my aunt Jo, uncle Bob, and my cousins Jonathon and Jesse joined the party. Jo was the "JoFuterman" who Anaïs had located on Twitter when she was searching for me. All the relatives had a good laugh trying to figure out who was who.

With everyone gathered, it was time for a Champagne toast. Jacques and Patricia had brought two bottles of Champagne from France—not sparkling wine, but true Champagne. It was thrilling to toast our new family. This was my ultimate dream, my ultimate fantasy—having our families together in the same place. It wasn't that I wasn't feeling claustrophobic with so many people milling about. There were moments in which I took refuge in the kitchen, pretending to be cooking. When I'm home, I like to cook to calm myself down. The chopping of vegetables and constant watching of the pot calms my nerves and forces me to focus on that one thing, concentrate while my brain processes the rest of the sensory overload coming from the rest of the house. My sister was being incredibly courteous in the living room, answering all the questions and pretending like she wanted to be there, although I knew that she'd probably have preferred to be taking a big ol' nap.

Every year for as long as I can remember, my father starts making his famous turkey soup the Sunday before Thanksgiving. I'd always wake up to the aroma of a turkey being boiled to oblivion and the sound of the dogs going crazy in the kitchen, feasting off of my dad's mess. As the soup simmered, he'd watch football between stirs, the all-American father. I would go to the kitchen every hour to check the soup's progress myself, and sneak a spoonful or two from the pot in my taste test. For the next few days after Thanksgiving, there would be turkey soup for breakfast, afternoon meals, evening meals, and snacks. Nobody complained—it was that good.

This year, my mom was worried about making the seating arrangement for twenty-two people. She wanted to satisfy everybody. So she decided to draw names from a hat and placed them at the table randomly. I rearranged Anaïs's and my names, even though I was cheating the system. There was no way we weren't going to be seated together. How else would I pick off her plate?

Dad took the turkey out of the oven, but there was still a half hour to go. I made a side dish/appetizer of kale marinated in balsamic vinegar and champagne vinaigrette, with roasted pumpkin seeds, dried cherries, and roasted butternut squash. Despite reservations on the part of some family members, it turned out to be a huge hit. My aunt ate three servings and offered full compliments. It was the perfect holdover until the turkey, stuffing, and mashed potatoes could get to the table.

The Bordiers' first Thanksgiving seemed to be a success. Eating, seeing my sister eat her turkey and stuffing, my dad burning the tops of the marshmallows on top of the canned yams—memories I'd never forget. It was just as I had imagined. And the dogs were staring at us longingly from the kitchen to get any tiny scraps of food.

We finished up the meal just before the sun went down, leaving us time for a quick game of football in the street. I wanted Anaïs to play, as it was tradition, but after she got hit in the face with a ball as a child, she preferred to just watch. The rest of us were running around in the street like children, screaming and yelling in good fun. I personally caught the winning touchdown, making my brothers proud. I did, however, take a chunk out of my hand when I toppled onto the sidewalk. What's a little football in the street with brothers without a few scrapes and bumps?

Because Thanksgiving is so close to my birthday, dessert is always a birthday cake for me. This year was no exception, and the best part was that I got to share it with my sister. As Anaïs and I were blowing out the candles, I remembered I had again forgotten to make a wish. But what more could I wish for? Everyone I needed was right there in the room with me.

The Friday after Thanksgiving, both sets of parents, Anaïs, my brothers, and I drove into New York to see the Christmas Spectacular at Radio City Music Hall. When we got to the helix that brought traffic into the entrance of the Lincoln Tunnel, the entire Manhattan skyline was visible across the Hudson River. Anaïs started *ooh*ing and *aah*ing at the breathtaking view. It was funny—I always felt like it was so crazy romantic that she had grown up with the Eiffel Tower in her backyard. I guess I was so used to my city that I took my own landmarks for granted. In the skyline, the Empire State Building, decked out in red and green lights from top to bottom, had its own impressive statement to make.

Everyone wanted to see the World Trade Center site as well as the newly finished Freedom Tower, the tallest building in the United States, so we headed to lower Manhattan. The site is still so humbling, while being such a testament to our ability to start over. In 2001, we came together for our city like never before, and we may have even felt quite protective of our right to be more horrified than those farther from Ground Zero, as we had experienced it with such immediacy and had felt the public and private pain of so many people. The number of tourists from foreign countries coming to pay their respects was truly astonishing.

We went for lunch at Southern Hospitality, Justin Timberlake's restaurant on Ninth Avenue and Forty-Fifth Street in Hell's Kitchen. How could we not go to his restaurant, loving his "Mirrors" song as much as we did? As seemed to be the pattern, portions were pretty massive compared to the servings at French restaurants. Anaïs and I loved the collard greens in particular, something else we had in common!

After lunch, we went to Rockefeller Center to take selfies in front of the world-famous Christmas tree, even though it hadn't been lit yet, then on to Radio City Music Hall for the Rockettes. Everyone must see the Christmas Spectacular once in their life! It certainly gets you in the holiday spirit. Anaïs and I could never be on this stage, high-kicking with the statuesque ladies on the chorus line—we were more than a foot shorter than the standard five ten.

After the show, we all walked over to Fifth Avenue and stopped into Saint Patrick's Cathedral. It was covered in scaffolding, which detracted from its elegance. After Notre Dame, all churches and cathedrals seemed pretty lame. The fact that Notre Dame was almost seven hundred years older than Saint Patrick's made Saint Patrick's seem that much less important.

At the Korean BBQ restaurant later, Anaïs and I ordered dinner for everyone. Her parents were a little put off by the whole "sharing" thing that Koreans and Americans do in these types of restaurants. Just as Anaïs started getting annoyed with them for not understanding, my father irritated me by saying he didn't really like Korean food. I assured him that it was the same cuts of beef he eats—brisket was the same piece of meat we eat at Passover, except this one was sliced thin and grilled right in front of you. Ugh. I started scolding him, and I turned around to see my sister was doing the same thing with her parents—except in French.

After dinner, Anaïs and I went downtown to meet some friends of mine for a drink and when we were close enough for me to point out the bar where they were inside waiting, Anaïs started running toward the bar, leaving me behind. I couldn't believe it. My sister was hilarious and simply bolted, just like her foster mother had done in Korea. When I got inside, there she was, giggling and waving to people who thought they knew her. We thought it was fun, but I think my friends were a little bit uncomfortable with the whole charade.

While in New York, Anaïs also wanted to go to MoMA, the Museum of Modern Art off Fifth Avenue. I had never seen her so excited. She'd grab my wrist and say, "You have to look at this artist!" I was so impressed with how much she knew about the artists and their intentions. She had a grasp on art history that was astonishing. I confess, sometimes I love to find the meaning behind paintings, but other times I admire them solely because they are pretty. I like the colors and textures of Pop Art, but Anaïs is more receptive to the ink paintings. She has a dark side, an introverted love of dark art. Pop Art gives me instant gratification, an exciting and thrilling feeling. Depressing art brings me down. But my sister loves that stuff. Hey, even identical twins have differences.

When the time came, I didn't want Anaïs to go, and she was equally distraught. Here was the long-distance relationship part again. . . . "So, we won't see each other for a while," "I'll call!" "I'll see you in April!" and all the other promises that went with it. I tried to think of reasons we'd reconnect before then. We were working together on the book and documentary, so we had those two things that might bring us together. I knew I'd see her all the time on Skype. That was the beauty of contemporary life—she was just a click away. I'd already woken up to her text messages every single morning since we first connected, so we knew we were not that far apart. Still, it was not the same as waking up to my sister's face, my face! I loved pulling her pillow away from her head in an annoying fashion until she woke up.

On our final night together, we stayed up talking pretty much until morning. Maybe it was good we didn't grow up together, because we would have never slept! I imagined hearing my parents yelling, "Girls! Lights out!" I imagined we would then have gone under the covers with flashlights, where my sister would draw while I staged our bedtime story.

My sister. I never thought I would say that. Matt and Andrew were my brothers, and that had been it, the three of us, two boys and a girl. I also have a birth mother. There is a woman out there who I may or may not meet one day. Sometimes, I still wonder if her intentions toward Anaïs and me were malicious. What if she had separated us on purpose? What if she never wanted Anaïs and me to find out about each other? But I guess that is irrelevant. No matter what her intentions were, they turned into something amazingly positive, and to me, that couldn't have been done without love.

By separating us, our mother gave two families each the gift of a lifetime. She gave the Bordiers a daughter to love until their dying days. And my family got me! No matter what she had in mind in the beginning, it didn't change what we had now. If Anaïs and I ever meet her, maybe she can fill in our storybook with more detail, but our abstract is absolutely beautiful as it is now.

I love my birth mother. She gave me life. She gave me a life with my family. She gave me my sister. Because of her, I got the best of both worlds.

19

SAM AND ANAÏS

dr. nancy l. segal's research results

By late fall, the results from Dr. Segal's studies were finally ready to review. She had collected all the data, analyzed all the testing, and conducted her final interviews, and she had prepared a comprehensive report about us to be published in the journal *Personality and Individual Differences*. We couldn't wait to see how nature and nurture had affected our personalities.

Dr. Segal found us to be remarkably similar. One of the first things she noted was how quickly we warmed to each other, even before our initial meeting. We had even created a pet name that we shared—Pop—within our first few online communications. Dr. Segal was struck by our physical similarities and mannerisms. She noted that we shared the same shy smile, similar giggle, crazy sense of humor, and delightful disposition. We were both artistic and creative and had pursued careers to use those talents. We were also both hardworking and independent.

Dr. Segal was not present at our reunion in London, but she found our initial responses to each other to be very typical of some other reared-apart twins meeting each other for the first time. We were cautious and curious. We didn't embrace, but poked each other to make sure the other was real. After all, we really were strangers to each other. We both grew up in Caucasian families, so even though there was no question we were adopted, we both wondered if anyone anywhere in the world looked like us. We had a longing for that physical connection that would make us secure in our identity. In London, when we first met, we were suddenly looking at our mirror image, no surprise that we would be inclined to just stare.

With the testing, Dr. Segal covered eight areas—life history, special cognitive abilities, personality traits, IQ, self-esteem, job satisfaction, medical history, and social relationships. Some of these tests were administered when we were together, others when we were apart. Whenever possible, Anaïs was given hers in French.

For the life history, Dr. Segal used the interview administered to participants of the Minnesota Study of Twins Reared Apart. She covered items concerning the circumstances of our adoption, the families that adopted us, and our educational background and our work histories.

In order to assess our general intelligence, the Wechsler Adult Intelligence Scale-IV (WAIS-IV) was administered to each of us, one week apart, in September 2013, Sam's in Los

Angeles and Anaïs's in Paris. This test measured verbal comprehension, perceptual reasoning, working memory, and processing speed scales, as well as general intelligence indexed by IQ. We also completed thirteen special metal ability tests.

Consistent with previous reared-apart twins, we were close in everything but "working memory." Dr. Segal speculated that Sam's superior performance on the memory tasks was consistent with her memorization of theatrical dialogue and food requests. Sam's acting and waitressing required good memory, social comprehension, and problem-solving skills. Anaïs outperformed Sam on four of the five visual-spatial tests, consistent with the idea that fashion designers benefit from good visual skills. It was likely that Anaïs exercised various visual-spatial skills as she imagined the look and movement of sizes and shapes.

Dr. Segal said that Sam's many skills required by her two jobs might also explain the difference in the IQ scores. Sam obtained an IQ score of 129, while Anaïs obtained a score of 112. The twins' seventeen-point difference slightly exceeds the test's standard deviation of fifteen. This discrepancy could variously reflect unknown differences in our prenatal environment (e.g., unequal nutrition), the different skills demanded of our jobs, and other life history or birth factors. Dr. Segal also pointed out that there is a phenomenon called "regression to the mean." So, if we were to retake the test, our scores might grow closer. In other words, Sam may have been really strong that one day of testing, and Anaïs may not have been feeling well. On another day, the test results might be different. In individual cases, people could show some change on different occasions.

Dr. Segal said the beauty of our situation was that being raised in different countries provided a glimpse into how culture interacted with common genes to produce some observable differences. We took three personality questionnaires. The first included two hundred items organized into twenty-one personality dimensions and the Big Five Personality Traits—openness, conscientiousness, extroversion, agreeableness, and stability, which was the reverse of neuroticism. The second personality inventory included three hundred adjectives we checked if the term was self-descriptive. The third questionnaire was a sixty-item personality inventory that also yielded scores on the Big Five.

It was surprising to detect some substantial differences in our Big Five personality trait profiles. The biggest differences between us occurred in the neuroticism and extroversion categories, with Anaïs scoring higher in neuroticism and Sam scoring higher in extroversion.

Dr. Segal said the reasons for these differences were unclear. Anaïs had recently completed a graduate program and taken a new job in France, so she suggested that perhaps a relatively lower score in extroversion reflected this life transition. Another possibility was prejudiced encounters while growing up. However, our scores were nearly identical for openness, conscientiousness, and agreeableness.

The testing showed that we both seem to have good self-esteem. On a range where "good" is fifteen to twenty-five, Sam obtained a score of twenty-four, and Anaïs obtained a score of fifteen. Our scores were at the upper and lower ends of this range, which, according to Dr. Segal, was a departure from our similarities.

To determine our job satisfaction, Dr. Segal gave us the Minnesota Job Satisfaction Questionnaire. We used a scale of one to five to indicate our satisfaction with twenty job-related items. We showed very similar profile patterns in terms of overall job satisfaction. Anaïs's score showed she was slightly more satisfied with her job than Sam. Regardless, our satisfaction with our work was consistent with genetic influence on job satisfaction.

We also completed a medical history, covering illnesses, injuries, and hospitalizations. We were very similar in height and weight, although Anaïs was 0.75 inches taller than Sam. We were both right-handed, although Anaïs could use both hands. We were generally healthy, but showed similarities across various symptoms and complaints, mostly gastrointestinal. Both of us were lactose intolerant, but we ate cheese despite the consequences. We both suffered from headaches. Sam controlled hers with over-the-counter medications, while Anaïs used prescribed medicines. Sam's headaches were "bothersome," whereas Anaïs's were more debilitating, sometimes requiring bed rest or stopping normal activities. We both had allergies, thirst, and dry mouth, bruised easily, wore contact lenses or glasses, and took oral contraceptives. In 2012, Anaïs experienced neuralgia in her left shoulder, a symptom Sam experienced in her leg.

We also had some different health-related problems. Sam

had sinus trouble and was allergic to antibiotics. She had to be hospitalized for the removal of her wisdom teeth. Anaïs was allergic to insects, seafood, and aspirin. She experienced low blood pressure, heart palpitations, joint pain, and teeth-grinding.

As much as we hate to admit it, we both smoke on occasion. Sam had her first cigarette at age eleven, and never smokes more than one cigarette every two weeks. Anaïs had her first cigarette at age nineteen and is more inclined to have at least one cigarette every day. She has never smoked more than half a pack in one day.

During a joint interview, which was videotaped at Cal State–Fullerton, we talked about all sorts of topics, from our reunion to our artistic fields of work, to our observations about our similarities. We admitted that we had come across many surprises at how similar we are, considering how different our lifestyles have been. Sam felt more "feminine" with Anaïs, relative to how she felt when among her brothers. Most important, we couldn't wait to share time together for the rest of our lives.

Each of us took away something different from Dr. Segal's findings and expertise. We both were most fascinated by points where we deviated from similarity. Sam was interested in mirror-image effects in twins, social coordination tests, and IQ. Anaïs was interested in the complications of test-taking—i.e., the language of the test, our participation in a larger study, and IQ. First and foremost, we were interested in IQ. We each prepared a few thoughts.

Sam: I wasn't sure of what the outcome would be on any of the tests, especially the ones that measured mental abilities. I was afraid that Anaïs and I would have wildly different scores, and I, being the dumb American actress, would have embarrassingly lower scores. But my sister assured me that in the Minnesota Study of Twins Reared Apart, the twins had scored on average about seven points apart, and some twins did not differ at all. However, some twins differed by more than seven points, and one pair differed by twenty-nine points. I was surprised to learn that, but even more surprised when we got our results. The three personality profiles were astounding. We were quite parallel in every way, except the ones concerning extroversion and neuroticism. One chart based on the third personality inventory was completely non-parallel in that respect. And although it's not surprising for an actress and a designer to have opposing intro/extroversion, it was still shocking to me that it would be so different. In my expression of work, aka acting, I am free and open with my feelings, yet when it comes to my actual emotions, I am quite pulled back. I don't say much until I have to. Or at least, that's what I perceive myself as doing.

To my excitement, my official IQ score came back in my favor! The French can never call us "dumb Americans" again! I was surprised, being that Anaïs had just finished graduate school and had had many more years in the classroom than I. And I never did my homework. I wasn't even remotely inter-ested in academics until my sophomore year of college. Relief to know that those college loans were worth it!

The results of the physical testing to see if we were "mirror twins" were not all that surprising, since they solidi-fied what we already thought we knew. In the physical test-ing, we were being checked to see whether we showed any opposite or reverse features. The phenomenon only occurs in identical twins, when the fertilized egg splits eight or more days after conception, which is relatively late. Twins showing mirror image effects exhibit reversed physical features. One might be right-handed, the other left. They might have similar birthmarks, but on opposite sides. They might even have hair curls that twist in opposite directions. Only about a quarter of identical twins show such reversed features.

It turned out that Anaïs and I mirrored each other in some things, but not all. I am right-handed, and Anaïs is ambidextrous. She only uses her right hand about a quarter of the time. I don't know if Dr. Segal's testing considered that Anaïs had been encouraged to use her right hand in school, part of French educational aversion to left-handedness. When she broke her right arm riding her horse at age fifteen, she had no choice but to write with her left hand. Anyway, she is considered ambidextrous, and I am right-handed. Also, our eyes are a bit opposite. My strong eye is her weak eye and vice versa.

In the hand-eye coordination test, we were thrown Ping-Pong balls and asked to catch them a bunch of times with only one hand. Anaïs wasn't fully able to catch the ball in one hand, but it left a comical moment in our memory. I was catching the ball in one hand, left or right, with no juggling or hesitation at all. That was not surprising—I grew up playing sports like softball and basketball, thanks to brothers, whereas Anaïs only did horseback riding and ballet.

Also, for those out there who think all Asians are good at math, our IQ scores say differently.

Anaïs: I was familiar with Dr. Segal's findings in her books and articles. I had looked online and read every document that she had sent to my sister and me. I wanted to know anything and everything about twins. Therefore, I was somewhat prepared for what the testing would involve.

Even though many of the tests were in French, my first language, I had been studying in London for quite a few years then, and I was working hard on my studies in English. So when I had to do vocabulary and writing skills, I was nervous that I had forgotten how to put things properly in French. Funny, you'd think I'd be able to speak more freely in my native tongue!

For the personality testing, I thought it was weird to see the questions rephrased. It seemed as though they had been translated, and sometimes I wasn't sure if I was supposed to be finding nuances in the exact meanings. I was probably overthinking it, but I would look at the English double, just to try to make sure that it all made sense. Even today, I can get lost in translation!

Not to my surprise, Sam's memory was a bit stronger than mine, although memory was a talent of mine as well. On the other hand, I was more visual, which made a lot of sense as I was staring at designs all day long. I must admit, I was a little disheartened by my IQ score, for I found out I was the stupid one. I'm sure my sister was thrilled, since we French always poke fun at the Americans! But it was a specific IQ test, and it was created by Americans. We have to take one made by the French in order for it to be accurate. I challenge my sister to a rematch.

epilogue

let things fall as they may

Our finding each other has changed not only our lives but the lives of everybody in our families. Each set of our parents has themselves a new "daughter"; each daughter has a new set of "parents." We asked our parents to put their thoughts on paper. We were so heartened to see what they wrote that we wanted to share their words here, followed by thoughts of our own:

JACQUES BORDIER

I was very cautious when I first heard about Sam as Anaïs's possible twin sister. Anaïs was, naturally, so moved by the event, and I knew her so well that, as a father, I wanted to avoid any terrible disappointment that would send her low in her spirits.

I, myself, as an "ordinary Caucasian" citizen, had been tempted to find similarities between Asian faces (the *they all look alike* syndrome), although I knew I would be able to recognize my daughter, even if she had been circled by a billion Korean and other

Asian faces. Several times I had encountered young
Asian ladies who I thought bore some traits
resembling Anaïs's. When Anaïs was about eight
years old, I vividly remember seeing an Asian young
lady, probably from Korean origin, who was about
eighteen or twenty years old. I thought that was
exactly how Anaïs would look when she turned
twenty. It was a real shock to me, like seeing a film,
a projection of the same person, ahead in time. So
impressed was I that I still remember that moment.

There was an actress in a Korean film I had just
watched, too, "looking like Anaïs," but obviously
with no possible family ties. Therefore, when we
learned about Sam, I wasn't prepared to admit that
she would be Anaïs's sister. I was skeptical myself,
and I wanted to "cool down" Anaïs's spirits.

After all, chances were thin. There is a saying in
Korean for when things are impossible, "It's like
finding Mr. Kim in Seoul," knowing that one-fifth
of the Korean population bears the family
name "Kim." So, how difficult it would be to find
the "Kim sisters"—Kim is Anaïs's Korean family
name—scattered about the entire world, one in
France, one in the USA, if the Koreans themselves
could not find "Mr. Kim" in Seoul?

Funny enough, when Anaïs provided Google
evidence of Sam's and Anaïs's obvious similarities,
like being born in Busan on November 19, etc.,
etc., the first website I checked on showed

Samantha Futerman being born on November 1. I stopped checking on Google and immediately reported to Anaïs that Sam could not be her sister . . . usual father shortcuts . . .

Of course, Anaïs encouraged me to carry on my investigations . . . and I was really taken aback when I watched "How It Feels to Be Adopted . . . I Am Sam," Sam's short video. I watched it over and over again, and this time, I indeed really thought Anaïs had good reason to feel what she was feeling, although rationally I could not accept the idea, as:

a) Patricia and I felt so confident about the Korean Association, which had taken care of Anaïs after she was born, and we trusted what they had told us about the situation with Anaïs's biological mother (a totally different story than we heard about Sam's).

b) we were asked whether we would accept twins, and we, of course, had answered yes, so why would twin sisters have been separated?

c) the chances of having two babies born from the same womb, scattered over the world, then finding each other were so slim, we would have had more chance to become millionaires in the European lottery games, as a statistical expert would have showed us rationally.

But this was no time for rationality. Still, my sixty-two-year-old rational mind was not ready to accept that kind of evidence. Time passed, and every week was bringing new facts, showing against all odds there was more to it than just resemblance.

Anaïs was so excited, but I wanted her to concentrate on her final exams and the fashion show she had to prepare. I was not pleased to learn funds were already being raised to create a documentary when no one even knew if the girls were twins. I had never heard of Kickstarter before, and did not know how it worked. Of course, we subscribed, like Sam's parents did and a lot of friends, as well as so many unknown, generous persons, moved by the story, which had started to spread all over the world in newspapers, magazines, blogs.

We were very happy when we learned Sam would be coming over to London in May with her family, and we all could meet. So much happy news!! How could it be possible? But my own rational mind was also feeling a little bit of guilt: What about if Sam and Anaïs were not twin sisters? I was so eager to have DNA tests performed so my rational mind would be at peace. If not, I felt we would have cheated those generous persons, and that was contrary to my personal and family ethics. And a few weeks later, there we were all in London. It wasn't the perfect spring season, but who cared. I shall remember this until my last moment.

I did not watch Sam and Anaïs reuniting, as my wife, Patricia, did—I was at work most of the day—but I received an SMS from my wife on my mobile phone that said, "No doubt, we now have two daughters."

At our hotel that evening, I was having dinner with my wife. Anaïs was showing Sam her *université* grounds, and Patricia and I contemplated having a quiet evening together, as we were planning to meet Sam, her parents, and brothers the next day for a tour of London. Then, all of a sudden, there was a mobile phone message from Anaïs saying they were going to "drop by" for a few minutes on their way home from school. I did not have time to prepare for our encounter—hardly a few minutes later, here Sam was, standing in front of us, a lovely, smiling, already familiar face, with Anaïs bearing her sister "accomplice" smile.

When I held Sam in my arms to greet her, my heart fainted and all my rational prejudices faded away instantly: I did not need a DNA test anymore to know the extraordinary had happened. The two separated sisters were reunited again! The following day we met Sam's family and visited London. It was amazing how we instantly got

on well with them, so that was an additional joy
for us.

PATRICIA BORDIER

When Anaïs told me about an American actress
who was looking very similar to her and born on
the same day in the same Korean town, I
immediately thought she could be her twin. . . .
Soon, Jacques and I were watching on YouTube the
video by Samantha called "How It Feels to Be
Adopted . . . I Am Sam." I thought at the moment
that the girl speaking English with an American
accent was Anaïs. I watched it three times
nonstop. I was amazed, the same smile, same way
of speaking, same gestures . . . same everything.
At that particular moment, I was sure they were
twins!

In London, I was with Anaïs when she physically
met Sam for the first time. Anaïs entered the flat
and went to Sam. I stayed at the entrance. The
two girls were looking at each other, laughing,
touching their fronts, their cheeks, their lips, their
fingers . . . and I was seeing "two Anaïses." When
I took Sam in my arms, I felt like I was taking in
my arms a second daughter. Immediately, I felt
good! I sent a message to my husband: "We now
have two daughters."

At night, the results of the DNA test were
supposed to be given by a doctor from L.A. via

Skype. I was sure that **the result** would be positive. I did not want to think what disappointment it would be for Anaïs, and certainly for Sam, if they were not twins . . . and, of course, it was positive!

The next day we met Sam's parents and her two brothers, and immediately we felt like a family. We share a lot of similar feelings, and the main one is the joy to see the two girls so happy together.

JUDD FUTERMAN

On February 21, 2013, Samantha texted me and said, "Dad, twin?" After talking with her, I learned that she had been contacted by a young lady who had been born in Busan, Korea, on November 19, 1987—the same date and location of Samantha's birth. Samantha had not yet spoken to this young lady, but she had seen her picture and said to me, "Dad, twin?"

As I spoke to my daughter, I got a chill through my body. Could this be? Could my beautiful twenty-five-year-old daughter truly have a twin somewhere in the world? WOW, could that be?

As the days progressed, Samantha began to receive pictures from Anaïs (her twin?). To me, it was obvious that my baby had a twin, and that she lived in England. WOW, what could I say? Finally someone of the same blood as Samantha, WOW.

Everyone said, "Be careful" until the DNA is completed. "Don't get your hopes up." But not me. I knew that this beautiful young lady in England was Samantha's twin (and my other daughter).

Samantha arranged a trip for us to go to London, England, to meet Anaïs and her parents. I couldn't wait to meet my new daughter and her mom and dad. How exciting this was going to be for all of us, but mostly for Samantha and Anaïs.

Upon our arrival in London, we took the train to one block from our hotel. It was eleven thirty p.m., and we were tired. As we approached the hotel, much to my surprise, Samantha came running out and hugged Jackie, Matt, and myself. Then, Samantha came out of the hotel. I looked twice and realized that this beautiful, lovely girl who had hugged me first was Anaïs and not Samantha. WOW.

In the days that followed our first meeting, I quickly learned to love my other daughter with such love that no one could imagine. My daughters are beautiful, smart, lovely, charming, funny, and the most that any father could ever hope for.

The day after our arrival in London, we met two of the loveliest people on Earth, Patricia and Jacques Bordier, Anaïs's other parents—although I guess that Jackie and I are her other parents, while Patricia and Jacques are her real parents— two lovely, warm, charming, and wonderful people.

To this day, I know that GOD came down upon me
and provided these three wonderful people to
allow Samantha and all of my family to enjoy utter
happiness.

JACKIE FUTERMAN

I know it was silly, but I felt rather responsible for
Anaïs before we met her. I worried that she'd had a
good childhood, that I would like her parents. Not
"like" as people, but "like" as in the type of
parents they had been (like I was supermom or
something!!). I think Patricia said something
similar about us. Because Judd and I had agreed to
take twins if they "came up," I rather felt as if
Anaïs was mine in some odd way.

Spending those first days with Anaïs and Sam, I
felt as if I had always known her, because her laugh,
body language, sense of humor, and voice were so
much like Sam's. I liked her immediately and loved
her very quickly, because it was like just extending
what I felt for Sam over to Anaïs. However, once we
got home from London, I started to feel as if I
hadn't really met the true Anaïs, because the girls
were always together, there was a crowd of people,
and we had no alone time. So I wondered if I hadn't
just transferred Sam over to Anaïs.

When she came to New York, Judd and I got to
spend time with her alone. We got to talk to her
and hear her opinions, etc. I think I have a better

feel for the differences between the two girls now, as well as the similarities. Their uniqueness is coming out more.

As for Jacques and Patricia, the more we interact, the more I like them. We parents are in a strange, maybe even odd position. There's no term for us, such as "in-laws." There's no term for our daughter's sister as she relates to us. Jacques and Patricia are not just new friends. They are very important people in the life of my daughter's sister. This sister has become a very important person in my daughter's life. By extension, we have all become very important to each other. I know all four of us parents have a sense of responsibility toward the other daughter and to each of us. Thank heavens for the Internet. It not only brought us all together, it *keeps* us together.

SAM

I could have had a mental breakdown when I found out about Anaïs. I could have gone into a deep depression about the meaning of life, how cruel it was for a mother to separate her twin girls, with, I'm assuming, the hope that what she had done would never be found out. But what would be the point? When I least expected it, I have found someone to be happy with for the rest of my life. I have been given a gift, and I choose to see the

good. I will take it and transform it into
something useful.

I see so many adopted children and teenagers in
the world who are sad and question their adoption,
focusing on the negative. They can't get away from
the feeling of being abandoned, that they weren't
wanted. Yet, without that birth, who knows if
they'd even be on this earth? Who knows if they
would have been able to give their parents and
families and friends the happiness they feel when
they are around?

I can't imagine what life would have been for
Anaïs and me if we hadn't been separated. Would
we have grown up in Korea together? Would we
have hated each other because people would have
lumped us into one identity . . . "them" . . . "the
twins" . . . "the girls"? Would we have been able
to be fashion designers and actresses? Would we
love croissants and cheese? But most importantly,
would Patricia and Jacques have had a daughter to
love and care for the rest of their lives?

I can't imagine Patricia and Jacques without
Anaïs. She is their pride and joy. You can just tell.
She gives them the meaning of life. I hope that
one day I have children of my own, biological and
adopted. I want to continue life and teach them
all the good things in the world. I want to take
them everywhere and watch them play sports and

do the school plays and teach them to ski. And
what would my parents have without me?!
Nothing, nor me without them.

My parents are amazing. I don't know anyone
else who would take the time to drive everyone
back and forth to a billion different restaurants,
shows, sites, and airports throughout the New York
area over Thanksgiving. There were so many people
to accommodate, and yet they did it selflessly.
How much they do is really insane, but they taught
me to do everything you can for the people you
love. It was something that was never verbally
explained to me, but shown through their actions.

I hope I will be as caring for my family and
friends as they have been for theirs. I always miss
my mom the moment I'm not with her. She annoys
me like nobody else, but I love her like nobody
else. She taught me how to treat people and how
to make chicken cutlets. My mom, my superhero,
does it all.

ANAÏS

I grew up as an only child. Now, not only do I have
a sibling, I have a twin sister! I was never
expecting that to happen in my twenty-fifth year,
when I was finishing my schooling, breaking out
on my own, establishing my identity. By purest
coincidence, and Kelsang, of course, all that
changed. After graduation, I could go anywhere in

the world I wanted. In fact, my field was the perfect choice to be able to live in so many great cities. By chance, I had an interview that led to a job that brought me home to Paris. Even though I had not intended to move back, I guess you should sometimes let things happen and be open to where they lead.

In a way, I think it felt comforting to know I would go home, close to my parents, too. After all that had happened this past year, I felt like I needed to be close to them. I understood how much family mattered. Sometimes when you get angry, or you want to grow and go your own way, you also need to feel at home somewhere. I think everything that happened left me in a state of shock for a long time after discovering Sam. When your life changes so profoundly, so suddenly, you need something familiar. You need a bit of order no matter how happy the upheaval might be.

When I found out Sam had brothers, I was not jealous. I was definitely curious about how she felt about them, especially brothers who were biological children of her parents, whereas she was adopted. I was very happy for her that she had them, but I did not feel that I had been deprived. They were part of her life, plus, I now had them as my own. Sam's parents are my family, too, but maybe like an aunt and an uncle. They aren't my parents; they are Sam's parents. The part that is so wonderful is that everybody is on the same side.

Even after finding Sam, I wouldn't change anything about my first twenty-five years. You can't have better parents than mine, just not possible. My parents support me in everything I try, they have taken me around the world several times and have encouraged me to never let a boundary keep me back. Even though they are as French as it gets, they are international people in their souls and spirits. They embrace the world and all its cultures, languages, religions, politics, and people, and they have taught me to do the same. They love me unconditionally, and I love them.

Once in a great, great while, for a fleeting moment, I think about the woman who gave birth to me. I have no idea how to imagine what she looks like or what type of person she is. How old is she? Does she have other children? Was she really a rice plantation worker? Does she still live in Busan? SWS has investigated a little bit, although I was not so keen on discovering her or her story. Everyone has a theory about how the separation might have happened to Sam and me.

I have my own theories how we came to be, like we are robots, or clones sent from outer space, but apart from that, the story could be anything from the simplest to the most complicated and dramatic story ever. I guess I used to need to know why I

had been abandoned. Now, Sam is here, and
nothing else matters anymore. Samantha and
I lived the same story once, and then we were
separated, and now we can just go further ahead
and live happy lives together. We don't really need
to look backward. With regard to our birth parents,
that is their story, not ours.

acknowledgments

From Samantha:

To my documentary team—Kanoa Goo, Ryan Miyamoto, Lisa Arendarski, Eileen DeNobile, Michael Allen, Yamato Cibulka, Tomas Yoo, Marie Roullion, Jenna Ushkowitz, Jeff Consiglio, Dan Matthews, Steve Brown—thank you for sticking by my side, challenging me, always believing in me and being part of this insane adventure.

Kanoa Goo, you have kept me grounded through every crazy moment. Thank you.

Ryan Miyamoto, thank you for sharing my journey and giving me endless support. You are completely irreplaceable. I will always love you.

Lisa Arendarski, thank you for being my support from accounting to vacuuming and everything in between. You keep my head above water.

Scott Moore, Kelsang Dorjee Dongsar, James Yi, Justin Chon, Relativity Media, Lauren Arps, Kevin Wu: Without you guys, I would have never met my sister. The universe brought us together, and now I know why.

Ben Sommers, Shinhye Kang, SooJoo Kim, and Sue Jeong: The amount of information you have been able to uncover and the amount of support you provide is life-changing.

Eileen DeNobile: Thank you for protecting me throughout all these years and always sticking by my side. You have nurtured my talents from the beginning and are a huge part of who I am today.

To my foster mom, Shin Ja Kim: Thank you for nurturing me at my first and most crucial moments. Without you, I would have never had the strength or nourishment I needed in order to survive.

Mom and Dad: I love you a billion times. I would have nothing without you. Mom, you are my hero. Your encouragement and love give me the strength to be where I am today. Thank you for holding my hand, picking the carrots out of my soup, and making my dreams possible. Dad, you have taught me to be the determined woman I am today and to go above and beyond for my family. Thank you for always believing in me and allowing me to know that I can be whatever I want to be in this world.

Matt and Andrew: You are my protectors and my best friends, through all those years of video games, stickball in the streets, crammed car rides to Maine, and collectively making fun of our parents. You are both annoying as crap, but you are the best big brothers a girl could ever ask for. I love you.

Grandma, Uncle Bob, Aunt Jo, Jill, Jonathon, Jesse, Tom, Uncle Chic, Aunt Nancy, Laura, Cindy, Richard, Uncle

Danny, Aunt Joanne, Rachel, Max, and my big brother Jeremy: Thank you for making me the crazy person I am today. I love you all. I would have never been outgoing enough to put myself on YouTube without all those years of being forced to sing the Chanukah song.

Patricia and Jacques: You have helped me further understand the meaning of love by accepting me into your family. Thank you for loving my sister. I love you, and I look forward to our endless dinners of foie gras, wine, and dessert, together as family.

To my sister: I have always thought of every possible event that could occur in my lifetime. Discovering you was something I would have never imagined. It is possible that the universe was guiding us to each other and that we were yearning to be together, but without your courage and willingness to explore the unknown, I may have experienced this life without your existence. If that were the case, then I would have never known what happiness truly means. You have expanded my vision of the world into a place with endless possibilities and you constantly remind me of everything that is good. Whether it is through an embrace, an emoji, or simply just knowing that you are alive in this world, you give me the comfort and the strength to take on any challenge that life may offer. Thank you for giving me the opportunity to truly understand the meaning of life, love, happiness, and family. I am nothing without you. I love you. Pop.

From Samantha and Anaïs: Steve Ross, Kerri Kolen, Ellen Gilbert, Rachel Altman, Domina Holbeck, Victoria Shaffer, Pamela Fisher, and Eric Suddleson—thank you for being on our team and always supporting our decisions through all this insanity. We couldn't have asked for a better team.

Lisa Pulitzer: There are few in this world who will truly understand our experience. You are a kind, inspiring woman. There is no one better in this world to help tell our story. Thank you for becoming part of our family and allowing us to express our ideas to the fullest extent.

Martha Smith: You and Lisa have been on this project since Day One. Your hard work and dedication are greatly appreciated.

Dr. Segal: You have given us more than we could have ever asked for. We are eternally grateful for your work conducting our DNA testing and so much more. You have been an incredible resource and friend.

Spence-Chapin Adoption Services, Holt International Children's Services, Kickstarter, *Good Morning America*, Samsung, Facebook Stories, YouTube, and IKAA: You have helped make all of our dreams come true.

To whoever gave us birth: It takes two, and we're very glad you both did it. We are happy as ever, thank you.

To our Kickstarter backers: You made our reunion possible. Your kindness and donations gave us the chance to stand in the same room for the very first time. Thank you for believing in us and being part of our journey.

From Anaïs:
To Kelsang Dorjee Dongsar, or the "hand of God": You will always remain my fashion master, teaching me all your tricks, being a wonderful cook, and taking such good care of me.

You are the most generous and selfless person I have ever met, and I will forever be thankful for your YouTube addiction. I love you.

Marie Rouillon and the amazing Jase Warner, my best friends and flat mates, for their moral support, all the cooking, the cleaning, the music, and wonderful memories of our year sharing a flat. To my two other great flat mates, Rory Crawford and Rafa Villalobos, with his uncanny Internet skills and opera concerts in the shower. And, thank you to my previous flat mates, Mátyás, Patrick, and Oliver.

To my little brother of the heart, Jonathan Dubreuil, and his mum, Anne: We have known each other since we were kids. You came after work to meet my sister, traveling all the way from the other side of London. I have met amazing people thanks to you, and I will always be here for you, as you have been here for my sister and me.

And to William van Hinloopen: Although I barely knew you when everything started, you have been here for me since. Thank you for not freaking out on my nail-biting and teeth-grinding. Your daily support on our professional and personal projects means so much to me.

To Lucas Gloppe, who was with me on the bus when all the elements started mixing and coming together. Maxence Parache for sending the first tweet and attracting my sister's attention, and Fabienne Fong Yan for being so supportive and patient. This journey would never have started without you and your help.

Jewon Lee and Jennifer Lee, thank you so much for introducing me to Korean culture, for all the Korean food, all the K-pop songs I discovered, and for making me proud of South Korea.

Justin Chon and Kevin Wu for being well-known actors and shooting with my sister. Lisa Arendarski, Tomas Yoo, Ryan Miyamoto, Kanoa Goo, James Yi, my sister's friends, who accepted me and let me enter their lives and were part of our trips. Even if you had not been my sister's friends, I hope we would have met someday and become friends, because you are gold.

Anaïs Lelong and Charles Constant for being my older "adopted" sister and brother of the heart.

To Racines Coréennes, Franck Leroy, and Holt Children's Services, a huge *merci* for your help in our search and investigation in Korea.

Eui-Soo Moon, my foster mum, I am so grateful you took care of me when I was just an infant. You cared and you were obviously one of the first people in my life, and thus you are one of the most important people to me.

To the whole Futerman family: You are incredible people, you welcomed my parents and me into your home and family, you accepted us, and we felt like home, even a thousand miles away.

Jackie and Judd, you have been great parents to my "little" sister. Thanks for accompanying and showing her the way. There are no words to express how happy it makes me to see who she has become thanks to you.

Andrew and Matt, I am so glad to have two brothers now, and that we are past our teenage years. I hope I will grow to be a nice sister to you both.

Pépé and Mémé, Gaston Bordier and Madeleine Bordier, you are gone already, but from where you are, you must have watched us. Thank you for giving me a dad, and thanks to Grand-père and Grand-mère, Jacques and Simone Wach, for giving me a mum and a wonderful uncle, Mgr. Gilles Wach.

Maman and Papa, thanks for being my parents, taking care of me, consoling me, teaching me, feeding me, playing with me, loving me whatever I did. Maman, you have always been understanding. Thanks for leaving your career to be a full-time mum. Papa, thanks for always pushing me further and going beyond my limits and showing me that with good-will I can do whatever I want. You found the trick to entice me to learn English by putting a Harry Potter book on my bedside table. You have supported my decision to follow my passion to study the arts and to pursue my studies in London, where it changed my life.

To my sister: I will never know if it was you I was missing when I was a little kid, but all I know is that feeling you are in this world any second makes me the happiest every day. It comforts me to know we found each other after so many years, and I love to believe we were meant to find each other. I am so thankful for our lives to have suddenly changed like this in ways I could never have even dreamed of. I will remain amazed every day at the fact we randomly fell upon each other via social media, and so thankful for the love it brought to our lives. Your daily joy, enthusiasm, jokes, and messages are a gift every day. I have nothing to fear now since you are here. I love you, my little sister.

kindred:
the foundation for adoption

Kindred: The Foundation for Adoption is an American foundation established by Samantha Futerman in 2014, after she and Anaïs Bordier discovered that they were identical twins separated at birth. When their reunion garnered worldwide attention, Samantha heard countless stories from fellow adoptees. They were all worth hearing and sharing and they instilled in her a desire to aid adoptees in a myriad of situations.

Kindred's initiative is to provide international and domestic adoptees and their families (both adoptive and biological) with services such as travel, translation, and therapy for those who wish to reunite; easily accessible hotlines; introduction to art and encouragement of artistic expression; and programs set in native countries to aid orphans living within the foster care and government systems. No matter how big or small the need, the foundation's goal is to aid adoptees and their families in finding stability and happiness.

Love and family is extendable not only to those with whom we share our DNA, but to whomever we choose to accept into our lives.

For more information on Kindred, visit:
www.kindredadoption.org
www.facebook.com/kindredadoption
www.twitter.com/kindredadoption